W9-BZY-515

HAPPINESS IS
BAKING

MAIDA HEATTER

HAPPINESS IS
BAKING

Foreword by
DORIE GREENSPAN

CAKES, PIES, TARTS, MUFFINS, BROWNIES, COOKIES
—
Favorite Desserts from
the Queen of Cake

Illustrations by
ALICE OEHR

LITTLE, BROWN AND COMPANY
New York | Boston | London

Copyright © 2019 by Maida Heatter
Foreword © 2019 by Dorie Greenspan
Illustrations by Alice Oehr

Hachette Book Group supports the right to free expression and
the value of copyright. The purpose of copyright is to encourage writers and artists
to produce the creative works that enrich our culture.

The scanning, uploading, and distribution of this book without permission is a theft of
the author's intellectual property. If you would like permission to use material from the book
(other than for review purposes), please contact permissions@hbgusa.com.
Thank you for your support of the author's rights.

Little, Brown and Company
Hachette Book Group
1290 Avenue of the Americas, New York, NY 10104
littlebrown.com

First Edition: April 2019

Little, Brown and Company is a division of Hachette Book Group, Inc.
The Little, Brown name and logo are trademarks of Hachette Book Group, Inc.

The recipes in *Happiness Is Baking* have been assembled from Maida Heatter's previously published books,
including *Maida Heatter's Cakes, Maida Heatter's Cookies, Maida Heatter's Book of Great Chocolate
Desserts, Maida Heatter's Book of Great Desserts, Maida Heatter's New Book of Great Desserts,*
and *Maida Heatter's Book of Great Cookies*. They have been occasionally updated or modernized from
their original forms for consistency, for ease of use, and in instances where Maida's personal notes on
her books have improved a recipe after its original publication.

The publisher gratefully acknowledges Connie Heatter for her assistance in
preparing this book, and the many friends of Maida who graciously shared their own
favorite desserts as these recipes were selected for publication.

The publisher is not responsible for websites (or their content) that are not owned by the publisher.

The Hachette Speakers Bureau provides a wide range of authors for speaking events.
To find out more, go to hachettespeakersbureau.com or call (866) 376-6591.

ISBN 978-0-316-42057-0
LCCN 2018959912

Design by Toni Tajima

10 9 8 7 6 5 4 3 2 1

WOR

Printed in the United States of America

Happiness is baking cookies.

Happiness is giving them away.

And serving them, and eating them,

talking about them, reading and

writing about them, thinking about them,

and sharing them with you.

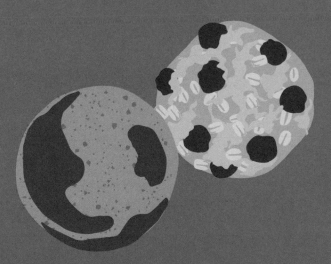

contents

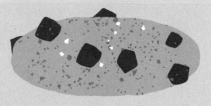

foreword

The one time I saw Maida Heatter was at Lincoln Center in New York City. The occasion was a James Beard Foundation Awards ceremony, and while I can't remember the specific reason she was being honored — the possibilities for celebrating her are many — I'll never forget the moment. She accepted her award, then moved to the edge of the stage, her white hair gleaming under the lights, her smile as broad as one of her crescent cookies, reached into a bag she'd brought with her, and began throwing brownies to the adoring crowd. I didn't get one, but had I, I'm sure I could have taken a quick look and told you which one of her many brownies it was — and I might even have been able to recite the recipe. That's how well I knew her work.

In our house, Maida Heatter, who might as well have been a kitchen god, was always given full title, as in, "Is that another Maida Heatter recipe?" Or, "This is so wonderful, it must be a Maida Heatter recipe." Or, most often, "Another fabulous dessert from Maida Heatter." Long before the internet, long before people cooked or baked their way through a book and shared their adventures with their followers, I baked my way through *Maida Heatter's Book of Great Desserts* and shared everything I baked with my husband, my friends, my workmates, and the men who ran the elevator in our apartment building. Everyone was grateful and, soon, discriminating. When I offered something that wasn't perfect, they'd say, "This isn't a Maida Heatter recipe," and they'd be right. Teach me for straying.

Maida Heatter helped make me a baker. When I got the first of her books, I was married, working, and going to graduate school. No matter how busy the day, I came home and baked. I didn't know much about the craft then, but I wanted to learn, and it was Maida Heatter who taught me. Her instructions were so good, so complete, and so meticulous and superbly thought out that it was easy to follow her and right to trust her. Her directions were also encouraging. As I worked my way through each recipe, I had the feeling that she was cheering me on.

Whenever someone tells me they want to start baking, I tell them to turn to Maida Heatter. I can't even count how many of her books I've given to beginning bakers. And now, there is this new edition, its recipes culled from Maida Heatter's archives and chosen by people who, like me, have been touched by her work. It makes me indescribably happy to know that a new generation of bakers will have the pleasure of being guided by this knowing and generous teacher.

One day, I hope that bakers will look back on this book and find, as I have in all of my Maida Heatter books, the notes that they scribbled alongside each recipe. My notes say things like, "Fantastic!" "Delicious and easy to make." "Make again!" "A knock-out!" Yours will too.

— Dorie Greenspan

introduction

Years ago I heard a doctor talking on television about the dangers of stress. It can kill you. It can cause a heart attack or a stroke. The doctor listed ways of coping with stress. Exercise. Diet. Do yoga. Take a walk.

I yelled, "Bake cookies."

I often talk to the television. I yelled it again and again. The doctor went on with his list of 12 ways to reduce stress...and he never once mentioned my surefire treatment.

Baking is a great escape. It's happiness. It's creative. It's good for your health. It reduces stress.

If you are reading this book, chances are you know what I mean. You have probably baked something delicious. You could probably tell me a thing or two about what fun it is. But if you have *not* baked even cookies, then let me tell you: Bake some cookies! Happiness is baking cookies.

The one question I am asked most often is, "What do you do with all the desserts you make while writing a cookbook?" Frankly, we eat an awful lot of them. And we have friends and neighbors, and delivery men, garbage men, gardeners, mailmen, and the butcher, the baker, and the candlestick maker...who hope I never stop testing recipes.

Some people (especially me) will stop at nothing to track down the recipe for a dessert they have tasted or heard about. Many, many years ago I bought a certain chocolate cake from a New York patisserie and fell madly in love with it. I simply had to have the recipe, but I could not get it. I tried to duplicate it at least 30 or 40 times with no luck. Since I thought that the particular brand of chocolate used in the cake might have been a clue to its unusual flavor, I hung around on the street in front of the shop for many days, hoping to see a chocolate delivery truck. I had the cake sent to all the good cooks and pastry chefs I knew around the country to see if they could help me analyze it. I wrote to all the publications that seem to be able to get recipes when no one else can. I even asked my husband to flirt with the lady who baked the cake to try to get the recipe. I told him, "Do anything necessary — just don't come home without it." When the lady realized his motive, she immediately threw him out of her shop. P.S. — I still do not have the recipe and haven't given up.

One more word about this book — about any cookbook — before you get down to the serious (fun) business of making the recipes. A cookbook should be treated like a school textbook. When reading it, or cooking from it, keep a pencil handy for notations. Underline things you especially want to remember, make notes — just don't be afraid to write in it. Write your experiences with the recipes and any changes you make. (For instance, "bake 3 minutes longer," "use pecans instead of walnuts," "cut these thinner," or "these are the ones I made when S and G came to dinner." Or "divine" or "troublesome.") In the future you will find that your own notes have added to the book and made it more valuable to you.

Special-effort cooking is truly one of the creative arts. You create something and share it with joy with those you love. You can't ask more of life than that.

Maida Heatter

before you bake

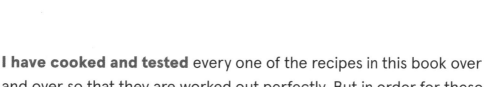

I have cooked and tested every one of the recipes in this book over and over so that they are worked out perfectly. But in order for these recipes to work for you as they do for me, it is of the utmost importance that you follow every direction exactly. Many instructions might seem trivial, arbitrary, or unimportant, but there really is a practical reason for everything.

If a recipe says to line a cookie sheet with aluminum foil, it is not because I am a fuddy-duddy and care about keeping cookie sheets clean. In some recipes, you would encounter disaster without the foil. With it, if you are like me, you will squeal with joy at the ease, fun, and satisfying excitement of peeling the foil from the smooth, shiny backs of the cookies.

If a recipe includes directions to refrigerate for at least 10 hours or longer, it is because the custard would collapse if it were served sooner. With adequate baking and chilling time it will hold its shape like a smooth cheesecake, and serving it (to say nothing of eating it) will be a sensuous thrill.

If brownies are not allowed to stand for the specified time after they come out of the oven, they will squash when you cut them into portions.

I could go on and on, but please, take my word for it. Read the recipes carefully and follow them exactly.

I wish you good luck with this book. I have had pleasure, satisfaction, moments of pride, and even some of sheer ecstasy with these recipes. And I wish you the same.

Before You Bake

1   Read the recipe completely. Make sure you have everything you will need, including the correct-size baking pan.

2   Remove butter, cream cheese, and eggs from the refrigerator.

3   Adjust oven racks and preheat the oven.

4   Prepare the pan according to the directions.

5   Grind or chop nuts.

6   Sift flour (and other dry ingredients) onto a large piece of wax paper or baking parchment.

7   Crack open the eggs (and separate them if necessary).

8   Measure all the other ingredients and organize them into the order called for in the recipe.

Ingredients

BUTTER
Whenever butter is called for it means unsalted (sweet) butter.

CHOCOLATE
Unsweetened chocolate is also called baking chocolate or bitter chocolate.

Sweet, semisweet, bittersweet, and **extra-bittersweet chocolates** are generally interchangeable in cooking and baking, depending on your taste and on the availability of chocolates.

Semisweet chocolate morsels, chips, or **bits:** Made by Nestlé, Hershey, and others. I seldom use them (although many people do with excellent results), except in cookies — and for making one of the greatest cookies of all, Toll House Cookies. The recipe for those cookies is printed on the package of Nestlé's Chocolate Morsels. Of course, that did not stop me from including my own Positively-the-Absolutely-Best-Chocolate-Chip Cookies on page 124.

Milk chocolate: I seldom use milk chocolate in cooking or baking. When I do, it is used cut up, like morsels (for chocolate chip cookies).

Compound chocolate: Real chocolate contains cocoa butter. Compound chocolate contains some shortening rather than cocoa butter. Real chocolate should be tempered to prevent discoloring or streaking after melting and cooling — compound chocolate does not need to be tempered and will set up (harden) faster than real chocolate. I use compound chocolate most especially for making Mushroom Meringues (page 181) and Chocolate Cigarettes (page 101). These can also be made with real chocolate but not as easily (unless the chocolate is tempered, which is a long story).

→ *To Melt Chocolate*
When melting chocolate with no other ingredient, the container *must* be absolutely dry. Even the merest drop of moisture will cause the chocolate to "tighten" or "seize." (If it should tighten, stir in 1 tablespoon vegetable shortening for each 3 ounces of chocolate.) Melt chocolate by stirring it slowly in the top of a double boiler over hot, but not boiling, water. The reason for this is that boiling water might bubble up and get into the chocolate. People who have a microwave tell me that it is the best way of all to melt chocolate.

Chocolate should melt slowly — it burns easily. To be sure chocolate doesn't get overheated and burn, it is always advisable to remove it from over the hot water before it is completely melted and then stir it until it is entirely melted and smooth.

COCOA

Any unsweetened cocoa may be used in baking and cooking, but I prefer Dutch-process cocoa. It has nothing to do with Holland or the Dutch — it is cocoa that has been treated with alkali to neutralize the natural acids. It is darker than other cocoa and, to my taste, has a richer and better flavor. I use Droste.

In some recipes, it's best to strain the cocoa before use. To do so, push it through a fine sieve or strainer.

COFFEE

Instant espresso or coffee in a recipe means dry — powdered or granules.

Instant coffee powder will dissolve more easily than granules. If you happen to have granules on hand, it is easy to powder it yourself. Whirl some in the blender, then strain it and return the coarse part to the blender to grind until it is all powdered. Medaglia d'Oro instant espresso is finely powdered and works very well. It is generally available at specialty food stores and Italian markets.

CREAM

Half-and-half has from 10½ to 18 percent butterfat. Light cream and coffee cream both have from 18 to 30 percent butterfat. Whipping cream has 30 to 36 percent. And heavy whipping cream has 36 to 40 percent.

→ To Whip Cream

Heavy cream may be whipped with an electric mixer, a rotary beater, or a large, balloon-type wire whisk (the same kind as described for beating egg whites, page 17). It will whip more easily and give better results if the cream, bowl, and beaters are cold. The bowl should be metal (but not copper), as that gets and stays colder. Place the bowl and beaters in the refrigerator or the freezer just before using them; they should be thoroughly chilled. If the room is very warm, the bowl in which you are whipping the cream should be placed in a larger bowl of ice and water.

Do not overbeat or the cream will lose its smooth texture; if you beat even more it will turn into butter. If you use an electric beater, a handy safeguard is to stop beating before the cream is completely whipped and then finish the job with a wire whisk. This allows less chance for overbeating.

EGGS

These recipes are all based on the use of large eggs, or occasionally extra-large or jumbo.

If directions call for adding whole eggs one at a time, they may all be cracked open ahead of time into one container and poured into the other ingredients, approximately one at a time. Do not crack eggs directly into the batter — you wouldn't know if a piece of shell had been included.

→ To Separate Eggs

A new bride, when faced with the direction "separate eggs," placed them carefully on the table about 4 inches apart, and wondered how far they should be from one another...

Eggs separate best (that is, the yolks separate most readily from the whites) when they are cold. Place three small bowls in front of you, one for the whites and the second for the yolks. The third may not be needed, but if you should break the yolk when opening an egg, just drop the whole thing into the third bowl and save it for some other use. When

cracking the shell it is important not to use too much pressure or you will break the yolk at the same time.

Some cooks open the egg directly onto the palm of a hand and let the white run through their fingers into a bowl while the yolk remains in their hand. But the most popular method is to tap the side of the egg firmly on the edge of a bowl to crack the shell. Then, holding the egg in both hands, separate the two halves of the shell, letting some of the white run out into a bowl. Now pour the yolk back and forth from one half of the shell to the other, letting all of the white run out. Drop the yolk into the second bowl.

→ To Beat Egg Whites

Egg whites may be beaten with an electric mixer, a rotary eggbeater, or a large balloon-type wire whisk. Both the bowl and beater must be perfectly clean and dry. Just a bit of oil or grease will prevent the whites from inflating properly.

If you use an electric mixer or a rotary beater, be careful not to use a bowl that is too large, or the whites will be too shallow to get the full benefit of the beater's action. Also, if you use an electric hand mixer or rotary beater, keep moving it around in the bowl. If you use a mixer on a stand, use a rubber spatula frequently to push the whites from the sides of the bowl into the center. If you use a wire whisk and a bowl, an unlined copper bowl is best, though you may use glass, china, or stainless steel. Do not beat egg whites in an aluminum or plastic bowl.

The beaten whites will have a better — creamier — consistency if you beat some of the sugar into the whites as they begin to hold a shape.

Do not beat egg whites ahead of time. They must be folded in immediately after they are beaten. If it is a cake that you are making, it must then be placed in the oven right away.

Do not overbeat the whites or they will become dry and you won't be able to fold them in without losing the air you have beaten in. Beat only until they hold a shape or a point — "stiff but not dry."

FLOUR

With only a few exceptions, these recipes call for *sifted* flour. This means that it should be sifted immediately before it is measured. If the flour is not sifted, or if it is sifted long before it is used, it packs down and 1 cup is liable to contain a few spoonfuls more than 1 cup of flour that has been sifted immediately before measuring.

→ To Sift Flour

If you have one, use a double or triple sifter (which forces flour through multiple layers of fine mesh); otherwise sift the flour twice using a fine-mesh sieve. Sift onto a piece of wax paper or baking parchment, sifting a bit more than you will need. Use a metal measuring cup. Spoon the sifted flour lightly into the cup. Do not shake the cup or pack the flour down; just scrape any excess off the top with a metal spatula or any flat-sided implement. It is not necessary to wash a flour sifter, just shake it out firmly and store in a plastic bag.

SUGARS

When sugar is called for in these recipes, unless otherwise stated, it means granulated white sugar.

Sugar should be measured in the same metal cups as those recommended for flour. If granulated sugar is lumpy it should be strained before use. Brown sugar and confectioners' sugar are best strained also. (Hard lumps in brown sugar will not disappear in mixing or baking.) Unlike flour, sugars may all be strained ahead of time and you may do several pounds at once. Use a very large strainer set over a large bowl and press the sugar through with your fingertips.

→ Brown Sugar

Most brown sugars are made of white granulated sugar to which molasses has been added. Dark brown has a slightly stronger flavor than light brown sugar, but they may be used interchangeably.

You can make your own brown sugar by blending together ½ cup granulated sugar with 2 tablespoons unsulphured molasses. The yield is equivalent to ½ cup brown sugar.

Brown sugar is moist; if it dries out it will harden. It should be stored airtight at room temperature. If your brown sugar has hardened, place a damp paper towel or a slice of apple inside the bag and close the package tightly for 12 hours or more.

→ Confectioners' Sugar

Confectioners' sugar and powdered sugar are exactly the same. They are both granulated sugar that has been pulverized very fine and has had about 3 percent cornstarch added to keep it in a powdery condition. Of these, 4X is the least fine and 10X is the finest; 10X is now the most common. They may be used interchangeably. Store it airtight.

NUTS

I've given weights as well as volume measure for nuts weighing over 2 ounces. If only volume is given, the weight is under 2 ounces.

→ To Store Nuts

All nuts should be stored in the freezer or refrigerator. Always bring them to room temperature before using, and smell them and taste them — rancid nuts would ruin a whole cake or an entire batch of cookies.

→ **To Blanch Nuts**

To blanch almonds: Cover almonds with boiling water. Let them stand until the water is cool enough to touch. Pick out the almonds one at a time and squeeze each one between thumb and forefinger to squirt off the skin. As each one is skinned, place it on a towel to dry. Then spread the almonds in a single layer in a shallow baking pan and bake in a 200-degree oven for half an hour or so, until they are dry. Do not let them brown. If the almonds are to be split or sliced or slivered, cut them immediately after removing the skin and bake to dry as above.

To blanch hazelnuts: Spread the hazelnuts on a rimmed cookie sheet and bake at 350 degrees for 15 minutes, or until the skins parch and begin to flake off. Then, working with a few at a time, place them on a large coarse towel (I use a terry-cloth towel). Fold part of the towel over to enclose the nuts and rub firmly against the towel. Or hold that part of the towel between both hands and roll back and forth. The handling and the texture of the towel will cause most of the skins to flake off. Pick out the nuts and discard the skins. Don't worry about the few pieces of skin that may remain. This is not as quick and easy as it sounds.

To blanch pistachios: In a small saucepan, bring a few inches of water to a boil. Drop the nuts (no more than ¼ to ½ cup at a time, as the skin is difficult to remove after the nuts have cooled) into the boiling water and let them boil for only a few seconds. They will lose their color if boiled for too long. Remove one nut and pinch the skin off with your fingers. If it slides off easily, immediately drain them all and turn them out onto a paper towel. While they are still warm, pinch off the skins. Now they may be either slivered with a small paring knife or chopped into pieces that are coarse or almost as fine as a powder, when they make a fine decoration.

→ **To Grind Nuts**

When the instructions say to grind nuts, it means that the nuts should be reduced to a powder, the consistency of coarse flour. *Chopped* nuts are much less fine and are left in visible pieces. To grind nuts in a food processor, use the metal chopping blade; you can also use a nut grinder or blender. If possible, always add some of the flour called for in the recipe. It will help to prevent the nuts from becoming oily. If the recipe does not have any flour, add some of the sugar called for. And do not overprocess.

DATES AND RAISINS

Raisins and dates must be fresh and soft — baking will not soften them. They may be softened by steaming them in a vegetable steamer or a strainer over boiling water, covered, for about 5 minutes. Dates and raisins should be stored in the refrigerator or freezer.

ORANGE AND LEMON ZEST

When grating orange or lemon zest, if your grater has a variety of shaped openings, it is best to grate the zest on the side with the small, round openings, rather than the diamond-shaped ones.

Equipment

DOUBLE BOILER

Some directions call for a double boiler, perhaps a larger or smaller one than you have. If necessary, you can create a double boiler by placing the ingredients in a heatproof bowl over a saucepan of shallow hot water. The bowl should be wide enough so that its rim rests on the rim of the saucepan and the bowl is supported above the water.

ELECTRIC MIXER

Mixing and beating in these recipes may be done with different equipment — an electric hand mixer, any type of stand mixer, or by hand. I use a stand mixer. Susan, my mother's cook for thirty-five years, beat egg whites with a tree branch, in spite of a fantastically well-equipped kitchen. In the country she picked a fresh one as she needed it; in the city, she always washed it carefully and put it away.

Because I use a stand mixer, I have given directions for beating times based on this type of mixer; a handheld mixer might take longer. If you are not using a stand mixer, when directions call for "small bowl of electric mixer," use a bowl with a 7-cup capacity. When directions call for "large bowl of electric mixer," use one with a 4-quart capacity.

Some of these recipes would be too much work without a mixer. Others, especially many of the cookies, may be made using your bare hands for creaming and mixing. Don't be afraid to use your hands.

MEASURING EQUIPMENT

Success in baking depends on many things. One of the most important is correct oven temperature. I suggest that you buy an oven thermometer, preferably a good one. Hardware stores and quality cookware stores sell them. All oven temperatures in this book are in Fahrenheit.

→ Measuring Cups

Glass measuring cups with the measurements marked on the sides are only for measuring liquids. With the cup at eye level, fill carefully to exactly the line indicated. To measure dry ingredients, use the cups that come in sets that include at least four sizes: ¼ cup, ⅓ cup, ½ cup, and 1 cup. Fill to overflowing and then scrape off the extra with a flat spatula or large knife. If you are measuring flour, do not pack it down — but do pack down brown sugar.

→ Measuring Spoons

Standard measuring spoons must be used for correct measurements. For dry ingredients, fill to overflowing and then scrape off the excess.

PASTRY BAGS

Although most bakers prefer the convenience of disposable pastry bags, canvas bags are still available online and at high-end kitchen shops. If you use canvas bags, they should be washed in hot soapy water after use, then just hung up to dry.

It is easier to work with a bag that is too large rather than one that is too small. When filling a pastry bag, unless there is someone else to hold it for you, it is generally easiest if you support the bag by placing it in a tall and wide glass or jar.

PASTRY BRUSHES

There are different types of pastry brushes. Use a good one, or the bristles will come out while you are using it. Sometimes I use an artist's watercolor brush in a large size; it is softer and there are times when I prefer it.

ROLLING PINS

If you have many occasions to use a rolling pin (and I hope you will), you really should have different sizes and shapes. Sometimes a very long, thick, and heavy one will be best; for other doughs you will want a smaller, lighter one. The French style, which is extra-long, narrow, and tapered at both ends, is especially good for rolling dough into a round shape, as for a pie crust, while the straight-sided pin is better for an oblong shape.

However, in the absence of any rolling pin at all, other things will do a fair job. Try a straight-sided bottle, tall jar, or drinking glass.

RUBBER SPATULAS

Rubber spatulas are almost indispensable — do not use plastic; they are not flexible enough. Use rubber spatulas for folding, for some stirring, for scraping bowls, pots, etc. I suggest that you have several. Most spatulas manufactured now are synthetic and heatproof.

TURNTABLE OR LAZY SUSAN

If you ice a cake — either occasionally or often — you will be able to do a much better job (it will be smooth and professional-looking in no time) if you have a cake-decorating turntable. You will be glad if you

do. If you don't have one now, you will thank me if I influence you to get one. You will say, "Wow — this is a joy — how did I get along without it — why didn't you tell me sooner?"

A cake-decorating turntable allows a cake to rotate freely as you decorate it. Not that you can't ice a cake without it, but it will not look the same. It works on the same principle as a lazy Susan and, although a lazy Susan can be used in place of a turntable, it usually does not turn quite so easily.

Turntables are available at specialty kitchen equipment shops and at restaurant and bakery suppliers. They do not have to be expensive. The thing to look for is one that turns very easily. There is no reason why a turntable, if it is not abused, should not last a lifetime or two.

I put the cake on a cake plate and then put the plate on the turntable.

First put the icing on freely just to cover the cake. Then hold a long, narrow metal spatula in one hand, with the blade at about a 30-degree angle against the side or the top of the cake. With your other hand, slowly rotate the turntable. Hold the spatula still as the cake turns and in a few seconds you will have a smooth, sleek, neat-looking cake. It is fun. And exciting.

I also use the turntable when trimming and then fluting the edge of pie crust (you will love using it for this).

Techniques

FOLDING

Many recipes call for folding beaten egg whites and/or whipped cream into another mixture. The whites and/or cream have air beaten into them, and folding rather than mixing is done in order to retain the air.

This is an important step and should be done with care. The knack of doing it well comes with practice and concentration. Remember that you want to incorporate the mixtures without losing any air. That means handling them as little as possible.

If one of the mixtures is heavy, first actually stir in a bit of the lighter mixture. Then, with a rubber spatula (or occasionally on the lowest speed of an electric mixer), gradually fold the remaining light mixture into the heavier mixture as follows:

Place some of the light mixture on top. With a rubber spatula, rounded side down, cut down through the center to the bottom, then toward you against the bottom of the bowl, then up against the side, and finally out over the top, bringing the heavier ingredients from the bottom over the top. Rotate the bowl slightly with your other hand. Repeat, cutting with the rounded side of the spatula down, rotating the bowl a bit after making each cut. Continue only until both mixtures are combined. Try to make every motion count; do not handle any more than necessary.

TO PREPARE A CAKE PAN

To grease a pan: I use butter, which I spread on the pan with a piece of crumpled wax paper or plastic wrap. Occasionally I also spray the buttered pan with nonstick cooking oil spray.

To dust a pan: For most recipes (but not all), I prefer to coat the buttered pan with bread crumbs rather than flour, because in those recipes there is less chance of sticking if you use crumbs rather than flour. Put a few spoonfuls of crumbs (or flour, when specified) into the buttered pan. Holding the pan over a piece of paper, tilt it in all directions. Tap the pan and shake it back and forth until it is completely coated. Invert the pan over the paper and shake out the excess crumbs or flour. It should be a thin, even coating. Use unseasoned bread crumbs, or make your own.

To dust a pan for a dark cake: It is best to use dark crumbs or dark flour. Simply mix enough unsweetened cocoa powder into fine dry bread crumbs or flour to give the mixture a medium-brown color. It is handy to keep a jar of these already mixed. They last well.

To make homemade bread crumbs: Use sliced white bread with or without the crusts. Place the slices in a single layer on cookie sheets and bake in a 225-degree oven until the bread is completely dry and crisp. (If the bread is so stale that it is completely dry, it is not necessary to bake it). Break the slices into coarse pieces and grind them in a food processor or blender until the crumbs are rather fine, but not as fine as powder. Strain the crumbs through a coarse strainer and return any chunks to the processor and repeat. Store bread crumbs in an airtight container.

To line a pan with parchment: Some recipes call for using baking parchment to line pans. Baking parchment has been coated on both sides with silicone to prevent sticking. It comes in sheets or in a roll and is available in hardware stores and most kitchen shops. To line a pan, place the pan right side up on the paper and trace around it. If it is a tube pan, stick the pencil into the tube and trace the opening. Cut the paper with scissors. After you have cut the opening for the tube, cut short lines radiating from the tube hole about ½ inch deep and ¼ inch apart to ensure a smooth fit.

BAKING A CAKE

The minute you put the cake into the oven, set a timer and write down the time that it should be finished. Good insurance.

It is important not to overbake cakes, or they become dry. There are several ways to test for doneness, but the tests vary with different cakes. (All of the recipes here indicate which test or tests to use.) Some cakes will come slightly away from the sides of the pan when done, the top of others will spring back when touched lightly with your fingertip, while others must be tested with a cake tester or a toothpick. Insert it gently straight down into the middle of the cake, going all the way to the pan. If it comes out clean, the cake is done. In most cases, if some moist batter clings to the tester, the cake needs to be baked longer. Test in two or three places to be sure.

FREEZING A CAKE

All of the cakes in this book may be frozen before icing (individual layers should be wrapped separately or they will stick together), and most of them can also be frozen after, except where indicated in individual recipes (for instance, 7-Minute Icing doesn't freeze). Iced cakes should be frozen unwrapped and then, when firm, wrapped airtight — plastic wrap is best for this. If you freeze a cake on a plate and then want to remove it from the plate to wrap it, be sure to put wax paper or baking parchment between the cake and the plate or else the cake will stick.

Having frozen every freezable recipe in this collection, I find that contrary to general opinion it is better to thaw iced cakes *before* removing the wrapping. They sweat while thawing. If they have been unwrapped the moisture collects on the cake. If they have not been unwrapped, the moisture collects on the outside of the wrapping.

FREEZING COOKIES

Most cookies freeze quite well. It is always extremely handy (I think it is a luxury) to have cookies in the freezer for unexpected company; they usually thaw quickly, and many can be served frozen direct from the freezer.

(Almost always, when I need a gift for someone, my first thought is cookies. And if they are in the freezer, individually wrapped, all I have to do is plan some attractive packaging for them.)

The same rule about thawing cakes applies to cookies — thaw before unwrapping.

Any cake or cookies that may be frozen may be thawed and refrozen — even several times. I do it often. I would rather refreeze it immediately than let it stand around and get stale.

Label the packages in your freezer — if not, you might wind up with a freezer full of UFOs (Unidentified Frozen Objects).

PREPARING A CAKE PLATE

When you are ready to ice a cake, begin by tearing off a 10-inch length of wax paper or baking parchment. Fold it crossways into four parts, then cut through the folds with a knife, making four 10 x 3-inch strips. Place them in a square on the cake plate, and put the cake on top, making sure the entire edge is touching paper. As soon as the cake is iced remove the paper, pulling each strip out by a narrow end and leaving the cake plate clean.

Using Ingredients

→ To Bring Ingredients to Room Temperature
In individual recipes I have indicated the very few times I actually bring ingredients to room temperature before using. Otherwise they may be used right out of the refrigerator. If butter is too hard, cut it into small pieces, and let it stand only until it can be worked with.

→ To Add Dry Ingredients Alternately with Liquid
Always begin and end with dry ingredients. The procedure is generally to add about one-third of the dry ingredients, half the liquid, the second third of the dry, the rest of the liquid, and finally the last third of the dry.

Use the lowest speed on an electric mixer for this. After each addition mix only until smooth. If your mixer is the type that allows for a rubber spatula to be used while it is in motion, help the blending along by using the rubber spatula to scrape around the sides of the bowl. If the mixer does not have the room, or if it is the handheld kind, stop it frequently and scrape the bowl with the spatula.

A Final Word

I once put a cake in the oven and then realized that I had forgotten to use the baking powder that the recipe called for. I learned the hard way that it is necessary to organize all the ingredients listed in a recipe — line them up in the order they are called for — before you actually start mixing. As you use an ingredient, set it aside. That way, nothing should be left on the work surface when you are through. A quick look during and after mixing will let you know if something was left out.

EVERYDAY
CAKES

BLACK AND WHITE POUND CAKE

NOTES
↓
Stir the chocolate syrup before using — the heavy part settles if it has been standing for a while.
↓
Some pound cakes form a too-heavy top crust; covering the cake with foil for the first half hour of baking helps prevent this.

Makes 16 portions I have made this cake many times. And always — I can hardly wait to cut into it, because the design inside is different every time. It is a white cake with a chocolate tunnel. The tunnel is never the same. But it is always spectacular — and delicious.

- 1 pound (4 sticks) unsalted butter
- 1 tablespoon vanilla extract
- 3⅓ cups sugar
- 10 large eggs
- 4 cups *sifted* unbleached all-purpose flour
- ½ teaspoon almond extract
- ¼ teaspoon baking soda
- 2 tablespoons instant espresso or coffee powder
- ¾ cup Hershey's chocolate-flavored syrup (see Notes)

Adjust an oven rack one-third up from the bottom of oven. Preheat the oven to 350 degrees. Butter a 10 x 4-inch tube pan, line the bottom with baking parchment, butter the paper, and dust it all lightly with fine, dry bread crumbs.

In large bowl of electric mixer, beat the butter to soften it a bit. Beat in the vanilla and gradually add the sugar. Beat on moderate speed for 2 to 3 minutes, scraping the bowl with a rubber spatula as necessary.

Add the eggs, two at a time, beating after each addition until thoroughly incorporated. On lowest speed, very gradually add the flour, continuing to scrape the bowl with the rubber spatula and beating only until the flour is incorporated.

Remove half (or about 5 cups) of the batter and set aside. Mix the almond extract into the remainder and turn it into the prepared pan. Level the top by rotating pan briskly back and forth.

Return the other half of the batter to the mixer bowl and add the baking soda, instant coffee, and chocolate syrup. Beat on low speed, scraping the bowl with a rubber spatula and beating only until smooth.

Pour evenly over top of white batter. Level by rotating pan briskly back and forth. Cover the top of the pan with a piece of aluminum foil large enough to turn down loosely around the sides of the pan.

Bake for 30 minutes. Open oven door just enough to reach in and remove the aluminum foil. Continue baking for an additional 1 hour and 20 minutes. (Total baking time: 1 hour and 50 minutes.) The cake is done when the top springs back when gently pressed with fingertips and cake tester comes out dry. Remove from oven. Cool in pan for 10 to 15 minutes.

Cover with a rack and invert. Remove pan and paper. Cover with another rack and carefully invert again to finish cooling right side up.

THE KING'S POUND CAKE

Makes 2 (10-inch) loaf cakes This is adapted from a recipe that was Elvis Presley's favorite pound cake. They say he often ate a whole one (or two) all by himself. It is simply — and unequivocally — the best! Moist, tender, juicy, irresistible. With a smooth, fine, silky texture. And it is easy to make and it keeps well.

- 8 ounces (2 sticks) unsalted butter
- ⅛ teaspoon mace
- ½ teaspoon salt
- 1 teaspoon baking powder
- 2 teaspoons vanilla extract

- 3 cups sugar
- 7 large eggs
- 3 cups *sifted* cake flour
- 1 cup heavy cream

NOTE

↓

Just for your interest and so you can see what a difference it makes to sift: 3 cups of unsifted cake flour equals 12 ounces...3 cups of sifted cake flour equals 9 ounces.

Adjust an oven rack one-third up from the bottom of the oven and preheat the oven to 350 degrees. You need two loaf pans that should not be dark metal, which makes this cake too dark. They should each have at least a 7-cup capacity and should measure about 10 x 3¾ x 3¼ inches. Butter the pans and dust them all over with fine, dry bread crumbs. Invert over paper to allow excess crumbs to fall out.

In the large bowl of an electric mixer, beat the butter with the mace, salt, baking powder, and vanilla until mixed. Gradually add the sugar and beat for about 5 minutes. Then beat in the eggs one or two at a time, scraping the bowl with a rubber spatula and beating only until incorporated after each addition.

Then add half of the flour and stir/fold it in with a large rubber spatula (to prevent splashing) or beat on low speed to incorporate. Gradually add the cream and stir or beat on low speed to incorporate. Add the remaining flour and stir or beat to incorporate. Finally, beat only until smooth.

Divide the batter between the two pans. Jiggle the pans just a little to slightly level the tops. (The cakes will really level themselves during baking.)

Bake for 1 hour and 15 or 20 minutes, until the loaves begin to come away from the sides of the pans.

Let the loaves cool in the pans for 25 to 30 minutes. Then cover one pan with a cake rack. Turn pan and rack upside down. Remove pan. With your hands, very gently and carefully turn the loaf right side up. Remove the second loaf from the pan the same way. Let the loaves cool on racks.

BUTTERMILK SPICE CAKE

Makes 12 to 16 portions To make your own buttermilk, warm 1½ cups of regular milk over low heat until room temperature (about 70 degrees). Place 1½ tablespoons of lemon juice in a 2-cup glass measuring cup. Then fill it to the 1½-cup line with the room-temperature milk, stir, and let stand for 10 minutes. Now you have 1½ cups buttermilk.

NOTE
↓

Do not freeze this cake after it has been iced—the icing will become wet when thawed.

3 cups *sifted* cake flour

1½ teaspoons baking soda

1 teaspoon salt

1½ teaspoons ground cinnamon

¾ teaspoon ground nutmeg

¼ teaspoon ground cloves

6 ounces (1½ sticks) unsalted butter

1 teaspoon vanilla extract

1¼ cups firmly packed light brown sugar

1 cup granulated sugar

3 large eggs

1½ cups buttermilk

Finely grated zest of 1 lemon

Adjust rack one-third up from the bottom of the oven. Preheat oven to 350 degrees. Butter a 13 x 9 x 2-inch pan and dust it all lightly with fine, dry bread crumbs.

Sift together the flour, baking soda, salt, cinnamon, nutmeg, and cloves. Set aside. In large bowl of electric mixer, beat the butter to soften it a bit. Add the vanilla and then, gradually, both sugars and beat for 1 to 2 minutes. Add the eggs individually, scraping the bowl as necessary with a rubber spatula and beating well after each. On lowest speed, alternately add sifted dry ingredients in three additions and buttermilk in two additions, scraping the bowl with the spatula and beating only until smooth after each addition. Remove from mixer and stir in lemon zest.

Turn into pan and spread level.

Bake for 50 to 55 minutes, until the top springs back when lightly touched and the cake begins to come away from sides of pan.

Let cake cool in the pan on a rack for about 15 minutes. Cut around sides to release. Cover with a rack or a cookie sheet and invert. Remove pan. Cover with a rack and invert again to finish cooling.

When the cake is completely cool, prepare the icing.

Brown Sugar Icing

1 cup firmly packed light brown sugar

⅓ cup heavy cream

2 tablespoons unsalted butter

Pinch of salt

½ teaspoon vanilla extract

In a medium saucepan over moderately low heat, stir the brown sugar and cream to slowly dissolve the sugar, brushing down the sides occasionally with a wet brush to remove any sugar granules. Stirring constantly, slowly bring the syrup to a boil and let boil for exactly 1 minute. Transfer to small bowl of electric mixer. Add the butter and stir to melt. Add the salt and vanilla and beat until creamy and slightly thickened. It will still be warm.

Immediately pour the icing over the cake and, with a long, narrow metal spatula, spread to cover.

JOAN'S PUMPKIN LOAF

Makes 14 to 16 slices The first time I ate this, there was also a huge tray piled high with California crabs and a marvelous string bean salad, and although the whole meal was memorable, I especially remember getting up for more and more slices of this pumpkin loaf that made me an addict with the first bite. It is so good, there ought to be a law...

My neighbor uses this recipe to make mini muffins for Thanksgiving. They bake for about 15 minutes, or until a toothpick comes out clean.

2½ cups *sifted* unbleached all-purpose flour

2 teaspoons baking soda

½ teaspoon salt

1½ teaspoons ground cinnamon

1 teaspoon ground ginger

½ teaspoon ground nutmeg

¼ teaspoon ground cloves

2 large eggs

2 cups granulated sugar or firmly packed light or dark brown sugar

½ cup canola oil

16 ounces (2 cups) canned pumpkin (solid packed)

8 ounces (1 cup) pitted dates, each date cut into 2 or 3 pieces — no smaller

4 ounces (generous 1 cup) walnuts, chopped or broken into medium-size pieces

Adjust an oven rack one-third up from the bottom of the oven and preheat oven to 350 degrees. Butter a 10 x 5 x 3-inch loaf pan, or any other loaf pan that has a 10-cup capacity, measured to the very top of the pan; dust the pan with fine, dry bread crumbs and tap over a piece of paper to shake out excess crumbs.

Sift together the flour, baking soda, salt, cinnamon, ginger, nutmeg, and cloves and set aside.

It is not necessary to use an electric mixer for this although you can if you wish (I do). In any large bowl, beat the eggs just to mix. Add the sugar and oil and beat lightly just to mix. Mix in the pumpkin and then the dates. Now add the sifted dry ingredients and stir, mix, or beat only until they are smoothly incorporated. Stir in the nuts.

Turn into the prepared pan and smooth the top.

Bake for 1½ hours, until a cake tester gently inserted into the middle comes out just barely clean.

Cool in the pan for 15 minutes. Cover with a rack, turn over the rack and the pan, remove the pan, and then turn the loaf right side up again on a rack. Let stand until cool.

Now if you can wait, wrap the loaf in plastic wrap and refrigerate for a day or two, or freeze.

To serve, cut into slices a generous ½ inch thick. If you do not wait for the loaf to age a day or two, it is best to cut it with a serrated bread knife.

CHOCOLATE INTRIGUE

Makes 2 small loaves, about 8 portions each Gloria and Jacques Pépin and some of their friends came to our home for a visit one afternoon while I was working on this recipe. They all said yes, they would like some. When it was served they all raved about it, more than I expected since it is a plain little loaf. They all asked what the exotic flavor was. I asked them to guess. Jacques guessed many spices — a mixture of spices — some of which I had never heard of. And they never did guess what it was. When I told them that it was just a little bit of black pepper, they thought I was kidding; they thought that there must be more to it. Incidentally, they all loved the cake and had seconds.

It is a moist cake with a fine texture and an extremely generous amount of chocolate. It keeps well (preferably in the refrigerator), slices beautifully, and is quick and easy to make.

You need two small loaf pans, preferably 8 x 4 x 2½-inch pans with a 5-cup capacity, but I have also used 8½ x 4½ x 2¾-inch pans with a 6-cup capacity; the cakes were equally delicious in the larger pans, although not quite as high.

3 ounces semisweet chocolate	¼ cup unsweetened cocoa powder (preferably Dutch-process)	4 ounces (1 stick) unsalted butter
2 ounces unsweetened chocolate	1½ teaspoons baking powder	1½ teaspoons vanilla extract
1 tablespoon instant espresso or coffee powder	1 teaspoon salt	2 cups sugar
1⅓ cups boiling water	½ teaspoon finely ground black pepper (preferably freshly ground)	3 large eggs
1¾ cups *sifted* unbleached all-purpose flour		OPTIONAL: Bittersweet Chocolate Sauce with Cocoa (page 38) and/or ice cream

Adjust an oven rack one-third up from the bottom and preheat the oven to 325 degrees. Butter two 5-cup loaf pans (see headnote) and dust all over with chocolate bread crumbs (see Notes on next page), tap over paper to remove excess crumbs, and set aside.

In a small saucepan over moderate heat, place both chocolates with the espresso or coffee and boiling water. Whisk frequently until the chocolates are melted and the mixture is smooth. Transfer to a small pitcher that will be easy to pour from (i.e., a 2-cup measuring cup) and set aside to cool to lukewarm.

Sift together the flour, cocoa, baking powder, salt, and pepper and set aside.

continues ↘

In the large bowl of an electric mixer, beat the butter until soft. Beat in the vanilla and then gradually add the sugar and beat well until incorporated. Add the eggs and beat until smooth. Then, on low speed, alternately add the sifted dry ingredients in three additions and the chocolate mixture in two additions. Scrape the bowl as necessary and beat until smooth.

Pour the mixture (which will be very liquid) into the prepared pans.

Bake both pans on the same rack for 1 hour and 10 to 15 minutes; cover the pans loosely with foil after about 40 minutes of baking. Bake until a cake tester gently inserted comes out clean; since the cake forms a hard crust on top, it is best to insert the cake tester on the side of the top edge, where there is no crust.

Let the cakes cool in the pans for about 15 minutes. Then cover each pan with a rack, invert the pan and rack, remove pan, and let the cake cool upside down (the bottom of the cake is moist and tender at this stage).

It is best to wrap the cakes in plastic wrap and refrigerate them for several hours or overnight.

To serve: Cover the top of the cake with a generous layer of unsweetened cocoa powder, sprinkling it on through a wide but fine strainer. Refrigerate.

Work next to the sink so that you can hold the knife under hot running water before making each cut. With a long and sharp knife, cut the cake into small portions. Since it is so light and delicate, work carefully. With a wide metal spatula, transfer the pieces to cake plates.

Serve plain. Or, as an important dessert, serve with Bittersweet Chocolate Sauce with Cocoa (page 38) and, if you wish, ice cream as well. Pour the sauce on one side of a portion of cake and place the ice cream on the other side.

NOTES
↓

To coat a pan for a dark cake it is best to use dark crumbs or dark flour. Simply mix enough unsweetened cocoa powder into fine dry bread crumbs or flour to give the mixture a medium-brown color. It is handy to keep a jar of these already mixed. They last well.

↓

To serve this after freezing, thaw it covered in the refrigerator for at least 5 or 6 hours.

continues ↘

Bittersweet Chocolate Sauce with Cocoa

Makes 1½ cups

1 cup strained unsweetened cocoa powder (preferably Dutch-process)

¾ cup sugar

1¼ teaspoons instant espresso or coffee powder

Pinch of salt

1 cup boiling water

1 tablespoon plus 1½ teaspoons dark rum

In a heavy 5- to 6-cup saucepan, stir the cocoa, sugar, espresso or coffee, and salt to mix. Add the water and stir with a wire whisk.

Place over moderate heat and stir and scrape the pan constantly with a rubber spatula until the mixture comes to a boil. Immediately reduce the heat to low and let barely simmer, stirring and scraping the pan constantly with a rubber spatula, for 3 minutes.

Remove from the heat. Strain. Stir in the rum. Place in a covered jar and refrigerate.

Check the sauce ahead of time. If it has become too thick to serve, let it stand at room temperature and stir it a bit.

Pour the sauce into a pitcher and serve quickly while it is cold.

86-PROOF CHOCOLATE CAKE

Makes 12 to 24 portions This is an especially moist and luscious dark chocolate cake, generously flavored with bourbon and coffee. Sensational! It is made in a fancy pan and is served without icing. I have made this at demonstrations all around the country. It is one of my favorite cakes to teach because people can't wait to make it.

5 ounces unsweetened chocolate	Boiling water	2 cups sugar
	Cold water	3 large eggs
2 cups *sifted* unbleached all-purpose flour	½ cup bourbon (or rum, Cognac, or Scotch whiskey)	OPTIONAL: additional bourbon
1 teaspoon baking soda		OPTIONAL: confectioners' sugar
¼ teaspoon salt	8 ounces (2 sticks) unsalted butter	
¼ cup instant espresso or coffee powder	1 teaspoon vanilla extract	

Adjust rack one-third up from bottom of the oven and preheat oven to 325 degrees. You will need a 9-inch Bundt pan (this is the smaller size; it is called a mini Bundt pan) or any other fancy tube pan with a 10-cup capacity. Butter the pan (even if it is a nonstick pan) and dust the whole inside of the pan with fine, dry bread crumbs. Invert over a piece of paper and tap lightly to shake out excess crumbs. Set the pan aside.

Place the chocolate in the top of a small double boiler over warm water on low heat. Cover and cook only until melted; then remove the top of the double boiler and set it aside, uncovered, to cool slightly.

Sift together the flour, baking soda, and salt and set aside.

In a 2-cup glass measuring cup, dissolve the coffee in a bit of boiling water. Add cold water to the 1½-cup line. Add the bourbon. Set aside.

Cream the butter in the large bowl of an electric mixer. Add the vanilla and sugar and beat to mix well. Add the eggs one at a time, beating until smooth after each addition. Add the chocolate and beat until smooth.

Then, on low speed, alternately add the sifted dry ingredients in three additions and the coffee mixture in two additions, adding the liquid very gradually to avoid splashing, and scraping the bowl with a rubber spatula after each addition. Be sure to beat until smooth after each addition, especially after the last. It will be a thin mixture.

continues ⌄

Pour into the prepared pan. Rotate the pan a bit briskly, first in one direction, then in the other, to level the top. (In a mini Bundt pan the batter will almost reach the top of the pan, but it is OK — it will not run over, and you will have a beautifully high cake.)

Bake for 1 hour and 10 or 15 minutes. Test by inserting a cake tester into the middle of the cake and bake only until the tester comes out clean and dry.

Cool in the pan for about 15 minutes. Then cover with a rack and invert. Remove the pan, sprinkle the cake with a bit of optional bourbon, and leave the cake upside down on the rack to cool.

Before serving, if you wish, sprinkle the top with confectioners' sugar through a fine strainer.

This is a simple, no-icing cake, wonderful as is. Or with a spoonful of vanilla- or bourbon-flavored whipped cream.

CHOCOLATE POUND CAKE

Makes 12 to 16 (or more) portions If they had a chocolate pound cake Olympics, this would win a gold medal. It is almost five pounds of dense, dark, delicious chocolate pound cake. And the chocolate icing is as smooth and shiny as a mirror.

NOTE

Pound cakes should be served in thin slices, two or three slices to a portion. It is best to let pound cake stand overnight before slicing. When completely cool, wrap in plastic wrap or aluminum foil and let stand at room temperature.

3 cups *sifted* unbleached all-purpose flour

1 tablespoon baking powder

½ teaspoon salt

8 ounces (2 sticks) unsalted butter

1 tablespoon vanilla extract

½ teaspoon almond extract

2 tablespoons plus 1 teaspoon instant espresso or coffee powder

3 cups sugar

3 large eggs

1 cup strained unsweetened cocoa powder (preferably Dutch-process)

1¾ cups milk

CHOCOLATE ICING

9 ounces sweet or semisweet chocolate

4½ ounces (1 stick plus 1 tablespoon) unsalted butter, at room temperature

Adjust oven rack one-third up from the bottom of the oven. Preheat oven to 350 degrees.

Butter a 10 x 4-inch tube pan, line the bottom with baking parchment cut to fit, butter the paper, and coat lightly with fine, dry bread crumbs.

Sift together the flour, baking powder, and salt. Set aside.

In large bowl of electric mixer, beat the butter to soften it a bit. Add the vanilla and almond extracts, the instant coffee, and then, gradually, the sugar. Scrape sides and bottom of bowl with a rubber spatula as necessary all during mixing. Beat in the eggs one at a time, beating after each until it is incorporated. On lowest speed, gradually add cocoa. Alternately add milk and sifted dry ingredients, each in three additions; in this case, start with the milk since the batter is rather heavy at this stage. Beat only until smooth after each addition. Finish as usual with dry ingredients. Turn into prepared pan. Jiggle the pan briskly several times to level top.

Bake for 1½ hours, or until the top springs back when lightly touched and the cake comes away slightly from the sides of the pan. Let the cake cool in the pan on a rack for 10 to 15 minutes. Cover with a rack and invert. Remove pan and paper. Let cool.

When completely cool, prepare the icing.

continues ↘

For the icing:

Break up the chocolate and place it in the top of a small double boiler over hot water on medium heat. When it is almost completely melted, remove the top of the double boiler and stir the chocolate with a small wire whisk until smooth. Add the butter, 1 to 2 tablespoons at a time, stirring with the whisk until smooth after each addition. The icing might thicken with the first few additions of butter, but then it will thin out as the remainder is added.

Place four strips of wax paper or baking parchment around the outer edge of a cake plate. Place the cake on it.

Pour the icing over the top, letting some run down the sides. With a long, narrow metal offset spatula, quickly spread over the sides first, and then the top.

Remove wax paper strips by pulling each one out by a narrow end.

SOUR-CREAM BLACK-FUDGE LOAF CAKE

NOTE

↓

To make chocolate bread crumbs, simply mix enough unsweetened cocoa powder into fine dry bread crumbs or flour to give the mixture a medium-brown color. It is handy to keep jars of both regular and chocolate crumbs already mixed. They last well.

Makes 1 (10-inch) loaf cake When I was testing recipes for my first book, my daughter would peer into the kitchen and announce, "There's no dinner tonight. Mother's cooking!"

This recipe is for serious chocoholics.

1 cup plus 3 tablespoons *sifted* unbleached all-purpose flour

3 tablespoons unsweetened cocoa powder (preferably Dutch-process)

1 tablespoon baking powder

½ teaspoon salt

3½ ounces semisweet chocolate

2 ounces unsweetened chocolate

2 tablespoons instant espresso or coffee powder

2 tablespoons boiling water

4 ounces (1 stick) unsalted butter

1 teaspoon vanilla extract

1 cup firmly packed light brown sugar

2 large eggs

½ cup sour cream

SOUR CREAM–CHOCOLATE ICING

6 ounces semisweet chocolate

Pinch of salt

½ cup sour cream

Adjust a rack one-third up from the bottom of the oven and preheat the oven to 350 degrees. Butter an 8-cup loaf pan, preferably one that is long and narrow as opposed to one that is short and wide. The pan that measures 10 x 3¾ x 3¼ inches makes a beautifully shaped cake. Dust the pan with chocolate bread crumbs (see Note), tap over paper to remove excess crumbs, and set aside.

Sift together the flour, cocoa, baking powder, and salt and set aside.

Place both of the chocolates in the top of a small double boiler over hot water on moderate heat. Cover the pan with a folded paper towel (to absorb steam) and then the pan lid. Cook until the chocolate is about melted, then remove the top of the double boiler and stir until melted and smooth and set aside.

In a small cup, stir the espresso or coffee with the boiling water and set aside.

In the large bowl of an electric mixer, beat the butter until soft. Beat in the vanilla and

continues ↘

sugar and then the eggs, one at a time. Add the chocolate (which may still be slightly warm) and beat to mix. On low speed, beat in half of the sifted dry ingredients, then the sour cream and espresso or coffee, and finally the remaining dry ingredients. Scrape the sides of the bowl as necessary with a rubber spatula and beat only until smooth.

Turn into the prepared pan. Smooth the top. Bake for about 1 hour and 5 minutes, until a cake tester gently inserted in the middle comes out dry. Remove from the oven and let stand for 10 minutes. While standing, the cake will settle down slightly, but it will be OK.

Cover the pan with a rack, turn the pan and rack upside down, remove the pan, and let the cake stand upside down to cool.

Prepare a serving board or flat tray as follows. Cut a length of wax paper slightly longer than the cake. Fold the paper in half lengthwise and cut on the fold. Then fold each piece in half lengthwise. Place the two strips on the serving bowl or the tray, folded edges meeting in the center of the board or tray. Carefully transfer the cake to the lined board or tray.

Prepare the icing:

Place the chocolate in the top of a small double boiler over hot water on moderate heat, cover the pan with a folded paper towel (to absorb steam) and then with the pan lid, and cook until the chocolate is almost melted. Stir until melted and smooth. Remove the top of the double boiler and stir in the salt and the sour cream.

Spread the icing over the top and sides of the cake. Either smooth the icing with a long, narrow metal offset spatula or form it into swirls with the underside of a spoon. Or, if you wish, reserve some of the icing, smooth the balance all over the cake, and then, with a pastry bag and a fluted tube, decorate the cake as you wish.

Remove the strips of paper by slowly pulling each one out by a narrow end.

CALIFORNIA CARROT CAKE

Makes 16 portions Divine, moist, rich, solid, tantalizing, loaded with goodies, and as pretty as a picture (made in a fancy tube pan). You will love this. Make it as a dessert, a coffee cake, or a wonderful gift.

1½ cups *sifted* whole wheat flour

½ cup *unsifted* unbleached all-purpose white flour

2 teaspoons baking soda

2 teaspoons ground cinnamon

¾ teaspoon ground nutmeg

½ teaspoon ground allspice

½ teaspoon ground cloves

½ teaspoon salt

¾ pound carrots (to make 2 cups shredded)

3 large eggs

¾ cup canola oil

¾ cup buttermilk

1½ cups honey

1 (8-ounce) can (1 cup) crushed pineapple (packed in natural juice)

5 ounces (1 cup) raisins

4 ounces (generous 1 cup) walnuts, chopped or broken into medium-size pieces

OPTIONAL: confectioners' sugar

Adjust a rack one-third up in the oven and preheat the oven to 375 degrees. Butter a fancy-shaped 12-cup tube pan (I use the 10-inch Bundt pan) — butter it even if it has a nonstick finish — and dust it all over with fine, dry bread crumbs. Invert over a piece of paper and tap to shake out excess crumbs. Set aside.

Sift together the whole wheat and white flours, baking soda, cinnamon, nutmeg, allspice, cloves, and salt. Set aside.

Wash the carrots (do not peel them) and cut off the ends. Shred the carrots with a fine shredder — you can use a manual grater (on a 4-sided metal grater use the small round openings) or a food processor (use the fine shredding disk). You should have 2 cups, firmly packed. Set aside.

In a really large mixing bowl, beat or whisk the eggs just to mix. Gradually beat in the oil, buttermilk, and honey. Then stir in the carrots, pineapple (with its juice), raisins, and nuts.

Add the sifted dry ingredients all at once and stir/mix only until the dry ingredients are moistened. (Do not overmix; if the bowl is large enough and if you stir with a large rubber spatula, you will not overmix.) It will be a very liquid (thin) mixture.

Turn into the prepared pan and rotate the pan a bit to smooth the top.

Bake for 45 to 50 minutes, until a cake tester inserted in the middle comes out clean.

Let the cake cool in the pan for about 15 minutes. Then cover it with a rack, hold the pan and rack firmly together, and invert. Remove the pan and let the cake stand until it is completely cool.

Carefully, with two wide metal spatulas, transfer the cake to a plate. Before serving, sprinkle the top generously with the optional confectioners' sugar, shaking it through a fine strainer held over the top of the cake.

APPLE KUCHEN

Makes about 8 portions This recipe is from my first book. *Kuchen* is German for cake, and this is a fine cake with a crunchy caramelized apple topping and a beautiful appearance, despite its simplicity. It is perfect for a sweet breakfast or as a treat in the afternoon with a cup of coffee.

BATTER

⅓ cup light or dark raisins

1¼ cups *sifted* unbleached all-purpose flour

1½ teaspoons baking powder

½ teaspoon salt

¼ cup sugar

2 ounces (½ stick) unsalted butter

1 large egg

¼ cup milk

1 teaspoon vanilla extract

2½ ounces (¾ cup) walnuts, chopped into medium-size pieces

FILLING

4 medium-large Golden Delicious apples

2 ounces (½ stick) unsalted butter

¼ cup sugar

1½ teaspoons ground cinnamon

APRICOT GLAZE

½ cup apricot preserves

2 tablespoons sugar

For the batter:

Adjust rack to center of oven. Preheat oven to 400 degrees. Butter a 13 x 9 x 2-inch baking pan.

Place the raisins in a small strainer over a saucepan of shallow boiling water. Cover and let steam for 3 to 5 minutes. Remove from heat and set aside.

Sift together the flour, baking powder, salt, and sugar into a mixing bowl. With a pastry blender, cut in the butter until the mixture resembles coarse crumbs.

In a cup or a small bowl, stir the egg just to mix and then stir in the milk.

Add the egg, milk, and vanilla to the flour mixture, stirring with a fork only until the dry ingredients are thoroughly moistened.

Spread the batter evenly in the prepared pan — it will be a thin layer. Sprinkle with the raisins and nuts and set aside.

For the filling:

Peel, quarter, and core the apples. Cut each quarter into about six very thin wedges. Place them, overlapping, in three rows down the length of the cake. If there is a space between the rows, it may be filled in with additional slices placed in the opposite direction. If the apples are small, use one or two more and make four rows of slices.

Melt the butter and brush it over the apples. Mix the sugar and cinnamon, and sprinkle over the butter. Cover the pan loosely with a cookie sheet or a large piece of aluminum foil.

continues ⬎

Bake for 35 minutes, removing cookie sheet or foil for the last 5 minutes.

For the glaze:

Strain the preserves and stir in the sugar. In a small saucepan over moderate heat, bring the mixture to a boil, stirring constantly. Boil, stirring, for 3 minutes. Immediately brush over the apples.

Serve while still warm or at room temperature, but it is best while very fresh.

Cut cake into eight to ten portions. With a wide metal offset spatula, transfer portions to a cake platter.

WEST INDIES GINGER CAKE

Makes 1 (9-inch) loaf cake Gingerbread is said to be the oldest sweet cake in the world; *The Dictionary of Gastronomy* puts its creation at about 2800 BC in Greece and it has remained rather popular ever since. This Jamaican cake is not the usual ginger cake; this is made with chunks of preserved ginger (delicious), walnuts, honey, and sour cream. Serve it as a tea or coffee cake or as a dessert. It keeps well, it freezes well, it is a wonderful gift, it is a wonderful whatever.

2 cups *sifted* unbleached all-purpose flour

1 teaspoon baking soda

1 teaspoon ground ginger

½ teaspoon salt

8½ ounces (about ⅔ cup) preserved ginger with its syrup

4 ounces (1 stick) unsalted butter

½ cup firmly packed light brown sugar

2 large eggs, separated

½ cup sour cream

½ cup honey

3½ ounces (1 cup) walnuts, chopped into medium-small pieces

Adjust a rack one-third up from the bottom of the oven and preheat oven to 350 degrees. Butter a 9 x 5 x 3-inch pan, or any pan of a similar shape with an 8-cup capacity. Dust it all with fine, dry bread crumbs, and tap to shake out excess over a piece of paper. Set aside.

Sift together the flour, baking soda, ginger, and salt and set aside. Place pieces of the preserved ginger on a plate or board and, with a small, sharp knife, cut them one at a time into pieces ¼ to ⅓ inch in diameter (no smaller). Mix together the cut ginger and its syrup and set aside.

In the large bowl of an electric mixer, beat the butter until it is soft. Add the sugar and beat well for a few minutes. Add the egg yolks and beat well. On low speed, mix in about a third of the sifted dry ingredients, then all the sour cream, another third of the dry ingredients, all the honey, and then the remaining dry ingredients, mixing only until incorporated after each addition. Remove from the mixer and stir in the ginger, syrup, and nuts.

In a small bowl, beat the egg whites only until they hold a shape but not until they are stiff or dry. Fold them into the batter.

Turn the batter into the prepared pan, smooth the top, and bake for 1 hour and 15 minutes, until the top springs back when it is lightly pressed with a fingertip.

Cakes made with honey tend to become too dark on the top: about 20 minutes before this cake is done (or when it has formed a top crust, and it begins to look too dark), cover loosely with foil.

Let the cake cool in the pan for 15 minutes. Then cover it with a rack. Hold the pan and rack carefully together and turn them over, remove the pan, and very carefully (the cake is fragile now) turn the cake right side up to cool on the rack.

When the cake has cooled, wrap it in plastic wrap and place it in the freezer or refrigerator until it is well chilled before slicing it.

THE BEST DAMN LEMON CAKE

Makes 1 (8½-inch) loaf cake I remember when my husband, Ralph, took the first bite of this. The name stuck like frosting on a cake.

½ cup blanched (skinned) whole almonds

1½ cups *sifted* unbleached all-purpose flour

1 teaspoon baking powder

¾ teaspoon salt

4 ounces (1 stick) unsalted butter

1 cup sugar

2 large eggs

½ cup milk

1 ounce (2 tablespoons) lemon extract

Finely grated zest of 2 extra-large or 3 medium lemons

GLAZE

⅓ cup plus 2 tablespoons sugar

⅓ cup fresh lemon juice

NOTE
↓

For this cake, do not use a nonstick pan, a black metal pan, or a glass pan; it should be aluminum, preferably heavy weight. And do not double the recipe and bake it in one larger pan, it is not as good — it is better to make two or more cakes in the specified 6-cup loaf pan.

Adjust a rack one-third up from the bottom of the oven and preheat oven to 350 degrees. Butter an 8½ x 4½ x 2¼-inch loaf pan with a 6-cup capacity (see Note). Dust it all with fine, dry bread crumbs, invert over a piece of paper, and tap firmly to shake out excess. Set the pan aside.

The almonds must be ground very fine. It can be done in a food processor or nut grinder. Then set them aside.

Sift together the flour, baking powder, and salt, and set aside.

In a small, heavy saucepan over low heat, melt the butter. Transfer it to the large bowl of an electric mixer. Add the sugar and beat a bit to mix. On low speed, beat in the eggs one at a time, beating only to

mix well. Then, still on low speed, add the sifted dry ingredients in three additions alternating with the milk in two additions, scraping the bowl with a rubber spatula and beating until mixed after each addition. Mix in the lemon extract.

Remove from the mixer. Stir in the grated zest and then the ground almonds. It will be a rather thin mixture. Turn it into the prepared pan.

Bake for 65 to 75 minutes, until a cake tester carefully inserted into the center of the cake, all the way to the bottom, comes out just barely clean and dry. (If the pan is long and narrow, the cake will bake in less time than if it is short and wide. During baking, the cake will form a large crack or two on the top; the crack, or cracks, will remain light in color — it is OK.)

Two or 3 minutes before the cake is done, prepare the glaze.

For the glaze:

Stir the sugar and juice in a small, heavy saucepan over moderate heat only until the sugar is dissolved; do not boil the mixture.

When the cake is removed from the oven, let it stand for 2 to 3 minutes. Then, with a brush, brush the hot glaze very gradually over the hot cake; the glaze should not be applied quickly — it should take about 5 minutes to apply it all.

Let stand until tepid, not quite completely cool. Then, gently invert the cake onto a rack. (If the cake sticks to the pan, cover it loosely with foil or wax paper, turn it upside down onto one hand, tap the bottom of the pan with your other hand, and the cake will slide out.) Turn the cake right side up.

When the cake is completely cool, wrap it in plastic wrap or foil and let stand for 12 to 24 hours before serving. Or place it in the freezer for about 2 hours, or in the refrigerator for about 4 hours before serving.

EAST 62ND STREET LEMON CAKE

NOTE
↓

I have a Key lime tree. I have made this with ½ cup Key lime juice in the glaze in place of the ⅓ cup lemon juice and it is divine. (But you should continue to use the lemon zest in the cake itself.)

Makes 10 portions There are those among you who swear the best damn lemon cake is The Best Damn Lemon Cake. I thought so too...until this recipe was sent to me by my daughter, Toni, who lived on East 62nd Street when she began to make it. When I sent this recipe to my friend Craig Claiborne, he printed it in the *New York Times*. It became amazingly popular.

Devin, the young man who took care of our swimming pool, once even baked this cake on his charcoal grill (he didn't have an oven). It came out perfectly!

3 cups *sifted* unbleached all-purpose flour	2 cups sugar	**GLAZE**
2 teaspoons baking powder	4 large eggs	⅓ cup lemon juice
½ teaspoon salt	1 cup milk	⅔ cup sugar
8 ounces (2 sticks) unsalted butter	Finely grated zest of 2 large lemons	

Adjust an oven rack one-third up from the bottom of oven. Preheat the oven to 350 degrees. Butter a plain or fancy tube pan with an 11- to 12-cup capacity and dust it lightly with fine, dry bread crumbs.

Sift together flour, baking powder, and salt and set aside. In large bowl of electric mixer, beat the butter to soften it a bit. Add the sugar and beat for 2 to 3 minutes. Beat in the eggs individually, scraping the bowl as necessary with a rubber spatula to keep mixture smooth. On lowest speed, alternately add the dry ingredients in three additions and the milk in two additions, scraping the bowl with the rubber spatula as necessary and beating only until incorporated after each addition. Remove the bowl from the mixer. Stir in lemon zest. Turn the batter into prepared pan. Level top by rotating pan briskly back and forth.

Bake for 1 hour and 5 to 10 minutes, until a cake tester comes out dry.

Let cake stand in the pan for about 5 minutes and then cover with a rack and invert. Place over a large piece of aluminum foil or wax paper.

For the glaze:

The glaze should be used immediately after it is mixed: Stir the lemon juice and sugar together and brush all over the hot cake until absorbed.

Let cake cool completely. Use two wide metal pancake turners or a cookie sheet to transfer it to a cake plate. Do not cut for at least several hours.

CHOCOLATE APPLESAUCE CAKE

Makes 12 to 14 portions A tube cake with no icing — so lusciously moist it is almost a pudding, although it holds its shape and slices beautifully. The combination of applesauce, cinnamon, and chocolate is simply wonderful — everyone loves it. It is an unusual cake and unusually good. Although this is appropriate for any time of the year, it seems to belong especially to the Thanksgiving or Christmas holiday. It is a marvelous cake to bring to someone's house as a gift.

3 ounces (⅔ cup) raisins

1½ cups *sifted* unbleached all-purpose flour

2 teaspoons baking soda

½ teaspoon salt

1 tablespoon ground cinnamon

½ teaspoon ground nutmeg

¼ cup plus 1 tablespoon unsweetened cocoa powder (preferably Dutch-process)

6 ounces (1½ sticks) unsalted butter

2 cups granulated sugar

3 large eggs

16½ ounces (scant 2 cups) sweetened or unsweetened applesauce

6 ounces (1½ cups) walnuts or pecans, chopped or broken into medium-size pieces

OPTIONAL: confectioners' sugar

Adjust rack one-third up from bottom of the oven and preheat oven to 350 degrees. Butter a one-piece plain tube pan that measures 10 inches across the top. (The standard depth of this size pan is 4 inches. The cake will not be that deep, but it is all right to use a pan that size.) Line the bottom with baking parchment or wax paper cut to fit, butter the paper, dust the inside of the pan with fine, dry bread crumbs, and invert over a piece of paper to tap out excess. Set aside.

Cover the raisins with boiling water and let stand for about 5 minutes. Then pour into a strainer and let stand with the strainer over a cup, to allow any remaining water to run off.

Sift together the flour, baking soda, salt, cinnamon, nutmeg, and cocoa and set aside.

In the large bowl of an electric mixer, cream the butter. Add the sugar and beat well. Add the eggs one at a time, beating until thoroughly incorporated after each addition. Beat at high speed for about a minute after adding the last egg.

On low speed add the sifted dry ingredients in three additions, alternating with the applesauce in two additions, scraping the bowl with a rubber spatula and beating only until thoroughly mixed after each addition. (The applesauce will make the mixture look curdled — it's all right.)

Remove from the mixer and stir in the raisins and nuts.

Turn into the prepared pan and rotate the pan a bit one way, then the other, to smooth the top.

Bake for 1 hour and 25 to 30 minutes, until the cake begins to come away from the sides of the pan and the top springs back when lightly pressed with a fingertip. (The baked cake will fill the pan only a little more than halfway — that is correct; it will be about 2½ inches high.)

Cool in the pan on a rack for about 15 minutes. Cover with a rack and invert, peel off the paper lining, and let the cake cool. During cooling, cover the cake with a rack and turn it over briefly a few times just to make sure that it doesn't stick to the rack.

If you wish, the cake may be sprinkled with confectioners' sugar pressed through a fine strainer.

This is so rich and dense that it should be cut into small slices — two small slices for a portion.

BUDAPEST COFFEE CAKE

Makes 12 portions This is one of the most popular recipes in all of my books. I have received love letters and a variety of proposals and propositions all because of this cake. Watch out.

NUT FILLING

- ¾ cup firmly packed dark brown sugar
- 1 tablespoon ground cinnamon
- 1 tablespoon unsweetened cocoa powder (preferably Dutch-process)
- 2 to 3 tablespoons currants or raisins, coarsely chopped
- 3½ ounces (1 cup) walnuts, finely chopped

CAKE BATTER

- 3 cups *sifted* unbleached all-purpose flour
- 1½ teaspoons baking powder
- 1½ teaspoons baking soda
- ½ teaspoon salt
- 6 ounces (1½ sticks) unsalted butter
- 2 teaspoons vanilla extract
- 1½ cups granulated sugar
- 3 large eggs
- 2 cups sour cream

GLAZE

- 2 cups confectioners' sugar
- 1 teaspoon vanilla extract
- 2 to 3 tablespoons hot milk

For the filling:

In a small bowl, stir the brown sugar, cinnamon, and cocoa to mix thoroughly. Stir in the currants or raisins and then the walnuts, and set aside.

For the batter:

Adjust rack one-third up from the bottom of the oven. Preheat oven to 375 degrees. Butter a 10-inch (12- to 14-cup capacity) Bundt pan. (This is best baked in a Bundt pan, but a tube pan of similar size may be substituted.) Even if the pan is nonstick, it should be buttered for this recipe.

Sift together the flour, baking powder, baking soda, and salt. Set aside. In large bowl of electric mixer, beat the butter to soften it a bit. Add the vanilla and granulated sugar and beat for a minute or two. Add the eggs individually, beating until thoroughly incorporated after each. Scrape the bowl with a rubber spatula as necessary to keep the mixture smooth, and beat briefly at high speed for a minute or so until the mixture is very smooth.

On lowest speed, alternately add the sifted dry ingredients in three additions and the sour cream in two additions, continuing to scrape the bowl as necessary with the rubber spatula and beating only until smooth after each addition.

Spread a thin layer of the batter in the bottom of the pan. Sprinkle very generously with about one-third of the nut filling. Continue making layers, four of the batter and three of the filling. The top layer should be batter. It will take a bit of patience to spread the batter thin. It will be easier if the batter is placed on by many

continues ↘

spoonfuls and then spread with the back of the spoon, instead of just being dropped on in two or three large amounts.

Bake for about 1 hour, until a cake tester comes out dry and the top feels firm and springy. Be sure it is done. Remove from oven. Leave the cake in the pan for 5 minutes, no longer. The cake should be hot when the glaze is applied.

For the glaze:

In a small bowl, with a rubber spatula, mix the sugar with the vanilla and about 2 tablespoons of the hot milk. Very gradually add more milk, just a bit at a time, using only enough to make a semifluid mixture about as thick as thick cream sauce.

Cover the cake with a rack and invert over a large piece of wax paper or aluminum foil. Remove the pan. Immediately pour on the glaze — just pour it on quickly, don't spread it or work over it — and let it run down the sides unevenly.

When the glaze has set, use a large spatula to transfer the cake to a cake plate. Serve the cake while still slightly warm or after it has cooled completely — even the next day.

MILDRED KNOPF'S ORANGE PUFF CAKE

Makes 1 (10-inch) cake   In Mrs. Knopf's marvelous cookbook *The Perfect Hostess Cook Book* (published in 1950 by Alfred A. Knopf), there is a recipe for a sublime cake. For many years it was my father's favorite—I made it for him at least once a week. We called it Daddy Cake. It always brought forth a smiling "Ah, there's good news tonight."

The egg whites are beaten on a large platter (mine measures about 18 x 11 inches—it is a turkey platter) with a flat wire whip. It works, but I suspect you've never done it before. I never had.

The cake is as light as angel food but more moist. It is extraordinary! It is not quick or easy—but it is the greatest!

Alfred A. Knopf, the publisher, was Mildred's brother-in-law. And Mildred's husband, Edwin A. Knopf, was a famous Hollywood producer and director.

NOTES

↓

Most angel-food pans are equipped with small feet that allow the cake to "hang" (the pan is inverted but the cake does not touch the surface of the table). However, in case your pan is an ordinary tube pan and not a specially made angel-food pan, do not be discouraged. Insert a glass wine bottle into the tube and allow the pan to "hang" supported by the bottle until cool.

↓

At first glance, this cake may seem like a lot of trouble, but, believe me, this is the sort of adventure in baking that makes a cook's reputation. Just follow each direction separately, one at a time, and you will have it done before you know it. It is a superb achievement, and I heartily recommend it as one of the finest cakes in the entire collection.

1 overrunning cup egg whites (approximately 10 large egg whites)	7 large egg yolks
	Grated zest of 1 large, deep-colored orange
¼ teaspoon salt	¼ cup orange juice
1 teaspoon cream of tartar	1 cup pastry flour (I use cake flour)
1⅓ cups sugar	
⅔ cup water	

Preheat the oven to 325 degrees.

First, beat the egg whites with a flat wire whip with the salt on a large platter or in a large, wide bowl. When the whites are foamy, add the cream of tartar, sifting it into the whites through a small strainer.

Continue to beat until the mixture looks moist and shiny and forms peaks when the whip is lifted up.

continues ↘

Second, boil the sugar and water until it forms a thread when dropped from a silver fork. (That's 234 degrees on a candy thermometer.)

Third, pour the cooked sugar over the egg whites in a thin stream, holding the pan high enough so as not to scald or curdle the egg whites. This will happen if the sugar syrup is added to the whites too rapidly. Pour with one hand and blend with the other, using silver fork, not the wire whip.

Fourth, after all the sugar syrup has been added, set the platter or bowl in a pan of cold, shallow water. Continue beating with the flat wire whip until cool, always using a high, lifting stroke to achieve a light texture.

Fifth, beat the egg yolks until lemon-colored. Add the orange zest and juice. Mix well and fold gently into the meringue.

Sixth, sift the pastry flour. Measure and resift four times. Sift gently into mixture and fold in with a light, folding motion. Pour the mixture into an angel-food cake pan that has been rinsed in cold water, handling as little as possible. Use a rubber spatula to scrape the bowl clean, then cut through the mixture in the pan with a knife to clear away the air pockets. Bake at 325 degrees for 1 hour. Remove from oven and invert, allowing cake to "hang" until cool. (See Notes.) Do not place by open window or in drafts, as this causes the cake to shrink.

P.S.: I follow Mrs. Knopf's above directions — however, I use cake flour, and since I do not have a silver fork, I use a stainless steel one. I use a loose-bottomed aluminum (not Teflon) angel-food cake pan that measures 10 x 4 inches, and, although it does have small feet to raise it when inverted, I find it necessary to "hang" the cake over a bottle anyhow, as it has risen so high that the feet do not raise it enough. Incidentally, flat wire whips are generally available in specialty kitchen-equipment shops. (Some of my friends tell me that they make this cake in a large bowl with a large balloon-type whisk. Others make it in an electric mixer, but recently I tried an electric mixer and I do not recommend it for this cake.)

Use a serrated bread knife to cut the cake and handle very gently so as not to squash the light-as-air creation.

BLUEBERRY CRUMB CAKE

Makes 9 to 12 portions Especially wonderful!

TOPPING

⅓ cup *sifted* unbleached all-purpose flour

½ cup sugar

1 teaspoon ground cinnamon

2 ounces (½ stick) unsalted butter

CAKE

2 cups fresh blueberries

2 cups *sifted* unbleached all-purpose flour

2 teaspoons baking powder

½ teaspoon salt

2 ounces (½ stick) unsalted butter

1 teaspoon vanilla extract

¾ cup sugar

1 large egg

½ cup milk

Finely grated zest of 1 lemon

½ cup walnuts, chopped medium fine

OPTIONAL: confectioners' sugar

For the topping:

In a small bowl, mix the flour, sugar, and cinnamon. With a pastry blender, cut in the butter until the mixture resembles coarse crumbs. Set aside.

For the cake:

Adjust rack to the center of the oven. Preheat oven to 375 degrees. Butter a 9-inch square baking pan. Coat it well, bottom and sides, with fine, dry bread crumbs. Set aside.

Pick over and wash the blueberries in a large bowl of cold water. Drain in a sieve or colander. Turn them out onto a towel and pat lightly with towel to dry. Set aside in a single layer on the towel to dry completely.

Sift together the flour, baking powder, and salt. Place the blueberries in a large bowl. Sprinkle with about 1½ tablespoons of the sifted dry ingredients. Using a rubber spatula, toss and turn gently to flour the blueberries without crushing them. Set

aside both the floured berries and also the remaining sifted dry ingredients.

In the small bowl of an electric mixer, beat the butter to soften it a bit. Beat in the vanilla and sugar and beat for 1 minute. Add the egg and beat for 1 minute more. On lowest speed, alternately add the remaining sifted dry ingredients in three additions and milk in two additions, scraping the bowl with a rubber spatula and beating only until smooth after each addition.

Remove from mixer. Stir in the lemon zest. The batter will be stiff. Pour it over the floured blueberries. With a rubber spatula gently fold together until just mixed.

Turn the batter into the prepared pan. Spread smooth. Sprinkle the walnuts over the top, and then sprinkle the reserved topping over the nuts.

Bake for 50 minutes, or until the top is well browned. Cool in the pan for about 30 minutes.

continues ↘

Cut around sides of pan to loosen cake.

Cover the top of the pan with a piece of aluminum foil large enough to fold down around the four sides (in order not to lose any of the topping when the cake is inverted). Over the aluminum foil place a cake rack or cookie sheet. Invert and remove pan. Place a cake plate or board upside down on the cake and invert again. Remove the foil.

This may be served while still warm or at room temperature—it holds its heat for 1 to 1½ hours after being removed from pan. If you wish, before serving cover the top generously with confectioners' sugar sifted through a fine strainer.

CHOCOLATE GINGERBREAD

Makes 16 large squares or 32 small slices This is a thick, soft, moist, spicy, old-fashioned dark chocolate cake. It is quite plain. Marvelous between meals with milk or coffee, or with whipped cream as a dessert. Or anytime with ice cream and chocolate sauce.

2½ cups *sifted* unbleached all-purpose flour

1½ teaspoons baking soda

1 teaspoon salt

1 teaspoon ground ginger

1 teaspoon ground cinnamon

1 teaspoon ground allspice

2 ounces unsweetened chocolate

8 ounces (2 sticks) unsalted butter, cut into small pieces

1 cup boiling water or hot prepared coffee

1 cup firmly packed dark brown sugar

1 cup light molasses

4 large eggs

OPTIONAL: ⅓ cup finely chopped candied or preserved ginger

Adjust rack one-third up from the bottom of the oven and preheat oven to 325 degrees. Butter a shallow 13 x 9-inch baking pan; dust it with fine, dry bread crumbs and invert it over paper to shake out excess crumbs. Set aside.

Sift together the flour, baking soda, salt, ginger, cinnamon, and allspice, and set aside.

Place the chocolate in the top of a small double boiler over warm water on low heat. Cover until the chocolate is melted. Then remove the top of the double boiler and set it aside, uncovered, to cool slightly.

Place the butter in the large bowl of an electric mixer. Add the boiling water or hot coffee and mix until the butter is melted. Add the brown sugar and mix well. Then mix in the molasses. Add the eggs

all together and beat until well mixed. Mix in the chocolate. On low speed gradually add the sifted dry ingredients and beat only until they are incorporated. Stir in the optional ginger. The mixture will be thin.

Pour it into the prepared pan and tilt the pan to level the batter.

Bake for about 50 minutes, until the top of the cake springs back when it is gently pressed with a fingertip.

Cool in the pan for 15 to 20 minutes. Cover with a cookie sheet or a rack and invert. Remove the pan. Cover the cake again with a sheet or a rack and invert again, leaving the cake right side up to cool.

Cut the cake into 16 large squares or 32 slices.

SPECIAL OCCASION CAKES

COUNTY-FAIR CHOCOLATE LAYER CAKE

Makes 12 generous portions A dark and tender two-layer cocoa cake with a luscious dark chocolate filling and icing that stays rather soft and creamy. It is over 4 inches high and is quite easy for such an impressive and delicious cake.

2 cups *sifted* cake flour

1 teaspoon baking soda

½ teaspoon salt

6 tablespoons strained unsweetened cocoa powder (preferably Dutch-process)

4 ounces (1 stick) unsalted butter

1 teaspoon vanilla extract

1¼ cups sugar

2 large eggs

1 cup milk

CHOCOLATE ICING

5 ounces unsweetened chocolate

1 cup heavy cream

1¼ cups sugar

4 ounces (1 stick) unsalted butter, cut into pieces

1 teaspoon vanilla extract

Adjust rack to center of the oven and preheat oven to 350 degrees. Butter two 8-inch round layer-cake pans, dust them with flour, invert, and tap lightly to shake out excess, and then set aside.

Sift together the flour, baking soda, salt, and cocoa and set aside.

In the large bowl of an electric mixer, cream the butter. Add the vanilla and then the sugar and beat well. Beat in the eggs one at a time, scraping the bowl with a rubber spatula and beating well after each addition.

On low speed add the sifted dry ingredients in three additions alternating with the milk in two additions. Scrape the bowl with the spatula and beat only until smooth after each addition.

Divide the batter between the prepared pans and spread smooth.

Bake for 35 to 40 minutes, until the layers just begin to come away from the sides of the pans. Cool the layers in the pans for 5 to 6 minutes. Then, with a small, sharp knife, cut around the sides to release. Cover each layer with a rack, invert, remove the pan, cover with another rack, and invert again, leaving the layers right side up to finish cooling.

Prepare a flat cake plate or serving board by placing four strips of wax paper around the outer edges of the plate. Place one cooled cake layer upside down on the plate, checking to see that the papers touch the cake all around. If you have a cake-decorating turntable or a lazy Susan, place the cake plate on it.

For the icing:

Chop the chocolate into small pieces — it is all right for them to be uneven — and set aside.

In a heavy 2½- to 3-quart saucepan, stir the cream and sugar to mix. With a wooden or rubber spatula, stir over moderate heat until the mixture comes to a boil. Then reduce the heat and let simmer for exactly 6 minutes.

Remove from the heat, add the chocolate, stir until it is melted, then add the butter and stir until it is melted. Add the vanilla and stir.

Partially fill a large bowl with ice and water. Place the saucepan of icing in the bowl of ice water and stir frequently until completely cool. Then stir constantly until the mixture begins to thicken.

When the icing begins to thicken, remove it from the ice water and stir/beat briskly with a rubber or wooden spatula until it becomes smooth and thick enough to spread — or about like a very heavy mayonnaise. It should take only a few seconds or maybe a minute or so of stirring/beating. If the icing remains too soft, return it to the ice water briefly, then remove and stir/beat again.

When the icing is thick enough, quickly spread it about ⅓ inch thick over the cake on the plate. Cover with the second layer, placing it right side up (both flat sides meet in the middle), pour the remaining icing over the cake, and with a long, narrow metal spatula spread it over the top and sides of the cake. If you wish, form large swirls on top, using the spatula to indent the icing from the outer rim toward the center in a rather abstract daisy shape.

Remove the wax paper strips by pulling each one by a narrow end.

COCONUT LAYER CAKE

NOTES

↓

When serving, dip the knife in hot water before making each cut to prevent the icing from sticking to the knife.

↓

This icing does not freeze well. It is best to ice the cake the day it is to be served.

Makes 10 portions I love to see people enjoy eating. It's the Jewish-mother instinct in me. And baking brings out the ham in me. Having family and friends rave about my creations gives me great satisfaction. This is a delightfully light and airy cake, spread thickly with gorgeous white icing and apricot preserves and topped with shredded coconut. It will elicit oohs and aahs when brought out for dessert.

2½ cups *sifted* cake flour

1 tablespoon baking powder

¼ teaspoon salt

4 ounces (1 stick) unsalted butter

1 teaspoon vanilla extract

1½ cups granulated sugar

2 large eggs

1 cup milk

Finely grated zest of 1 large orange (or 2 small)

A few spoonfuls of melted and strained apricot preserves

FLUFFY WHITE ICING

4 large egg whites

¼ cup light corn syrup (e.g., Karo)

2 tablespoons water

2½ cups confectioners' sugar

Pinch of salt

1 teaspoon vanilla extract

¼ teaspoon almond extract

—

8 to 10 ounces (3 to 4 cups) shredded coconut

Adjust rack to center of oven. Preheat oven to 375 degrees. Butter two 9-inch round layer-cake pans. Line the bottoms with baking parchment cut to fit. Butter the paper and dust all over lightly with flour. Set aside.

Sift together the flour, baking powder, and salt and set aside.

In large bowl of electric mixer, beat the butter to soften a bit. Add the vanilla and granulated sugar and beat for a few minutes. Add the eggs and beat until smooth. On lowest speed, add the sifted dry ingredients in three additions — alternately with the milk in two

additions — scraping the bowl with a rubber spatula as necessary and beating only until smooth after each addition. Remove from mixer and stir in the orange zest.

Divide the batter between prepared pans. Tilt and shake pans gently to level batter. Bake for 25 to 30 minutes, until cakes come away from the sides of pans and tops spring back when lightly touched.

Let the cakes stand about 5 minutes. Cover with racks or cookie sheets and invert. Remove pans and papers. Cover with racks and invert again to cool right side up.

continues ↘

When layers have cooled completely, place four strips of wax paper or baking parchment around a cake plate and place one layer on the plate, upside down. Spread cake with a thin layer of smooth preserves, reserving some for second layer.

For the icing:

Mix the egg whites, corn syrup, water, confectioners' sugar, and salt in the top of a large double boiler; it must have at least an 8- to 10-cup capacity. Place over hot water on moderate heat. Beat with an electric mixer at high speed for 5 to 6 minutes, until mixture stands in peaks when beaters are lifted.

Immediately, in order to stop the cooking, transfer icing to large bowl of electric mixer. Add vanilla and almond extracts and beat at high speed for about 5 minutes more, scraping sides and bottom of bowl almost continuously with a rubber spatula, until mixture is smooth and very thick. Use immediately.

Spread one-third of the icing on the bottom layer. Sprinkle with one-third of the coconut.

Put on second layer right side up, so that the two cake bottoms meet in the middle. Spread the top with remaining apricot preserves. Use another third of the icing around the sides and then the remaining third on the top. Quickly spread with a long, narrow metal offset spatula to smooth the top and sides.

With the palm of your hand, press another third of the coconut onto the sides and sprinkle the remaining coconut evenly over the top.

Remove the wax paper strips by pulling each one by a narrow end.

DEVIL'S FOOD CAKE

Makes 8 to 10 portions A high, three-layer black cake with wonderful, fluffy 7-Minute Icing.

3 ounces unsweetened chocolate	2 teaspoons vanilla extract	**7-MINUTE ICING**
2½ cups *sifted* cake flour	2½ cups firmly packed dark brown sugar	4 large egg whites
2 teaspoons baking soda	3 large eggs	1½ cups granulated sugar
½ teaspoon salt	½ cup buttermilk	¼ cup plus 1 tablespoon cold water
4 ounces (1 stick) unsalted butter	1 cup boiling water	1 teaspoon cream of tartar
		⅛ teaspoon salt
		1½ teaspoons vanilla extract

Adjust rack to center of oven. Preheat oven to 375 degrees. Butter three 8-inch round layer-cake pans. Dust bottoms with fine, dry bread crumbs (see Notes on next page).

Melt chocolate in top of small double boiler over hot water on moderate heat. Set aside. Sift together the flour, baking soda, and salt. Set aside. In large bowl of electric mixer, beat the butter to soften a bit. Add the vanilla and brown sugar and beat for a minute or two. Beat in the eggs one at a time, scraping the bowl with a rubber spatula as necessary to keep the mixture blended. Continue to beat for 1 to 2 minutes after the last egg has been added. Beat in the melted chocolate. On lowest speed, add half of the sifted dry ingredients, then the buttermilk, and then the other half of the dry ingredients, scraping the bowl as necessary with the rubber spatula and beating only until smooth after each addition. Gradually beat in the boiling water.

Batter will be thin. Divide it among the prepared pans.

Bake for 25 minutes, or until tops spring back when lightly touched and cakes come away from sides of pans.

Cool cakes in pans for about 5 minutes. Cover with racks or cookie sheets and invert. Remove pans. Cover with racks and invert again to finish cooling right side up.

When layers have cooled completely, use a long, thin, sharp knife to cut off any rises in the tops, making them level.

Place the bottom layer on a cake plate protected with four strips of wax paper or baking parchment around the outer edge.

For the icing:

Mix everything except the vanilla in the top of a large double boiler; it must have at least an 8- to 10-cup capacity. Place over hot water on moderate heat. Beat

continues ↘

with electric mixer at high speed for about 5 minutes, until mixture stands in peaks when beaters are withdrawn. Immediately, in order to stop the cooking, transfer the mixture to large bowl of electric mixer. Add vanilla. Beat at high speed until mixture is smooth and stiff. Use immediately.

Stack and frost each layer, then cover sides and top of cake, pulling the icing up in irregular peaks, if you wish.

Remove paper strips, pulling each one out by a narrow end.

NOTES

↓

To add even more chocolate, shave some on top before serving.

↓

To coat a pan for a dark cake, it is best to use dark crumbs or dark flour. Simply mix enough unsweetened cocoa powder into fine dry bread crumbs or flour to give the mixture a medium-brown color. It is handy to keep a jar of each of these already mixed. They last well.

↓

7-Minute Icing does not freeze well. It is best to ice the cake the day it is to be served.

OLD-FASHIONED FUDGE CAKE

Makes 12 to 16 portions An old recipe for a large two-layer cake — dark-colored, light-textured, and delicate, with a thick layer of bittersweet chocolate filling and icing that stays soft and creamy. This is a delicious cake, and easy. So easy, in fact, that after I recommended the recipe to a young girl as her first experience in cake baking, she not only proudly brought me a slice, but started making it for friends and relatives. She was 11 years old.

NOTE

↓

Although I told an 11-year-old to do the following when measuring the vinegar, it is advisable for everyone. I do it myself. Pour the vinegar into a small cup first, then scoop it out with the measuring spoon. If you pour a clear liquid into a measuring spoon held over the mixing bowl, it is possible to easily splash in more than you mean to.

3 ounces unsweetened chocolate, chopped

1¾ cups *sifted* cake flour

1 teaspoon baking powder

1 teaspoon baking soda

½ teaspoon salt

4 ounces (1 stick) unsalted butter

1½ cups granulated sugar

2 large eggs

2 tablespoons plus 1½ teaspoons white vinegar (see Note)

1 teaspoon vanilla

1 cup milk

WHIPPED CHOCOLATE ICING

6 ounces unsweetened chocolate

4 ounces (1 stick) unsalted butter

2¼ cups confectioners' sugar

2 large eggs

3 tablespoons hot water

½ teaspoon vanilla extract

Adjust rack to center of the oven and preheat oven to 350 degrees. Butter two 9-inch round layer-cake pans, line the bottoms with baking parchment or wax paper cut to fit, butter the paper, dust with flour, then invert over a piece of paper and tap lightly to shake out excess. Set aside.

Place the chocolate in the top of a small double boiler over hot water on moderate heat. Cover until partially melted, then uncover and stir until completely melted. Remove from the hot water and set aside, uncovered, to cool slightly.

Sift together the cake flour, baking powder, baking soda, and salt and set aside.

In the large bowl of an electric mixer, cream the butter. Add the granulated sugar and beat to mix well. Add the eggs one at a time, beating until the egg is thoroughly incorporated after each addition. Mix in the vinegar and vanilla. The mixture will look curdled — it is OK. Add the melted chocolate and beat only until smooth.

continues ⌄

On low speed add the sifted dry ingredients in three additions, alternating with the milk in two additions. Scrape the bowl with a rubber spatula and beat only until smooth after each addition.

Place half of the mixture in each prepared pan and level the tops.

Bake for 40 minutes, until the layers begin to come away from the sides of the pans and the tops spring back when lightly pressed with a fingertip.

With a small, sharp knife, cut around the insides of the pans to release, pressing the sharp edge of the knife against the pan. Then let the layers stand in the pans for 5 minutes.

Cover each layer with a rack, invert, remove the pan, peel off the paper lining, cover with another rack, and invert again, leaving the layer right side up to cool.

Prepare a large, flat cake plate by lining the sides with four strips of wax paper. Place one layer upside down on the plate, checking to be sure that the papers touch the layer all around.

If you have a cake decorating turntable or a lazy Susan, place the plate on it.

For the icing:

Place the chocolate and butter in the top of a small double boiler over hot water on moderate heat. Cover until partially melted, then uncover and stir until completely melted.

Meanwhile, place all the remaining ingredients in the small bowl of an electric mixer. Beat briefly only to mix. Set the small bowl in a large bowl and fill the empty space left in the large bowl with ice and water, filling to about three-quarters the depth of the large bowl. (If you are using an electric mixer on a stand, use the large mixer bowl for the ice and water but adjust the stand for "small bowl.")

Add the melted chocolate and butter and beat until the mixture thickens slightly. Remove both bowls (together) from the mixer. With a rubber spatula, stir the icing over the ice and water until it thickens to the consistency of thick mayonnaise. Spread a scant third of the icing about ¼ inch thick over the bottom layer of cake. Cover with the other layer, placing it right side up (both bottoms meet in the middle). Spread the sides and the top with the remaining icing.

It may either be spread smoothly with a long, narrow metal offset spatula, or it may be formed into swirls.

Remove the strips of wax paper by gently pulling each one out by a narrow end.

FUDGE CAKE WITH FUDGE

Makes 12 to 16 portions There's something very special about chocolate. It all has something to do with love and sharing.

4 ounces unsweetened chocolate

½ cup hot water

1¾ cups sugar

2 cups *sifted* unbleached all-purpose flour

1 teaspoon baking soda

¼ teaspoon salt

4 ounces (1 stick) unsalted butter

1 teaspoon vanilla

3 large eggs

⅔ cup milk

FUDGE

3 cups sugar

1 cup milk

Pinch of salt

3 tablespoons light corn syrup (e.g., Karo)

4 ounces unsweetened chocolate, coarsely chopped

5⅓ tablespoons unsalted butter

2 teaspoons vanilla extract

Adjust racks to divide oven in thirds. Preheat oven to 350 degrees. Butter two 9-inch square cake pans.

Place chocolate and hot water in the top of small double boiler over hot water on moderate heat. Cook, stirring occasionally, until chocolate is melted and mixture is smooth. Mix in ½ cup of the sugar (reserve remaining 1¼ cups) and continue to cook 2 minutes longer, stirring with a rubber spatula to keep mixture smooth. Remove top of double boiler and set aside.

Sift together flour, baking soda, and salt. Set aside. In large bowl of electric mixer, beat the butter a bit to soften. Add vanilla and reserved 1¼ cups sugar and beat for about a minute or two. Scrape the bowl with a rubber spatula as necessary to keep mixture smooth. Beat in eggs one at a time, beating until thoroughly incorporated after each addition. On lowest speed, alternately add sifted dry ingredients in three additions and milk in two additions, scraping the bowl with the spatula as

necessary and beating only until smooth after each addition. Add the chocolate mixture (don't worry if it is still warm) and beat only until smooth.

Divide evenly between prepared pans. Tilt pans gently to level batter. Bake for 30 to 40 minutes, until the tops spring back when lightly touched and cakes come away from sides of pans.

Cool cakes in pans for 5 minutes. Cover with racks or cookie sheets and invert. Remove pans. Cover with racks and invert again to cool right side up.

Place the bottom layer upside down on a platter or board.

For the fudge (filling and icing):

Place sugar, milk, salt, corn syrup, and chocolate over moderate heat in a heavy saucepan with at least a 3-quart capacity (see Notes on next page). Bring slowly to a boil, stirring occasionally with

continues ⌄

a wooden spoon or spatula, until the sugar is dissolved and the chocolate is melted. Insert a candy thermometer in the saucepan and let the syrup boil until the temperature reaches 232 degrees (or until the syrup forms a very soft ball in cold water).

Immediately, in order to stop the cooking, transfer to a large mixing bowl. Cut the butter into small pieces and add. Replace the thermometer and let mixture stand without stirring until the temperature drops to 110 degrees. (This might take as long as 1 hour.)

Add the vanilla. With a heavy wooden spoon stir and beat for 3 to 5 minutes, until this heavy mixture thickens a bit more. Do not wait too long. You are making fudge; it will harden quickly and it must be spread before it hardens.

Work very quickly — spread about half the fudge roughly on the bottom layer, cover with the top layer placed right side up so that both flat sides meet in the center, and spread fudge on top. Do not try to spread it on the sides, but just let some of it run down unevenly.

NOTES

↓

If the saucepan for the fudge is too small, the syrup will boil over.

↓

If the fudge icing becomes too thick and stiff, add boiling water, a few drops at a time, to soften it to the right consistency.

↓

To make Fudge Squares, frost the separate cake layers with the fudge and do not stack them on top of each other. Cut into squares.

↓

Serve as is, or à la mode (with ice cream), or all the way — with a bowl of ice cream, a bowl of whipped cream, and a bowl of walnut halves or fresh strawberries. And chocolate sauce?

STAR-SPANGLED BANNER CAKE

Makes 20 portions   I made three of these for a big New Year's Eve party. After icing each cake I wrapped a shiny yellow ribbon around its middle, made big fluffy bows, inserted tiny yellow and white silk flowers into each bow, and taped a little "Happy New Year" sign onto one of the streamers of each bow. (I inserted a long bamboo skewer deep into the cake right under each bow to support its weight.)

The secret is to make the whole thing, ribbon, bow, and bouquet, ahead of time, using a cake pan as a dummy. Cut the ribbon at the side of the pan opposite the bow, then just "dress" this cake by taping the ribbon together at the back of the cake.

The cake was beautiful, but it is equally delicious and equally attractive without these decorations.

This is a big, bold, beautiful four-layer Southern banana-nut cake, 6 inches high, with a mountain of fluffy white icing and a shower of coconut. This is for occasions: birthdays, New Year's Eve, or the cover of a magazine. It is not difficult to make, there is nothing tricky, but stacking the four layers with the abundance of icing takes courage.

BANANA CAKE LAYERS

- 3 cups *sifted* unbleached all-purpose flour
- 2 teaspoons baking powder
- ½ teaspoon salt
- 6 ounces (1½ sticks) unsalted butter
- 1 teaspoon vanilla extract
- ¼ teaspoon almond extract
- 2 cups sugar
- 3 large eggs

- About 5 fully ripened large bananas (to make 2½ cups mashed)
- 1 teaspoon baking soda
- 6 ounces (1½ cups) pecans, finely chopped (not ground)
- ½ cup buttermilk

SOUTHERN FLUFFY WHITE ICING

- 3 cups sugar
- ⅓ cup light corn syrup (e.g., Karo)

- ¾ cup boiling water
- ¾ cup egg whites (from 6 large eggs; they may be whites that were frozen and then thawed)
- Pinch of salt
- 1 teaspoon vanilla extract
- ¼ teaspoon almond extract

- 7 ounces (2⅔ cups, loosely packed) moist shredded coconut

Adjust two racks to divide the oven into thirds and preheat the oven to 350 degrees. Prepare four 9-inch round layer-cake pans as follows: Butter the bottom and sides, line the bottoms with rounds of baking

continues ↘

parchment or wax paper cut to fit, then butter the paper, dust with fine dry bread crumbs, and invert over paper and lightly tap out excess crumbs. Set the pans aside.

Sift together the flour, baking powder, and salt and set aside.

In the large bowl of an electric mixer, beat the butter until it is soft. Beat in the vanilla and almond extracts and the sugar, beating only to combine well. Add the eggs one at a time, beating thoroughly after each addition. (The mixture might appear curdled — it is OK.)

Coarsely mash the bananas on a large plate with a fork (they should not be liquefied or pureed). Place them in a bowl and mix in the baking soda. Stir the bananas and then the nuts into the creamed butter mixture.

On low speed, add half of the sifted dry ingredients, then the buttermilk, and finally the remaining dry ingredients, beating only until mixed after each addition.

Divide the batter among the pans. Smooth the tops. The layers will be very thin.

Place two pans on each rack; do not place pans directly over or under others.

Bake for 28 to 30 minutes, until the tops spring back when pressed gently with a fingertip and the layers barely begin to come away from the sides of the pans.

Cover each layer with a rack, invert pan and rack, remove pan and paper lining, cover with another rack, and turn the layer over again, leaving it right side up to cool.

With a dry pastry brush, brush the sides of the cooled layers to remove loose crumbs.

Before icing the cake, place four 12 x 4-inch strips of baking parchment or wax paper in a square pattern around the sides of a large cake platter. Place one layer on the platter right side up and check to be sure that the papers touch the cake all around.

If you have a cake-decorating turntable, place the platter on it.

For the icing:

Place the sugar, corn syrup, and boiling water in a 2½- to 3-quart saucepan over moderate heat. Stir frequently with a wooden spatula until the sugar is dissolved. When the mixture comes to a full boil, remove it from the heat and set it aside briefly.

In the large bowl of an electric mixer, beat the egg whites with the salt until the whites stand up straight when the beaters are raised.

Transfer the hot syrup to a pitcher that is easy to pour from. Beating at high speed and holding the pitcher about 12 inches above the mixer bowl, pour the hot syrup in a threadlike stream into the whites. Pour slowly and scrape the sides of the bowl occasionally with a rubber spatula to keep the entire mass well mixed. It will look as though the bowl will not hold all of the icing; it will, but you must watch it carefully and reduce the speed if necessary to prevent the icing from overflowing.

After all the syrup has been beaten in, add the vanilla and almond extracts and continue to beat (at high speed, if possible) for about 15 more minutes, until the icing is very stiff and holds a straight peak when the beaters are raised. Remove the bowl from the mixer.

Spread a generous layer of the icing about 1 inch thick over the first layer of cake. Then place the second cake layer over the icing, also right side up. Cover it with another inch-thick layer of icing. Continue layering the cakes and the icing.

Spread a thick layer of the icing around the sides and then spread all the remaining icing (it will be a thick layer) over the top.

With a long, narrow metal offset spatula, smooth the sides and then the top (be sure the sides are straight and the top is flat).

Place the coconut on a large piece of paper right up against the cake platter. Take a handful of the coconut in the palm of your hand, then turn your hand to place the coconut on the side of the cake. Some of the coconut will stick to the cake and some will fall to the platter; with your fingers, transfer the fallen coconut to the pile of coconut on the paper. Pick up another handful and continue to coat the sides with the coconut. If there are spots on the sides near the bottom where there is no coconut, just fold the paper strips up against the cake and the coconut that has fallen to the strips will stick to the sides of the cake. Then sprinkle all the remaining coconut over the top of the cake.

Remove the paper strips gently by pulling each one out by a narrow end.

Let the cake stand at room temperature.

To serve, have dinner plates ready — cake plates are too small for this. Use a long, sharp knife and have a deep pitcher of very hot water to dip the knife into before each cut so you can cut with a hot, wet blade. Or if you prefer to serve on smaller plates, serve the two top layers first (making 10 two-layer portions) and then the two bottom layers (10 more portions).

VARIATION

Sprinkle a generous amount of light rum onto each layer when it is in place on the plate, just before icing it. If you do use the rum, use enough so you really taste it.

CHOCOLATE CUPCAKES

Makes 24 cupcakes These cupcakes and Brownies (page 186) are the desserts I usually make when I am asked to make something for a bake sale.

- 2 cups *sifted* unbleached all-purpose flour
- 1 teaspoon baking soda
- ¼ teaspoon salt
- ½ cup unsweetened cocoa powder (preferably Dutch-process)

- 5⅓ ounces (1¼ sticks plus 2 teaspoons) unsalted butter
- 1 teaspoon vanilla extract
- 1½ cups sugar
- 3 large eggs
- 1 cup milk

CHOCOLATE CUPCAKE ICING

- 6 ounces semisweet chocolate
- ⅓ cup heavy cream
- 1 tablespoon sugar
- 1½ tablespoons unsalted butter

Adjust two racks to divide oven into thirds. Preheat oven to 350 degrees. Butter the cups of two 12-cup standard muffin pans (with 2¾-inch-diameter cups). Sift a bit of flour or cocoa over them and shake out the excess. Or line the 24 cups with cupcake liners (see Notes). Set aside.

Sift together the flour, baking soda, salt, and cocoa. Set aside.

In large bowl of electric mixer, beat the butter

to soften a bit. Beat in the vanilla and sugar. Add the eggs one at a time, beating until smooth after each and scraping the bowl with a rubber spatula as necessary to keep mixture smooth. On lower speed, alternately add the sifted dry ingredients in three additions and the milk in two additions. Continue to scrape the bowl with the rubber spatula and beat only until smooth. Do not overbeat.

Spoon the batter into the prepared pans, filling the cups only two-thirds to three-quarters full. There is no need to smooth the tops — the batter will level itself.

Bake for 25 minutes, or until the tops spring back when lightly touched. Do not overbake. Cool in the pans for 2 to 3 minutes before removing to a rack to finish cooling.

For the icing:

Place all the ingredients in a small, heavy saucepan over moderate heat. Cook, stirring occasionally, until the chocolate is almost melted. Remove from heat. Continue to stir until the chocolate is completely melted and the mixture is smooth. Transfer to a very small, shallow bowl. Let stand, stirring occasionally, until the icing reaches room temperature.

Hold cupcakes upside down and dip the tops into the icing. Twirl slightly and then hold upside down for a few seconds for excess to drip off. Then, use a teaspoon to place a rather generous mound of icing on each cake — do not spread it.

Let stand for a few hours, or overnight if you wish, for the icing to set.

NOTES

When baking cupcakes, if you have only one pan with 12 cups, reserve the remaining batter and bake additional cupcakes after the first panful. If baking only one pan at a time, bake in the center of the oven.

Lining the pans with papers is a convenience and a time saver. The cakes take on a better shape and rise higher, and they stay fresh longer.

To freeze frosted cupcakes, let them stand until the icing is no longer sticky. Place them on a pan or tray in the freezer until frozen firm. Then place over them a large piece of plastic wrap, turning it down securely on the sides and under the bottom. Return to freezer. To thaw, remove from freezer, but do not remove plastic wrap until cupcakes have thawed.

BOSTON CREAM PIE

Makes 8 portions Long ago there was a famous American dessert called "pudding-cake pie." When the great Parker House Hotel opened in Boston, in 1855, they added a chocolate icing to the dessert and renamed it Boston Cream Pie. It immediately became, and has remained, one of America's most loved desserts. It is a plain white two-layer sponge cake (moist and tender) with a vanilla pastry-cream filling (like a vanilla pudding, creamy and delicate) and a thin layer of dark semisweet chocolate glaze on top: an addictive combination.

It looks so very simple and easy that you might think it should be easy to make, but simple-looking and plain things are often more difficult than elaborate things. Making this cake involves great care with folding in beaten whites and yolks and sifted dry ingredients and melted butter. And the filling calls for patience in making the custard carefully and slowly so you don't wind up with scrambled eggs.

But then — joy! It is a great accomplishment. My congratulations to you.

There are many recipes for Boston Cream Pie. This is the best I've ever had. We originally ate it in Boston; the recipe is adapted from one in the 1981 edition of the *Boston Globe Cookbook*. I don't know why this cake is called a pie.

VANILLA PASTRY CREAM

- 2 large eggs
- ¼ cup plus 1 tablespoon *sifted* unbleached all-purpose flour
- ¼ teaspoon salt
- ⅔ cup sugar
- 2 cups milk
- 1 teaspoon vanilla extract
- ¼ teaspoon almond extract
- 2 tablespoons unsalted butter, cut into small pieces

BOSTON SPONGE CAKE

- 1 cup *sifted* unbleached all-purpose flour
- 1 teaspoon baking powder
- 3 large eggs, separated
- ¼ teaspoon salt
- ⅔ cup sugar
- 1 teaspoon vanilla extract
- 1 tablespoon lemon juice
- 2 tablespoons cold water
- 3 tablespoons unsalted butter, melted

CHOCOLATE GLAZE

- ¼ cup whipping cream
- 4 ounces semisweet chocolate, coarsely chopped

For the pastry cream:

Unless you want to make the cake ahead of time and freeze it, make the pastry cream first in order to chill it well before using.

In a small bowl, beat the eggs lightly just to mix; set aside. Mix the flour, salt, and sugar in a heavy 2-quart saucepan. Gradually stir in the milk, then cook, stirring constantly over medium-low heat, until the mixture comes to a boil and begins to thicken.

Continue to stir and boil gently for a minute or two. The mixture should become as thick as a vichyssoise.

Remove the pan from the heat. With a ladle, add about ½ cup of the hot mixture to the eggs and stir well to mix. Repeat, adding ½ cup at a time, until you have added about half of the hot mixture to the eggs. Then, very slowly, stirring constantly, stir the egg mixture into the remaining hot milk mixture.

Place the pan over low heat and cook, still stirring constantly, for 2 minutes. Remove from the heat. Mix in the vanilla and almond extracts and the butter.

Immediately (to stop the cooking) pour the mixture into a bowl. Cut a round of wax paper to fit on top of the pastry cream (touching it), and place the paper directly on the cream. This will prevent a skin from forming.

Now, either let this stand until cool and then refrigerate for at least an hour, or save time by placing the bowl in a larger bowl of ice and water to cool quickly, and then refrigerate for at least an hour.

For the sponge cake:

Adjust a rack to the middle of the oven and preheat the oven to 350 degrees. Butter a 9 x 1½-inch round cake pan, line the bottom with a round of baking parchment or wax paper cut to fit, then butter the paper and dust all over with fine, dry bread crumbs. Invert the pan over paper and tap lightly to shake out excess crumbs. Set the pan aside.

Sift together the flour and baking powder and set aside.

Beat the egg whites and the salt in the small bowl of an electric mixer until the whites hold a soft shape. Reduce the speed to moderate and gradually add ⅓ cup of the sugar (reserve the remaining ⅓ cup of sugar). Then increase the speed again and continue to beat very briefly, only until the whites just hold a point when the beaters are raised. Do not let the whites become stiff or dry.

Transfer the beaten whites to the large bowl of the mixer. Scrape the beaters with your finger to remove most of the whites and scrape the bowl with a rubber spatula. (It is not necessary to wash the bowl or beaters.) Set aside.

Place the yolks in the small bowl of the mixer. Beat briefly, then gradually add the remaining ⅓ cup of sugar and continue to beat at high speed until the mixture is very light — almost white. Beat in the vanilla and lemon juice; then on low speed add the cold water, scraping the bowl as necessary and beating only until the mixture is smooth.

In about four additions, fold the yolks into the whites (do not handle any more than necessary and do not be too thorough, especially with the first few additions).

Place the dry ingredients in a sifter and hold the sifter over the bowl, sifting with one hand and folding with the other. The dry ingredients should be added in four or five additions. (Do not handle any more than necessary.)

continues ⌐

The melted butter may be slightly warm or it may have cooled to room temperature, but it must still be liquid. Add it all at once to the batter and fold gently only until barely (but not absolutely) incorporated.

Turn the batter into the prepared pan and smooth the top.

Bake for about 30 minutes, until the top springs back when pressed gently with a fingertip.

Remove from the oven. With a small, sharp knife, cut around the rim of the cake to release it. Let stand in the pan for 5 minutes. Then cover the pan with a rack, turn the pan and the rack over, and remove the cake pan — do not remove the paper lining, which should be clinging to the cake — cover the cake with another rack, and turn over again, leaving the cake right side up to cool.

The next step is to cut the cake into two thin layers. I think it is easiest and safest if you first chill the cake in the freezer for about 40 minutes or longer. Place the cold cake upside down on a flat cake plate. Remove the paper lining from the cake. If you have a cake-decorating turntable, place the cake plate on it. Use a long, thin, sharp knife (I use a ham slicer — or you might like to use a serrated knife) and carefully cut the cake into two thin layers.

Carefully remove and set aside the top layer.

Turn the chilled pastry cream onto the bottom layer of the cake. With a long, narrow metal spatula, spread the pastry cream to ½ inch from the edges of the cake. (If it goes any closer to the edges, the weight of the top layer might spread it out too far.)

Cover with the top layer. Refrigerate the cake while you make the glaze.

For the glaze:

Place the cream in a small, heavy saucepan over moderate heat until it begins to bubble. Add the chocolate, stir briefly until partly melted, then remove the pan from the heat and continue to stir until completely melted. Transfer the glaze to a small bowl and let stand for about 10 minutes, stirring occasionally.

Pour the glaze onto the cake; then, with a long, narrow metal spatula, smooth it just to the edges of the cake. Try to avoid having the glaze run down the sides of the cake, but if a bit does, leave it. Refrigerate and serve cold.

BULL'S EYE CHEESECAKE

Makes 10 portions "How did you do it?" — "I can't believe it." — "I never saw anything like it."

You will have two mixtures, one dark and one light. When you work your magic with them they will form a series of concentric circles (a bull's eye) of dark and light cheesecake to produce this photogenic and delicious creation. When you cut into the cake you will see gracefully curved, vertical stripes. This recipe is foolproof and not difficult. I think this is one of the most exciting and satisfying of all the baking recipes I know. It's a thrill to see it form those circles by itself.

Although this tastes perfectly delicious any time at all, the design will be more clearly defined after the cake has been refrigerated for at least 8 hours or overnight.

NOTES

↓

A professional cheesecake pan, the kind that is generally used by bakers and pastry chefs, is a one-piece pan, because cheesecakes are frequently baked in a pan of water. And they are deeper than layer-cake pans. They come in a variety of sizes.

↓

You may increase the number of circles when you feel comfortable with it. Once I had 13 circles plus the center dot!

2 pounds cream cheese (use Philadelphia brand; others don't all work the same), at room temperature

¼ cup sour cream

1 teaspoon vanilla extract

¼ teaspoon almond extract

¼ teaspoon salt

4 large eggs (a scant 7 ounces)

⅔ cup granulated sugar

⅔ cup firmly packed dark brown sugar

1 teaspoon instant espresso or coffee powder

2 teaspoons unsweetened cocoa powder (preferably Dutch-process)

About ¼ cup graham cracker crumbs

Adjust a rack one-third up from the bottom of the oven; preheat to 350 degrees. Butter a round 9 x 2-inch or 8 x 3-inch pan (see Notes), including the inside of the rim. You will also need a larger pan (for hot water) to place the cake pan in while baking; the larger pan must not be deeper than the cheesecake pan. Set aside.

In the large bowl of an electric mixer, beat the cheese until soft and smooth. Beat in the sour cream, then the vanilla and almond extracts and the salt. Beat in the eggs, one at a time, scraping the bowl and beating after each addition until incorporated.

continues ↘

You will have about 6 cups of batter. Place half in another bowl. Add the granulated sugar to one bowl and the brown sugar to the other. With a rubber spatula for each bowl, stir for about a minute, until the sugar has dissolved and the mixture has thinned.

To the brown sugar mixture, add the instant coffee and, through a fine strainer, the cocoa. Stir until they have dissolved and there are no visible specks.

Spray the buttered pan with nonstick vegetable oil spray.

You will have a scant 4 cups of each mixture. Pour a scant cup of one (it doesn't matter which) directly into the middle of the pan; it will spread to cover the bottom. Pour a scant cup of the other mixture directly into the middle of the first; it will spread out too. Repeat, alternating colors, with the remaining batter (for a total of four additions of each mixture, but see Notes). You will see the bull's eye pattern form.

Put a large pan (such as a roasting pan) in the oven. Handling the cake pan very carefully in order not to disturb the design, place it in the large pan. Pour hot water into the large pan to about half the depth of the cake pan. Bake for 1½ hours.

Set the cake on a rack to cool. Let it stand 3 hours at room temperature before unmolding. (The top, which rises during baking, will sink to the original level.)

Cover the top of the cake pan with plastic wrap and then a plate. Hold the cake pan and plate firmly together and turn them over. Remove the pan. Sprinkle the crumbs over the bottom of the cake.

Cover the cake with a serving plate and carefully turn it over again, leaving the cake right side up. (Don't press down on the cake; it is still soft.) Refrigerate to chill thoroughly. For the neatest slices, put the cake in the freezer for 4 or 5 hours before cutting and wipe the knife blade after each cut.

POLKA DOT CHEESECAKE

Makes 12 portions The design is quite unbelievable. You make a pattern of large dark polka dots on top of the cake with a pastry bag. When you cut portions and cut through the polka dots, you will be thrilled to see that there is a perfect round ball about the size of a golf ball of the dark mixture under each polka dot. Stunning. Anyone who bakes knows this: When you bake something like the Polka Dot Cheesecake, and you bring it to the table, and you cut it, and serve it, and everyone says, "This is wonderful!" or "This is spectacular!" or "This is magic!" then you know happiness.

If possible, make this a day ahead and refrigerate overnight.

2 ounces unsweetened chocolate	1 tablespoon vanilla extract	1¾ cups sugar
2 pounds cream cheese (use Philadelphia brand; others do not all work the same), at room temperature	¼ teaspoon almond extract	4 large eggs
		About ⅓ cup graham cracker crumbs

Adjust a rack to the lowest position in the oven and preheat oven to 350 degrees. Butter an 8 x 3-inch one-piece cheesecake pan all the way up to the rim and including the inside of the rim itself. You will also need a larger pan (for hot water) to place the cake pan in while baking; the larger pan must not be deeper than the cheesecake pan. Set aside.

In the top of a small double boiler over hot water on low heat, melt the chocolate and set it aside.

In the large bowl of an electric mixer, beat the cheese until it is completely smooth. During the beating, frequently scrape the sides and bottom of the bowl with a rubber spatula. When the cheese is smooth, beat in the vanilla and almond extracts and the sugar. Beat well and then add the eggs one at a time. After adding the eggs, do not beat any more than necessary to mix.

Remove the bowl from the mixer. Place one-third of the batter (2 cups) in the small bowl of the electric mixer. Add the melted chocolate and beat until smooth.

Spray the buttered cake pan with nonstick cooking oil spray, and then pour in the light-colored mixture.

Fit a large (about 16-inch) pastry bag with a plain #6 (½-inch) tube. Fold down a deep cuff on the outside of the bag and twist the tube end of the bag to prevent the mixture from running out.

Place the chocolate mixture in the bag.

Now, work at table height, not counter height (you will have better control at

continues ↘

table height). Place the cake pan on the table. Unfold the cuff on the pastry bag. Untwist the tube end of the bag. Place the tip of the tube in the center of the top of the cake, inserting it ¼ to ½ inch into the cake. Squeeze out some of the chocolate mixture. It will form a ball (tennis ball- or golf ball-size, precise and perfectly round) in the cake and will leave a dark polka dot about 2 inches wide on top of the cake.

Then, using the same procedure, squeeze out six balls around the rim. In order to space the six balls evenly, place the first one at twelve o'clock (straight up). The next at six o'clock (straight down). Then two on each side. Doing it this way, the chances are that the spacing will be quite even. The balls around the rim should be smaller than the one in the center, and they should not touch each other or the center ball. If you have some chocolate mixture left over, add it to the center ball; if you still have some left over, add a bit to each of the other balls.

The top of the cake will not be smooth and level now, but it will level itself during baking. When baked, the polka dot in the center will be about 2½ inches wide, the dots around the rim will be about 1½ inches wide.

Place the cake pan into the larger pan. Place it in the oven and pour hot water into the larger pan about 1½ inches deep. (If the larger pan is aluminum, add about ½ teaspoon cream of tartar to prevent the water from discoloring the pan.)

Bake for 1½ hours. The top of the cake will become golden brown and it will feel dry to the touch but the cake will still be very soft inside (it will become firm when it has cooled and been refrigerated).

Lift the cake pan out of the water and place it on a cake rack. Cool the cake in the pan for 2½ hours. (Do not cool in the refrigerator or the butter will harden and the cake will stick to the pan.)

Cover the pan with a piece of plastic wrap. Place a flat plate or small board upside down over the pan and invert the pan and the plate or board. Carefully remove the pan.

Carefully and evenly sprinkle the graham cracker crumbs over the bottom of the cake. Gently place another flat plate or small board upside down over the cake and carefully turn it all upside down again (without squashing the cake), leaving the cake right side up. Remove the plastic wrap.

Refrigerate for several hours or overnight.

To serve, dip a sharp knife in very hot water or hold it under running hot water before making each cut; shake off the water but do not dry the blade. Make the first cut through the middle of one of the smaller dots and the second cut (the one that will release the first portion) between two of the smaller dots.

COUNTESS TOULOUSE-LAUTREC'S FRENCH CHOCOLATE CAKE

Makes 10 portions Mapie, the Countess of Toulouse-Lautrec, wrote French cookbooks, food columns, and magazine articles about food, and she was the directress of a cooking school for young ladies at Maxim's restaurant in Paris. She was married to an admiral in the French navy who belonged to the same family as the artist (the artist was her father-in-law's cousin). Toulouse-Lautrec was also a gourmet and a fine cook himself. The Countess introduced this recipe to America in an article for *McCall's* magazine in 1959. Since then it has continued to grow in popularity under a variety of names and adaptions. (The "one tablespoon" measures of flour and sugar are correct.)

> **NOTE**
> ↓
> *Many recipes for this cake specify Baker's German's sweet chocolate. Jean Hewitt made a version of it for the* New York Times *and she used Maillard Eagle Sweet chocolate. Sue Britt, the home economist for the Nestlé Company, used semisweet morsels. I have used them all and they were all too good.*

This cake is not a cake by American standards. It is rather like a rich, moist, dense cheesecake — like unadulterated and undiluted chocolate. It is best to make it a day before serving or at least 6 to 8 hours before, or make it way ahead of time and freeze it. (Thaw before serving.)

- 1 pound semisweet chocolate (see Note)
- 5 ounces (1¼ sticks) unsalted butter, at room temperature
- 4 large eggs, separated
- 1 tablespoon *unsifted* all-purpose flour
- Pinch of salt
- 1 tablespoon sugar
- Accompaniments of choice

Adjust rack one-third up from bottom of the oven and preheat oven to 425 degrees. Separate the bottom and the sides of an 8-inch springform pan. (The cake will be only 1½ inches high on the sides, so the pan may be shallow or deep — either is all right. Or you could use an 8-inch round layer-cake pan that has a removable bottom.) Cut a round of baking parchment or wax paper to fit the bottom of the pan and butter it on one side. Butter the sides (not the bottom) of the pan. Put the bottom of the pan in place, close the clamp on the side, and place the buttered paper in the pan, buttered side up. Set aside.

continues ↘

Break up or coarsely chop the chocolate and place it in the top of a large double boiler over hot water on moderate heat. Cover until partially melted, then uncover and stir with a rubber spatula until completely melted. Remove the top of the double boiler from the hot water.

Add about one-third of the butter at a time and stir it into the chocolate with the rubber spatula. Each addition of butter should be completely melted and incorporated before the next is added. Set aside to cool slightly.

In the small bowl of an electric mixer, beat the egg yolks at high speed for 5 to 7 minutes, until they are pale-colored and thick. Add the tablespoon of flour and beat on low speed for only a moment to incorporate the flour.

Add the beaten yolks to the chocolate (which may still be slightly warm but should not be hot) and fold and stir gently to mix.

In a clean, small bowl, with clean beaters, beat the egg whites and the salt until the whites hold a soft shape. Add the sugar and continue to beat only until the whites hold a definite shape but not until they are stiff or dry. Fold about one-half of the beaten whites into the chocolate — do not be too thorough. Then fold the chocolate into the remaining whites, handling gently and folding only until both mixtures are blended.

Turn into the prepared pan. Rotate the pan a bit, first in one direction, then the other, to level the batter.

Bake for 15 minutes. The cake will be soft and you will think it is not done. But remove it from the oven. Do not throw the cake away now. You may think that is the only thing to do, but it is OK. (However, it might be wise not to let anyone else see it now.) It will be only about an inch high in the middle, the rim will be higher than the middle, and the top will be cracked. Don't worry — it's OK. Baking this cake longer will not prevent it from sinking.

With a small, sharp knife, carefully cut around the sides of the hot cake, but do not remove the sides of the pan. Let the cake stand in the pan until it cools to room temperature. Then refrigerate it for at least several hours or overnight. The cake must be firm when it is removed from the pan.

To remove the cake, cut around the sides again with a small, sharp knife. Remove the sides of the pan. Cover the cake with a small cookie sheet or the bottom of a quiche pan or anything flat, and invert. Then carefully insert a narrow metal spatula or a table knife between the bottom of the pan and the paper lining, moving it just enough to release the bottom of the pan. Remove the bottom and peel off the paper lining. Invert a serving plate over the cake and invert the plate and the cake, leaving the cake right side up.

The Countess served the cake just as it is. But you have several alternatives. The most obvious is to cover the top generously (excluding the rim) with whipped cream — see below.

continues ⬎

But if you do not plan to serve it all at once and you might want to freeze the leftovers, that is not the best plan. Instead, you can cover the top generously with large, loose, free-form chocolate shavings (shaved with a vegetable peeler from a thick piece of milk chocolate). If you do that, sprinkle confectioners' sugar over the top of the shavings. Or cover the top of the cake with a generous amount of fresh raspberries or strawberries, or chocolate-covered strawberries, and, if you wish, pass soft whipped cream as a sauce. Or cover the top with peeled and sliced kiwifruit and strawberries. Or cover the cake with whipped cream, cover the cream generously with chocolate shavings, and pass brandied cherries separately to be spooned alongside each portion. Or mound about two-thirds of the whipped cream on top of the cake. Cover the cream generously with chocolate shavings, or dot it with candied violets or rose petals. Fit a pastry bag with a star-shaped tube and use the remaining cream to form a border of rosettes around the rim of the cake. One final option: Cut the top of the firm, chilled cake, removing the raised rim and making the top smooth. Then serve the cake upside down, either just as is or with confectioners' sugar on top.

Serve the cake cold, in small portions — this is rich!

QUEEN MOTHER'S CAKE

Makes 12 portions This was in my first book and in my chocolate book. It is one of the most popular recipes in all of my books and is the one cake I make more often than any other. I originally got the recipe in 1962 from a food column by Clementine Paddleford in the *New York Herald Tribune*.

Jan Smeterlin, the eminent pianist, picked up the recipe on a concert tour in Austria. When the Queen Mother was invited to tea at the home of some friends of the Smeterlins, the hostess baked the cake according to Smeterlin's recipe. The Queen Mother loved it and asked for the recipe. Then — as the story goes — she served it often at her royal parties.

It is a flourless chocolate cake that is nothing like the flourless chocolate cakes that have become so popular. It is not as heavy or dense. This has ground almonds and the texture is almost light, although it is rich and moist. It is divine.

The cake may be frozen before or after it is iced, but while the icing is fresh it has a beautiful shine, which becomes dull if the cake stands overnight or if it is frozen. So to enjoy this at its very best, ice the cake during the day for the night. But I know several people who always have an un-iced Queen Mother's Cake in the freezer.

---

6 ounces (scant 1½ cups) blanched (skinned) or unblanched whole almonds

6 ounces semisweet chocolate, chopped into small pieces

¾ cup sugar

6 ounces (1½ sticks) unsalted butter

6 large eggs, separated

⅛ teaspoon salt

1 teaspoon lemon juice

ICING

½ cup whipping cream

2 teaspoons instant espresso or coffee powder

8 ounces semisweet chocolate, chopped into small pieces

OPTIONAL, FOR SERVING: Chocolate Cigarettes (below) or sweetened whipped cream and raspberries

---

First toast the almonds in a single layer in a shallow pan in a 350-degree oven for 12 to 15 minutes, shaking the pan a few times, until the almonds are lightly colored and have a delicious smell of toasted almonds when you open the oven door. Set aside to cool.

Adjust a rack one-third up in the oven and preheat oven to 375 degrees. Butter the bottom and sides of a 9 x 3-inch springform pan and line the bottom with a round of baking parchment cut to fit. Butter the paper. Dust the pan all over with fine, dry bread crumbs, invert over paper,

continues ↘

and tap lightly to shake out excess. Set the prepared pan aside.

Place the chocolate in the top of a small double boiler over hot water on moderate heat. Cover until partially melted, then uncover and stir until just melted and smooth. Remove the top of the double boiler and set it aside until tepid or room temperature. Place the almonds and ¼ cup of the sugar (reserve remaining ½ cup sugar) in a food processor fitted with a metal chopping blade. Process very well, until the nuts are fine and powdery. Stop the machine once or twice, scrape down the sides, and continue to process for at least a full minute. I have recently realized that the finer the nuts are, the better the cake will be. Set aside the ground nuts.

In the large bowl of an electric mixer, beat the butter a bit until soft. Add ¼ cup of the sugar (reserve remaining ¼ cup sugar) and beat to mix. Add the egg yolks one at a time, beating and scraping the sides of the bowl as necessary until smooth. On low speed, add the chocolate and beat until mixed. Then add the processed almonds and beat, scraping the bowl, until incorporated.

Now the whites should be beaten in the large bowl of the mixer. If you don't have an additional large bowl for the mixer, transfer the chocolate mixture to any other large bowl.

In the large bowl of the mixer, with clean beaters, beat the egg whites with the salt and lemon juice, starting on low speed and increasing it gradually. When the whites barely hold a soft shape, reduce the speed a bit and gradually add the remaining ¼ cup sugar. Then, on high speed, continue to beat until the whites just barely hold a straight point when the beaters are slowly raised. Do not overbeat.

Stir a large spoonful of the whites into the chocolate mixture to soften it a bit.

Then, in three additions, fold in the remaining whites. Do not fold thoroughly until the last addition and do not handle any more than necessary.

Turn the mixture into the prepared pan. Rotate the pan a bit briskly from left to right in order to level the batter.

Bake for 20 minutes at 375 degrees and then reduce the temperature to 350 degrees and continue to bake for an additional 50 minutes (total baking time is 1 hour and 10 minutes). Do not overbake; the cake should remain soft and moist in the center. (The top might crack a bit—it's OK.)

The following direction was in the original recipe, and although I do not understand why, I always do it. Wet and slightly wring out a folded towel and place it on a smooth surface. Remove the cake pan from the oven and place it on the wet towel. Let stand until tepid, 50 to 60 minutes.

Release and remove the sides of the pan (do not cut around the sides with a knife—it will make the rim of the cake messy). Now let the cake stand until it is completely cool, or longer if you wish.

The cake will sink a little in the middle; the sides will be a little higher. Use a long, thin, sharp knife and cut the top level. Brush away loose crumbs.

continues ↘

Place a rack or a small board over the cake and carefully invert. Remove the bottom of the pan and the paper lining. The cake is now upside down; this is the way it will be iced. Place four strips of baking parchment (each about 12 x 3 inches) around the edges of a cake plate. With a large, wide spatula, carefully transfer the cake to the plate; check to be sure that the cake is touching the papers all around (in order to keep the icing off the plate when you ice the cake).

If you have a cake-decorating turntable or a lazy Susan, place the cake plate on it.

For the icing:

Scald the cream in a 5- to 6-cup saucepan over moderate heat until it begins to form small bubbles around the edges or a thin skin on top. Add the espresso or coffee powder and whisk to dissolve. Add the chocolate and stir occasionally over heat for 1 minute. Then remove the pan from the heat and whisk or stir until the chocolate is all melted and the mixture is smooth.

Let the icing stand at room temperature, stirring occasionally, for about 15 minutes or a little longer, until the icing barely begins to thicken.

Then, stir it to mix, and pour it slowly over the top of the cake, pouring it onto the middle. Use a long, narrow metal offset spatula to smooth the top and spread the icing so that a little of it runs down the sides (not too much — the icing on the sides should be a much thinner layer than on the top). With a small, narrow metal offset spatula, smooth the sides.

Remove the strips of paper by pulling each one out by a narrow end.

⸺

Serve with Chocolate Cigarettes or whipped cream and fresh raspberries. Decorate the cake or individual portions with the Chocolate Cigarettes. Or place a mound of whipped cream (lightly sweetened with confectioners' sugar and lightly flavored with vanilla extract; see page 103) on one side of each portion on individual dessert plates, and a few raspberries on the other side of each portion.

Chocolate Cigarettes

These are long thin curls of chocolate that are used as a decoration. They look very professional. You can find compound or coating chocolate at kitchen supply stores, or online.

NOTE

If the room is too cold or the chocolate stands too long, it might not curl or it could crack when you form the cigarettes.

To make a very generous amount of chocolate curls (you can make much less) coarsely chop about 8 ounces of compound chocolate (see page 15). Melt the chocolate slowly in the top of a double boiler over hot water on moderate heat. When partially melted, remove from the water and stir until completely melted. Pour onto a marble work surface (such as a large marble cheese board), forming a ribbon about 3 to 4 inches wide and 10 inches long. The chocolate should be about ¼ to ⅜ inch thick. Let cool at room temperature until it is no longer soft or sticky.

To make the curls, use a long, heavy knife — I use a Sabatier chef's knife with a 12-inch blade. Hold it at a 45-degree angle across the width and right near the end of the chocolate. Cut down slowly and firmly. The chocolate will roll around itself as it is cut. Repeat, each time placing the blade very close to the cut end — the curls should be paper thin. Transfer them with a wide metal offset spatula to a shallow tray. Cover with plastic wrap and store either at room temperature, if it is not too warm, or in the refrigerator or freezer.

CHOCOLATE SOUFFLÉ CAKE

Makes 10 portions   At one time, one of the most talked-about chocolate cakes in New York City was the Chocolate Soufflé Cake from Fay and Allen's Foodworks (a fancy food store formerly on the Upper East Side). I had heard raves about it. It was described as a soft, moist, rich, dark chocolate mixture with a crisp, brownie-like crust.

In September 1980, my husband and I were on a tour to promote my chocolate book, and were in New York for only a few hectic days. As we were checking out of our hotel, I suddenly remembered the Chocolate Soufflé Cake. With the taxi waiting, I rushed to the phone to call Fay and Allen's, and to my surprise and joy, within a few minutes I had the recipe. I spoke to Mr. Mark Allen, the man who baked the cakes, and the son of the owner. He could not have been nicer or more agreeable. He told me that he got the recipe when he attended the Culinary Institute of America.

It is a flourless mixture similar to a rich chocolate mousse, baked in a large Bundt pan. During baking, a crisp crust forms on the outside; the inside stays quite wet.

The recipe calls for long, slow baking. It is best to serve it hot, right out of the oven. It is even better if you serve a few fresh raspberries and/or strawberries with each portion.

NOTE
↓
This cake will crumble a bit as you cut through the bottom (previously the top) crisp crust. (It did at Fay and Allen's, too.) Don't try to cut thin slices. Do try to cut with a serrated knife.

8 ounces semisweet chocolate, coarsely chopped

8 ounces (2 sticks) unsalted butter

2 tablespoons vegetable oil

8 large eggs, separated

1 cup granulated sugar

1 teaspoon vanilla extract

¼ teaspoon salt

Confectioners' sugar or Whipped Cream (below)

Adjust a rack one-third up from the bottom of the oven and preheat oven to 300 degrees. You will need a 10-inch Bundt pan or any other fancy-shaped tube pan with a 12-cup capacity. Butter the pan (even if it is nonstick): The best way is to use room temperature melted butter and brush it on with a pastry brush. Then sprinkle granulated sugar all over the pan; in order to get the sugar on the tube, sprinkle it on with your fingertips. Shake the pan to coat it thoroughly with sugar, then invert it over a piece of paper and tap to shake out excess. Then sprinkle 1 to 2 teaspoons of sugar evenly in the bottom of the pan. Set the pan aside.

Place the chocolate in the top of a large double boiler over hot water on moderate heat. Cut up the butter and add it and the oil to the chocolate. Cover and let cook until almost completely melted. Then stir, or whisk with a wire whisk, until completely melted and smooth. Remove from the hot water.

In a mixing bowl, stir the yolks a bit with a wire whisk just to mix. Gradually, in a few additions, whisk about half of the hot chocolate mixture into the yolks, and then, off the heat, add the yolks to the remaining hot chocolate mixture and mix together (the mixture will thicken a bit as the heat of the chocolate cooks the eggs). Add the sugar and vanilla and stir to mix. Set aside.

In the large bowl of an electric mixer, add the salt to the egg whites and beat until the whites hold a point but are not stiff or dry.

Fold a few large spoonfuls of the whites into the chocolate mixture. Then add the chocolate mixture to the whites and fold together gently until incorporated.

Gently turn the mixture into the prepared pan.

Bake for 2 hours and 15 minutes. During baking the cake will rise and then sink; it will sink more in the middle than on the edges. That is as it should be. It is OK.

Remove from the oven and, without waiting, cover the cake with an inverted serving plate. Hold the pan and the plate firmly together and turn them over. The sugar coating in the pan forms a crust and the cake will slide out of the pan easily.

Serve while still hot. If you wish, cover the top of the cake generously with confectioners' sugar, sprinkling it on through a fine strainer held over the cake. Brush excess sugar off the plate.

(A few years later, while in New York I went to Fay and Allen's to eat the cake there. I was thrilled to see that it was precisely the same as the ones I had made. They served it quite warm, just out of the oven, with a generous topping of icy cold whipped cream.)

Whipped Cream

2 cups heavy cream
¼ cup confectioners' sugar
1½ teaspoons vanilla extract

In a chilled bowl with chilled beaters, whip the cream, confectioners' sugar, and vanilla only until the cream holds a shape; it is more delicious If It Is not really stiff. (If you whip the cream ahead of time and refrigerate it, it will separate slightly as it stands; just whisk it a bit with a wire whisk before serving.) Serve the cream separately, spooning a generous amount over and alongside each portion.

HAZELNUT AND BOURBON CHOCOLATE CAKE

Makes 12 portions A chic and classy single layer of dense, intense chocolate-coffee-bourbon cake with a shiny, dark chocolate glaze. There are many chocolate cakes with ingredients similar to these, but this one has more chocolate per square inch than any other I know. The cake can be made a day before it will be served, but it is best to ice it the same day you will serve it.

NOTE
↓

To make chocolate crumbs, simply mix enough unsweetened cocoa powder into fine dry bread crumbs or flour to give the mixture a medium-brown color. It is handy to keep a jar of these already mixed. They last well.

- 12 ounces semisweet chocolate, finely chopped
- ¼ cup bourbon
- ¾ cup *sifted* unbleached all-purpose flour
- 1 tablespoon unsweetened cocoa powder (preferably Dutch-process)
- 2 teaspoons instant espresso or coffee powder
- 2½ ounces (½ cup) blanched (skinned) and toasted hazelnuts (see page 19)
- ½ cup sugar
- 4 ounces (1 stick) unsalted butter
- 3 large eggs, separated
- Pinch of salt

ICING

- 6 ounces semisweet chocolate, finely chopped
- ¼ cup whipping cream
- 1 tablespoon unsalted butter

OPTIONAL: 12 blanched and toasted hazelnuts

Sweetened softly whipped cream

Adjust a rack one-third up from the bottom of the oven and preheat the oven to 350 degrees. Butter an 8-inch springform pan, which may be 2 or 3 inches deep, although the cake will be only 1½ inches high. Line the bottom with a round of baking parchment cut to fit, butter the paper, and dust the pan all over with chocolate bread crumbs (see Note). Then, over paper, shake out excess crumbs; set the pan aside.

Place the chocolate and bourbon in the top of a large double boiler over warm water on low heat. Cover and let cook until partly melted. Then uncover and stir until completely melted and smooth. Remove and set aside the top of the double boiler.

Sift together the flour, cocoa, and espresso or coffee powder.

Place the hazelnuts in the bowl of a food processor fitted with the metal chopping blade. Add about one-third of the sugar (reserve the remaining sugar) and

continues ↘

2 generous tablespoons of the sifted dry ingredients (reserve the remaining sifted ingredients).

Process for 30 seconds, scraping the sides once, until the nuts are fine. Set aside.

In the small bowl of an electric mixer, beat the butter with one-half of the remaining sugar (reserve the remaining sugar) until thoroughly mixed. Add the egg yolks all at once and beat until mixed. Then beat in the chocolate mixture, which may still be warm (the mixture might look curdled, but it will be OK). Then add the ground-nut mixture and beat until incorporated.

Remove the bowl from the mixer and transfer the ingredients to the large bowl of the mixer.

Wash the small bowl of the mixer and the beaters (unless you have an additional bowl and additional beaters), and beat the egg whites with the salt until they barely hold a soft shape. On moderate speed, gradually add the remaining sugar. Then, on high speed, beat until the whites just barely hold a straight point when the beaters are raised. Remove the bowl from the mixer.

Sift the remaining sifted ingredients over the chocolate mixture, and turn the beaten egg white mixture over the sifted ingredients. With a rubber spatula fold everything together, folding only until you do not see any dry ingredients (you may see a bit of egg white that is not blended). Do not handle any more than necessary.

Turn into the prepared pan. Tilt the pan slightly to smooth the top.

Bake for 30 minutes. The center will still feel soft; the rim will just spring back when gently pressed with a fingertip.

Place the pan on a rack and let stand until cooled to room temperature.

Remove the sides of the pan. If the rim of the cake is higher than the center, it should be trimmed. If so, it is best to chill the cake (for only 10 to 15 minutes) in the freezer before trimming. If you have a cake decorating turntable, place the cake (still on the bottom of the pan) on the turntable, and use a long, thin knife (such as a ham slicer) to level the top.

To place the cake upside down on a cake plate, cover it with a wide and flat plate, turn the cake and the plate upside down, and then remove the bottom of the pan and the paper lining.

If the cake is going to wait overnight before being iced, cover it airtight with plastic wrap.

For the icing:

Place the chocolate, cream, and butter in the top of a double boiler over warm water on low heat. Cover until partly melted, then uncover and stir until melted and smooth. Remove the top of the double boiler and set aside for about 10 minutes, stirring occasionally.

Meanwhile, to protect the plate while icing the cake, slide four strips of baking parchment (each about 2½ x 9 inches) under the edges of the cake (you can gently raise the edge a bit with a wide metal offset spatula as you slide the papers under). The cake should touch the papers all around. If you have a cake-decorating turntable, place the cake plate on it.

Stir the icing and pour it all onto the top of the cake. With a long, narrow metal offset spatula, smooth the icing over the top of the cake, allowing a bit of it to run down the sides. Then, with a small, narrow metal offset spatula, smooth the icing (in a thin coat) on the sides.

Place the optional hazelnuts in a ring close to the rim around the top.

Remove the paper strips by pulling each one out by a narrow end of the strip.

Serve each portion with a large spoonful of whipped cream.

SEPTEMBER 7TH CAKE

Makes 12 portions I named this fabulous flourless cake for my birthday so I was sure to have it on my special day. Two thin, lightweight, dark layers are filled with white whipped cream and are thickly covered with a wonderful dark coffee-chocolate whipped cream. The cake has no flour; it is really a fluffy chocolate omelet that settles down like a hot soufflé when it cools. This may be made a day before or early in the day for that night, or the layers may be frozen before they are filled and iced.

On my 101st birthday, Hurricane Irma was approaching South Florida. As we hurriedly packed, my neighbors, the Fullers, came over at 9:00 a.m. for store-bought cake and coffee, and then everyone hastily left. For my 102nd birthday, I really would like to have this cake, please!

CAKE

- 6 extra-large eggs, separated
- ¾ cup granulated sugar
- ¼ cup plus 1 tablespoon strained unsweetened cocoa powder (preferably Dutch-process)
- ¼ teaspoon salt

FILLING

- ¾ teaspoon unflavored gelatin
- 1½ tablespoons cold water
- 1½ cups heavy cream
- ⅓ cup confectioners' sugar
- ¾ teaspoon vanilla extract

ICING

- 8 ounces semisweet chocolate, coarsely chopped
- 2 ounces (½ stick) unsalted butter
- 1 tablespoon instant espresso or coffee powder
- ¼ cup boiling water
- 2 cups heavy cream
- ¼ cup confectioners' sugar
- 1 teaspoon vanilla extract

Adjust rack one-third up from bottom of the oven and preheat oven to 375 degrees. Butter two 9-inch round layer-cake pans. Line the bottoms with rounds of wax paper or baking parchment cut to fit. Butter the paper, dust the inside of each pan all over with flour, and invert the pans and tap to shake out excess flour.

In the small bowl of an electric mixer, beat the egg yolks at high speed for 5 minutes, until they are light lemon-colored. Add about half (6 tablespoons) of the granulated sugar (reserve the remaining half) and continue to beat at high speed for 5 minutes more, until the mixture is very thick and forms a wide ribbon when the beaters are lifted.

Add the cocoa and beat on lowest speed, scraping the bowl with a rubber spatula, and beating only until the cocoa is completely mixed in. Remove from the mixer and set aside.

continues ↘

Add the salt to the egg whites in the large bowl of the electric mixer. With clean beaters, beat at high speed until the whites increase in volume and barely hold a soft shape. Reduce the speed to moderate while gradually adding the reserved granulated sugar. Increase the speed to high again and continue to beat until the whites hold a definite shape when the beaters are raised or when some of the mixture is lifted on a rubber spatula — they should not be stiff or dry.

In several additions, small at first (about a large spoonful), fold half of the beaten whites into the chocolate mixture. Then fold the chocolate mixture into the remaining whites. Do not handle any more than necessary.

Turn half of the mixture into each of the prepared pans. Gently smooth each layer.

Bake for 30 to 35 minutes, until the layers spring back when lightly pressed with a fingertip and begin to come away from the sides of the pans.

Remove from the oven. With a small sharp knife, carefully cut around the sides of the layers to release them. Cover each layer with a rack, invert pan and rack, remove pan, and peel off the paper lining. Cover layer with another rack and invert again to let the layers cool right side up.

While they are cooling, the layers will sink and the sides will buckle and look uneven, but don't worry. That is to be expected in this recipe. The filling and icing will cover them and they will be light, moist, and delicious.

When the layers are completely cool, prepare a flat cake plate as follows: Cut four strips of wax paper, each one about 10 x 3 inches. Place them around the outer edges of the plate.

Place one cake layer upside down on the plate and see that the wax paper touches all the edges of the cake.

For the filling:

Sprinkle the gelatin over the water in a small heatproof cup. Let stand for 5 minutes. Place the cup in a small pan containing about an inch of hot water. Set over moderate heat and let stand until the gelatin dissolves, then remove from the hot water and set aside.

Reserve 2 or 3 tablespoons of the cream and place the remainder in the small bowl of an electric mixer (if the room is warm, the bowl and beaters should be chilled). Add the confectioners' sugar and vanilla. Beat only until the cream has increased in volume and holds a soft shape. Then quickly stir the reserved tablespoons of cream into the warm dissolved gelatin and, with the mixer going, pour the gelatin all at once into the slightly whipped cream and continue to beat. The cream should be beaten until it is firm enough to hold a shape.

Place the whipped cream on the bottom cake layer. Carefully spread it evenly. Cover it with the other layer, placing the top layer right side up. Place in the refrigerator and prepare the icing.

For the icing:

Place the chocolate in the top of a small double boiler over hot water on moderate heat. Add the butter. In a large cup, dissolve the coffee in the boiling water and pour it over the chocolate. Stir with a rubber spatula until the mixture is melted and smooth. Remove it from the hot water and transfer it to a medium mixing bowl.

Now the chocolate must cool to room temperature. You can let it stand or, if you are very careful not to overdo it, stir it briefly over ice and water — but do not allow the chocolate to harden. In any event, the chocolate must cool to room temperature — test it on the inside of your wrist.

When the chocolate has cooled, place the cream, confectioners' sugar, and vanilla in the small bowl of the electric mixer. Beat only until the cream holds a soft shape. It is very important that you do not whip the cream until it holds a definite shape; that would be too stiff for this recipe and would not only cause the icing to be too heavy but would also give it a slightly curdled appearance. Everything about this cake should be light and airy, and the chocolate will stiffen the cream a bit more.

In two or three additions, fold about half of the cream into the chocolate, and then fold the chocolate into the remaining cream.

Ice the cake:

Remove the cake from the refrigerator. If you have a turntable for decorating cakes or a lazy Susan, place the cake plate on it.

Use as much of the icing as you need to fill in any hollows on the sides of the cake — use a spoon or a metal offset spatula — and then smooth the icing around the sides. If you are working on a turntable, rotate it while you hold a small metal offset spatula against the sides to smooth the icing.

Now the cake can be finished in one of two ways (depending on whether or not you want to use a pastry bag). You can either use all of the icing to cover the top very thickly, or you can spread it very thinly and reserve about 3 cups of the icing and decorate the top with a pastry bag and a star-shaped tube.

Place the icing on the top and spread it smooth. Then spread the sides again to make them neat.

To decorate the top, which will be completely covered with rippled lines of icing, fit a 15-inch pastry bag with a #6 (½-inch) star tube and fold down a deep cuff on the outside of the bag. Place the icing in the bag. Unfold the cuff. Close the top of the bag. To form the icing lines, begin at the edge of the cake farthest from you. Squeeze an inch or two of icing out of the tube in a line coming toward you. Continue to squeeze and, without stopping the flow of the icing, move the tube back away from you over about half the line you have just formed, making another layer of icing on the first. Still without stopping the flow of the icing, bring the tube toward you again and make another 1- to 2-inch line, then double back over half of the distance again. Continue across the whole diameter of the cake. The finished line will be along the middle of the cake. Make another, similar line to one side of the first, touching it. I find it easier to work from the middle — one side all the way and then the other side all the way — to entirely cover the top of the cake with these wavy lines.

Remove the strips of wax paper by pulling each one out by a narrow end.

Refrigerate for at least 6 hours or overnight and serve cold. To slice this cake without squashing it, insert the point of a sharp knife in the center of the cake. Then cut with an up-and-down sawing motion.

ABBY MANDEL'S BOULE DE NEIGE (SNOWBALL)

Makes 8 to 12 portions This is a dense, dark, moist chocolate mixture completely covered in tiny rosettes of whipped cream. It is in a class by itself — not a pudding, not a mousse, not a cake, yet vaguely like all three. It looks elegant, tastes divine, and is easy. It should be made at least a day before serving, or it may be refrigerated for 4 or 5 days; or it may be frozen, but the whipped cream should be put on the day it is served.

My neighbor Hope was asked to do a cake baking demo at a local community center. Since Boule de Neige was her favorite go-to recipe, she carried it off so well that the *Miami Herald* wanted to photograph the cake. Hope was too busy to bake another one, so she decorated an upside-down bowl with shaving cream and some artistic chocolate shavings (you know where this is going) and put it aside. When backs were turned, one of her houseguests scooped up a generous fingerful and got a hefty taste of Gillette Foamy.

NOTE
↓
Abby Mandel, the beautiful and talented Machine Cuisine cooking teacher, made this in a food processor (in about a minute) as follows: Break up the chocolate and place it with the coffee and sugar in a processor bowl that has been fitted with the steel blade. Turn the machine on and off four times to start the processing and then let the machine run until the chocolate is finely chopped. With the machine running, add the boiling water through the feed tube and process until the chocolate is melted. Add the butter in small pieces and process until blended. Add the eggs and Cognac or rum and process about 15 seconds, until well combined. Pour into the foil-lined bowl and continue the recipe.

- 8 ounces semisweet chocolate (if possible, use Baker's German's Sweet)
- 2 teaspoons instant espresso or coffee powder
- ½ cup boiling water

- 1 cup sugar
- 8 ounces (2 sticks) unsalted butter, at room temperature, cut into pieces
- 4 large eggs
- 1 tablespoon Cognac or dark rum

WHIPPED CREAM

- 1 cup heavy cream
- 2 tablespoons sugar
- 2 teaspoons Cognac or dark rum

Adjust rack one-third up from the bottom of the oven and preheat oven to 350 degrees. You will need a round, ovenproof mixing bowl (for baking this dessert) with a 6- to 8-cup capacity; it may

continues ↘

be glass, pottery, or metal, and it should preferably be deep and narrow rather than wide and shallow. (I use a stainless-steel bowl that measures 4½ inches high by 6 inches across the top and has an 8-cup capacity — although a smaller bowl would do.)

To line the bowl with aluminum foil, turn the bowl upside down, tear off a 12-inch square of foil, and center it over the inverted bowl. With your hands, press down on the sides all around to form the foil into a bowl shape. Then remove the foil, turn the bowl right side up, and place the bowl-shaped foil into the bowl. Press it firmly into place and set aside.

Break up the chocolate and place it in a small saucepan. Dissolve the coffee in the boiling water and add it to the chocolate along with the sugar. Stir over moderate heat until the chocolate is melted — the mixture does not have to be smooth.

Transfer to the large bowl of an electric mixer and beat on low speed until smooth. Gradually add the butter and continue to beat on low speed until smoothly blended. Add the eggs one at a time, beating until smooth after each addition. Add the Cognac or rum and beat on moderate speed for about a minute.

Pour the mixture into the lined bowl and bake for 55 minutes. When done the top will be puffy with a thick, cracked crust. (If you have used a bowl with an 8-cup capacity, the mixture will not rise to the top.)

Let the bowl stand at room temperature until the dessert is cool — it will shrink as it cools and will shrink more in the center than around the rim. This will leave a hollow in the middle, which should be eliminated. The following directions will seem unusual, but follow them. A few minutes after the dessert has been removed from the oven, place a piece of wax paper on top of the bowl, touching the dessert. With your fingertips, press down on the edges of the paper to flatten the raised rim of the dessert (the crust will crack — that's all right). Repeat several times while the dessert is cooling in order to flatten the top as much as possible.

When the dessert is cool, cover airtight and refrigerate overnight or for a few days, or freeze.

A few hours before serving, when you are ready to unmold the dessert and mask it with whipped cream, remove its covering. Invert a flat dessert plate over it (since the dessert will be solid white, a colored or clear glass plate will look better than an all-white one), invert the plate and bowl, remove the bowl, and then peel off the aluminum foil. Refrigerate.

For the whipped cream:

You will need a pastry bag about 13 inches long and a medium-small star tube, or about a #4. Insert the tube into the bag, fold down a deep cuff on the outside of the bag, and set aside.

In a chilled bowl with chilled beaters, whip the cream until it holds a soft shape. Add the sugar and Cognac or rum and continue to beat until the cream holds a definite shape, but be careful not to make it too stiff or it might curdle while you press it out of the pastry bag.

Transfer the cream to the pastry bag, unfold the cuff, and twist the top of the bag closed.

Now you completely cover the dessert with small pointed rosettes of whipped cream. Start at the center top and squeeze out one small rosette right in the middle. Then make a circle of rosettes touching one another around the one on top. Then another circle, etc. — the last circle should touch the plate.

Refrigerate.

(Traditionally, a Boule de Neige is decorated with a few crystallized violets and/or rose petals — if you use them, press them into the cream just before serving or they may run and discolor the cream.)

CRANBERRY UPSIDE-DOWN CAKE

Makes 8 portions If you like the tart flavor of cranberries you will be wild about this; I do and I am. It is a single layer of lovely, moist white cake covered with a generous topping of fresh cranberries that is brushed with red currant jelly after baking. It is shiny cranberry-red gorgeous. Although this is all quick and easy, I would be happy to serve it at a Thanksgiving dinner. This can be a luncheon or dinner dessert, or a brunch coffee cake, or a treat to serve with tea or coffee in the afternoon. You need fresh cranberries for this.

12 ounces (4 cups) fresh cranberries

5 ounces (1¼ sticks) unsalted butter, at room temperature

1 cup plus 2 tablespoons sugar

1¼ cups *sifted* unbleached all-purpose flour

1½ teaspoons baking powder

¼ teaspoon salt

1 large egg

1 teaspoon vanilla extract

⅔ cup milk

Finely grated zest of 1 large, deep-colored orange

⅓ cup red currant jelly

OPTIONAL, FOR SERVING: vanilla ice cream, sweetened whipped cream, or Ricotta Cream (below)

Adjust a rack one-quarter up from the bottom of the oven and preheat the oven to 350 degrees. You will need a 9 x 1½-inch round layer-cake pan (it should not be shallower).

Wash the cranberries briefly in cold water, discard loose stems, drain, and then spread the berries on a towel to dry a bit.

Use 4 tablespoons (½ stick) of the butter (reserve the remaining ¾ stick of butter) — it must be soft but not melted. Spread a bit of it on the sides of the pan and then, with the bottom of a spoon, spread the remainder (of the 4 tablespoons) over the bottom of the pan. Sprinkle ½ cup plus 2 tablespoons of the sugar (reserve the remaining ½ cup) over the butter. Sprinkle the berries over the sugar. They will almost fill the pan — it is OK. Set the pan aside.

Sift together the flour, baking powder, and salt with the remaining ½ cup of sugar and set aside.

In the small bowl of an electric mixer, beat the remaining ¾ stick of butter until soft. Beat in the egg and vanilla. Then, on the lowest speed, add the sifted dry ingredients in three additions alternately with the milk in two additions, mixing only until just combined (the mixture might appear slightly curdled — it is OK). Remove the bowl from the mixer, stir in the grated zest, and pour over the berries.

Smooth the top. The pan will be full —
it is OK.

Bake for 1 hour; the top will become quite
brown during baking.

Cool the cake in the pan on a rack for
20 minutes. After 10 minutes cut around
the sides with a small, sharp knife to
release the cake.

Meanwhile, place the jelly in a small pan
over moderate heat; stir occasionally until
the jelly melts and comes to a boil. Set
aside briefly.

After the 20 minutes are up, cut around
the sides of the cake again.

Cover with a flat cake plate, hold the pan
and the plate firmly together, and turn
them both over. Remove the pan.

Pour the melted jelly onto the cake and,
with the bottom of a spoon, spread it to
cover the top completely (right up to the
edges — if a bit runs over the sides it is OK,
but not too much).

Let stand until completely cool. Serve the
cake at room temperature.

If you serve this by itself it is really quite
tart, but with something bland and creamy
and icy cold it is divine. You could serve it
with vanilla ice cream, whipped cream (with
a bit of sugar and vanilla; see page 103), or
Ricotta Cream.

Ricotta Cream

**1 cup all-natural whole milk
ricotta cheese**

**2 teaspoons sugar (or 2 teaspoons
light honey)**

A few drops vanilla extract

In a food processor fitted with a
steel blade, process the ricotta for
a full minute (at least). Then add the
sweetener and vanilla and process to
incorporate.

Transfer to a covered container and
refrigerate for several hours or longer.

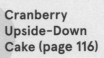

Cranberry
Upside-Down
Cake (page 116)

Pineapple
Upside-Down
Cake

PINEAPPLE UPSIDE-DOWN CAKE

Makes 6 to 8 portions This pretty cake is quick and easy, light and delicious, and although it is very old-fashioned, it never goes out of style. It makes a lovely dessert cake but is also wonderful as a coffee cake to serve at breakfast, brunch, or a kaffeeklatsch. Serve it while it is fresh; it is extra good while it is still hot and for several hours after it is baked.

TOPPING

- 2⅓ ounces (5⅓ tablespoons) unsalted butter
- ½ cup firmly packed light brown sugar
- 1 (20-ounce) can or 2 (8-ounce) cans sliced pineapple (packed in natural juice)

  OPTIONAL: pecan halves, canned black Bing cherries, stewed prunes, candied cherries, or maraschino cherries

CAKE BATTER

- 1 cup *sifted* unbleached all-purpose flour
- ⅓ teaspoon baking powder (measure 1 level teaspoon, mark it into thirds, return ⅔ to the box, and use the remaining ⅓)
- ¼ teaspoon salt
- 2 large eggs
- ⅔ cup granulated sugar
- 1 teaspoon vanilla extract
- 6 tablespoons drained pineapple juice from the canned rings

APRICOT GLAZE

- ½ cup apricot preserves

You will need a frying pan with a heatproof handle or a pie plate with an 8-cup capacity. (The average deep 10-inch frying pan or 12-inch pie plate should be the right size, but measure the capacity to be sure.)

Adjust a rack to the center of the oven and preheat oven to 350 degrees. Spray the pan or plate with nonstick cooking oil spray—this recipe works better with a nonstick spray than it does with a buttered pan.

Place the butter in a small pan over moderate heat to melt.

Pour the melted butter evenly over the bottom of the sprayed pan or plate. Sprinkle the brown sugar evenly all over the butter, then, with your fingers, pat the sugar to press it into an even layer, making sure it is all moistened with the melted butter.

Drain the pineapple, reserving the juice for the cake batter, and place the slices on paper towels to dry.

Now, with the pineapple rings, make a pretty design around the outside of the pan on top of the sugar. And if there is room, place one ring in the middle. If there is not room for a whole ring in the middle, you can use one half of a ring. Cut it into quarters and form a design with the pieces.

continues ↘

You will probably not use all of the pineapple slices.

Traditionally, pecan halves are arranged flat side up in a pattern in the spaces between the pineapple rings. And a black Bing cherry, a piece of stewed prune, or a maraschino or candied cherry is put in the middle of each ring.

Either arrange the fruit as described or make up your own pattern. My favorite design is as follows: Place one pineapple ring directly in the center. Cut the other rings in half, making two half circles from each ring. Place the half circles, touching each other (and touching the ring in the center) and fitting one against the other, all facing the same way — the cut sides of one against the round side of another, all around the pan.

Set the pan aside and prepare the batter.

For the batter:

Sift together the flour, baking powder, and salt and set aside. In the small bowl of an electric mixer, beat the eggs at high speed for about a minute. Gradually add the granulated sugar while beating and continue to beat (total beating time about 5 minutes) until the mixture is thick and pale. Add the vanilla and the pineapple juice and beat on low speed, scraping the bowl with a rubber spatula, beating only until smooth. Still on low speed, add the sifted dry ingredients, scraping the bowl and beating only until smooth.

Pour the batter evenly over the fruit.

Bake for 45 to 50 minutes, until the top just barely springs back when it is lightly pressed with a fingertip and a toothpick gently inserted into the middle comes out clean and dry. (The cake might begin to come away from the sides of the pan — another sign that it is done.)

While it is baking, prepare the glaze.

For the glaze:

The preserves should be bubbling hot and ready to be used as soon as the frying pan or pie plate is removed from the oven. Therefore, 5 or 10 minutes before the cake is done, melt the preserves in a small pan over moderate heat. Force them through a strainer. Return to the pan and bring to a boil.

To serve:

The very second that the cake comes out of the oven it must be removed from the pan. Cover the cake with a serving plate or board. If you have baked the cake in a frying pan, the handle might be in the way; use good pot holders and be careful. Center the plate carefully, and immediately turn over the plate and the frying pan or pie plate — hold it all firmly to prevent the cake plate from slipping. Having turned everything over, do not remove the frying pan or pie plate immediately; wait a minute or so to allow all of the butter/sugar topping to settle onto the cake. Remove the pan or pie plate carefully. If any nuts have slipped out of place on the cake, rearrange them.

With a pastry brush, brush the hot preserves generously over the top and sides of the hot cake.

Serve the cake hot or cooled.

Use a serrated knife for slicing, preferably the small one called a tomato knife.

COOKIES

POSITIVELY-THE-ABSOLUTELY-BEST-CHOCOLATE-CHIP COOKIES

Makes about 50 (3-inch) cookies A poll taken among food editors at newspapers and magazines found that chocolate chip cookies were the number-one favorite of all homemade cookies in America. (That's not news.)

Well, this recipe is the mother of all chocolate chip cookie recipes.

The following recipe is closely based on the original Toll House recipe. But I make a few changes: I use 2 teaspoons vanilla instead of 1. And I use 16 ounces of chocolate instead of 12. Also, instead of using morsels, I use semisweet or bittersweet chocolate bars, cut into pieces.

Do not sift the flour before measuring it! Just stir it a bit to aerate it.

8 ounces (2 sticks) unsalted butter

1 teaspoon salt

2 teaspoons vanilla extract

¾ cup granulated sugar

¾ cup firmly packed light brown sugar

2 large eggs

2¼ cups *unsifted* unbleached all-purpose flour

1 teaspoon baking soda

1 teaspoon hot water

8 ounces (2 generous cups) walnuts, chopped or broken into medium-size pieces

16 ounces semisweet or bittersweet chocolate bars, chopped into pieces

NOTES

↓

I was told that this is a big secret: Mrs. Fields refrigerates her chocolate chip cookie dough before shaping and baking. (Actually, Ruth Wakefield, who created the original Toll House recipe in the 1930s, did also.) The dough should be cold when the cookies go into the oven. The cookies have a much nicer and more even golden brown color.

↓

This method of dissolving the baking soda before adding it is the way Mrs. Wakefield did it. The Nestlé Toll House recipe sifts the soda with the flour. I do not know which method is better. I only know these are delicious this way.

↓

You may think 16 ounces of chocolate is too much to be incorporated into the dough. Just be patient. It's not too much.

Adjust two racks to divide the oven into thirds and preheat oven to 375 degrees. Line cookie sheets with baking parchment or with aluminum foil, shiny side up.

In the large bowl of an electric mixer, beat the butter until soft. Add the salt, vanilla, and both sugars and beat to mix. Add the eggs and beat to mix. On low speed, add about half the flour and, scraping the bowl with a rubber spatula, beat until incorporated.

In a small cup, stir the baking soda into the hot water (see Notes), then mix into the dough. Add the remaining flour and beat only until incorporated.

Remove the bowl from the mixer. Stir in the walnuts and the chocolate.

Spread out a large piece of aluminum foil next to the sink. Use a rounded tablespoonful of the dough for each cookie and place the mounds any which way on the foil.

Then wet your hands with cold water and shake off excess, but do not dry your hands. Pick up a mound of dough and roll it between your wet hands into a ball, then press it between your hands to flatten it to about a ½-inch thickness.

Place the cookies on the lined sheets about 2 inches apart.

Bake two sheets at a time, reversing the sheets top to bottom and front to back as necessary to ensure even browning. (If you bake one sheet alone, bake it on the upper rack.) Bake for about 12 minutes, until the cookies are browned all over. The cookies must be crisp; do not underbake.

Let the cookies stand for a few seconds, then transfer with a metal spatula to racks to cool.

Store in an airtight container.

David's Cookies
(page 129)

Big Sur Chocolate Chip Cookies

Positively-the-Absolutely-Best-
Chocolate-Chip Cookies (page 124)

$250.00
Cookies
(page 132)

Colorado Cowboy
Cookies (page 131)

BIG SUR CHOCOLATE CHIP COOKIES

Makes 12 to 15 very large cookies These California cookies are 6 inches in diameter — they are the largest homemade chocolate chip cookies I know (nothing succeeds like excess). They are crisp, crunchy, buttery, delicious. Too good. Irresistible. But because of their size, don't make them for a fancy tea party. Do make them for a barbecue or a picnic, or for any casual affair.

1½ cups *sifted* unbleached all-purpose flour

½ teaspoon salt

1 teaspoon baking soda

½ teaspoon ground cinnamon

6 ounces (1½ sticks) unsalted butter

1½ teaspoons vanilla extract

1 teaspoon lemon juice

⅔ cup firmly packed light brown sugar

⅓ cup granulated sugar

2 large eggs

¼ cup quick-cooking rolled oats

6 ounces (generous 1½ cups) walnuts, chopped or broken into medium-size pieces

6 ounces (1 cup) semisweet chocolate morsels

Adjust two racks to divide the oven into thirds and preheat oven to 350 degrees. Line cookie sheets with baking parchment or foil.

Sift together the flour, salt, baking soda, and cinnamon and set aside. In the large bowl of an electric mixer, cream the butter. Add the vanilla and lemon juice and then both of the sugars and beat to mix. Beat in the eggs one at a time. On low speed, add the sifted dry ingredients and then the rolled oats, scraping the bowl as necessary with a rubber spatula and beating only until mixed. Remove from the mixer and stir in the nuts and morsels.

Now work next to the sink or have a large bowl of water handy so you can wet your hands while shaping the cookies. Spread out a piece of wax paper or foil. Use a ¼-cup measuring cup to measure the amount of dough for each cookie. Form 12 to 15 mounds of the dough and place them any which way on the wax paper or foil. Wet your hands with cold water, shake the water off, but do not dry your hands; pick up a mound of dough, roll it into a ball, flatten it to about ½-inch thickness, and place it on the lined sheets. Do not place more than 4 cookies on a 15½ x 12-inch cookie sheet. These spread to gigantic proportions.

Bake two sheets at a time for 16 to 18 minutes, reversing the sheets top to bottom and front to back as necessary to ensure even browning. (If you bake only one sheet at a time, bake it on the higher rack.) Bake until the cookies are well colored; they must not be too pale. Watch these carefully; before you know it, they might become too dark.

When you remove them from the oven, let the cookies stand for about a minute, until

continues ↘

they are firm enough to be moved. With a wide metal spatula, transfer them to racks to cool. If the racks are not raised at least ½ inch from the work surface, place them on a bowl or cake pan to allow more air to circulate underneath.

When cool, wrap them with bottoms together, two to a package, in cellophane or wax paper or in plastic sandwich bags. If you do not plan to serve these soon, freeze them.

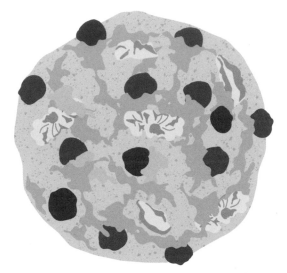

DAVID'S COOKIES

Makes 40 to 50 small cookies David's Cookies was the name of a small chain of bakeries in New York City and its suburbs that became wildly popular in the mid-'80s. These chocolate chunk cookies put them on the map.

David's trademark was that his cookies were made with coarsely chopped semisweet chocolate bars, instead of morsels. As far as I know, this recipe has been and still is a closely guarded secret—but here it is.

It is best to bake these on parchment. If you line the sheets with foil, or if you butter them, the cookies spread out too much and the edges become too thin and brittle. If you butter and flour the sheets, the cookies tend to burn.

NOTE

↓

To make these like David's, do not overbake. Actually, David underbaked them (6 to 8 minutes baking time), but I like 8 to 10 minutes or even longer if necessary. David's were very soft; mine are slightly crispier.

---

8 ounces semisweet or bittersweet chocolate

8 ounces (2 sticks) unsalted butter

½ teaspoon salt

½ teaspoon vanilla extract

1 cup firmly packed light or dark brown sugar

1 large egg

2 cups *sifted* unbleached all-purpose flour

OPTIONAL: 4 ounces (generous 1 cup) pecans or walnuts, chopped or broken into large pieces

---

Adjust two racks to divide the oven into thirds and preheat oven to 400 degrees. Line cookie sheets with baking parchment. Place the chocolate on a cutting board and, with a long, heavy, sharp knife, cut the chocolate first in one direction and then in the opposite direction, making uneven ¼- to ½-inch (or larger) pieces. Set aside.

In the large bowl of an electric mixer, beat the butter until soft. Beat in the salt and vanilla, then the sugar, until well mixed. Add the egg and beat, scraping the bowl with a rubber spatula, until mixed. Then, on low speed, add the flour and beat until incorporated. Remove from the mixer.

With a heavy wooden spoon, stir in the chopped chocolate and the optional nuts. The mixture will be thick and sticky. Use two teaspoons to shape the cookies, one for picking up dough and one for pushing it off. Use a rounded teaspoonful of dough for each cookie. Do not make these too large. Place the cookies 2 inches apart on the lined sheets.

Bake two sheets at a time for 8 to 10 minutes, reversing the sheets top to bottom and front to back as necessary to ensure even browning. Bake only until the

continues ↘

edges of the cookies start to brown (see Note). If some are done before others, remove them as they become ready and bake the rest as necessary. If they are too soft to handle, let them wait on the sheet for a few seconds and they will become firmer. With a wide metal spatula, transfer the cookies to racks to cool.

VARIATION

I have often made these huge, and they are wonderful. I make only 9 or 10 cookies with the full amount of dough. Here's how:

Preheat the oven to only 350 degrees (instead of the 400 degrees used for the smaller cookies).

Place a large piece of aluminum foil on the counter next to the sink. Use ¼ cup of the dough for each cookie (measure with a ¼-cup metal measuring cup) and place the mounds any which way on the foil. Wet your hands with cold water and shake the water off but do not dry your hands. Roll a mound of the dough between your cold, wet hands to form a ball, and then flatten the ball to about ½-inch thickness. Place only 3 cookies on each lined cookie sheet.

Bake the cookies for 20 to 22 minutes, reversing the sheets top to bottom and front to back as necessary to ensure even browning, until the cookies are lightly colored and just barely spring back when pressed lightly with a fingertip.

Let the cookies cool briefly on the paper until they are firm enough to be moved, and then use a wide metal spatula to transfer them to racks to cool.

COLORADO COWBOY COOKIES

Makes 36 cookies In Colorado any oatmeal cookie that contains chocolate chips is called a Cowboy Cookie. I've had many versions and no two were alike. The cowboy who gave me this recipe said, "There are enough for a cowboy and his horse." I halved his recipe (we don't have a horse), but you can multiply it by any number. These are deliciously crisp cookies that will keep very well in a cookie jar.

1 cup *sifted* unbleached all-purpose flour

½ teaspoon baking soda

¼ teaspoon baking powder

¼ teaspoon salt

4 ounces (1 stick) unsalted butter

½ teaspoon vanilla extract

½ cup granulated sugar

½ cup firmly packed dark brown sugar

1 large or extra-large egg

1 cup quick-cooking or old-fashioned rolled oats

3 ounces (½ cup) semisweet chocolate morsels

2 ounces (generous ½ cup) walnuts or pecans, chopped or broken into medium-size pieces

Adjust two racks to divide the oven into thirds and preheat oven to 350 degrees. Line cookie sheets with aluminum foil.

Sift together the flour, baking soda, baking powder, and salt and set aside. In the large bowl of an electric mixer, cream the butter. Add the vanilla and then both sugars and beat well. Add the egg and beat well. On low speed, gradually add the sifted dry ingredients and beat, scraping the bowl with a rubber spatula, until incorporated.

Remove the bowl from the mixer. Stir in the oats and then the chocolate morsels and nuts. Transfer to a small bowl for ease in handling. (The dough will be rather stiff.)

Use a well-rounded (slightly less than heaping) teaspoonful of the dough to make each cookie. Place the mounds 2 inches apart on the lined sheets. Bake for about 18 minutes, until the cookies are golden-colored. (If you bake only one sheet at a time, bake it on the upper rack.) During baking, reverse the sheets top to bottom and front to back to ensure even browning.

With a wide metal spatula, transfer the cookies to racks to cool. When completely cool, store them in an airtight container.

THE $250.00 COOKIE RECIPE

Makes about 54 cookies I heard a story that began with a lady and her daughter having lunch at Neiman Marcus in Dallas, Texas. For dessert they ordered the "Neiman Marcus Cookie." It was so delicious that the lady asked the waitress if she could have the recipe.

"I'm afraid not."

"Could I buy the recipe?"

"Yes."

"How much?"

"Two fifty."

The lady was pleased and asked the waitress to just add it to her bill.

A month later when she received her credit card statement she saw, "Cookie recipe — $250.00."

She spoke to the credit department at the store and asked them to take back the recipe and credit her account. The store people said they couldn't do that. They said that all of their recipes were very expensive so that everybody wouldn't get them and copy them.

The lady customer told the store people that she was going to spread the recipe all over the country. The store people said, "We wish you wouldn't do that." But she did. She said it was the only way she could get even.

2 cups *sifted* unbleached all-purpose flour	4 ounces milk chocolate	2 large eggs
1 teaspoon baking powder	8 ounces (2 sticks) unsalted butter	12 ounces (2 cups) semisweet chocolate morsels
1 teaspoon baking soda	¼ cup firmly packed light brown sugar	6 ounces (1½ cups) walnuts, chopped into medium-size pieces
½ teaspoon salt	½ cup granulated sugar	
2½ cups old-fashioned rolled oats	1 teaspoon vanilla extract	

Adjust two racks to divide the oven into thirds and preheat oven to 375 degrees. Line cookie sheets with baking parchment or aluminum foil, shiny side up; set aside.

Sift together the flour, baking powder, baking soda, and salt; set aside.

Place the oatmeal in the bowl of a food processor fitted with the metal chopping blade. Cut or break the milk chocolate into pieces and add it to the oatmeal. Process for 20 or 25 seconds, until the oatmeal and the chocolate are almost powdered. Set aside.

In the large bowl of an electric mixer, beat the butter until soft. Add both sugars and the vanilla and beat until mixed. Beat in the eggs. Then, add the sifted dry ingredients and the oatmeal mixture and beat on low speed, scraping the bowl with a rubber spatula as necessary and beating only until mixed.

Remove the bowl from the mixer and stir in the chocolate morsels and walnuts. (It will be a stiff mixture.)

Place a long piece of aluminum foil next to the sink. Use a rounded tablespoon of the dough for each cookie. Place mounds of the dough any which way on the foil.

Wet your hands with cold water. Shake them off a bit but don't dry them. Roll a mound of the dough between your hands to form a ball, flatten it a bit, and place it on a lined cookie sheet. Continue shaping the cookies and placing them about 2 inches apart on the lined sheets. Wet your hands as often as necessary.

Bake two sheets at a time for about 14 minutes, until the cookies are lightly colored and are just about firm to the touch. Reverse the sheets top to bottom and front to back as necessary during baking to ensure even browning. Remove the sheets from the oven. Let the cookies stand on the sheets briefly, then transfer them with a wide metal spatula to racks to cool.

Store in an airtight container.

CHOCOLATE HERMITS

Makes 24 large cookies Hermits are very old-fashioned cookies that usually have raisins, nuts, and spices. Some were made in a shallow, oblong pan and cut into squares; some were drop cookies. This yummy chocolate version is a drop cookie. They are large, thick, semisoft, dark, not too sweet, slightly spicy, full of raisins and nuts, and topped with a white sugar glaze. They keep well; they are great for a lunch box or a picnic, or for wrapping as a gift. Or for just having around.

3 ounces unsweetened chocolate

1¼ cups *sifted* unbleached all-purpose flour

2 teaspoons baking powder

¼ teaspoon salt

1 tablespoon unsweetened cocoa powder (preferably Dutch-process)

1 teaspoon ground cinnamon

1 teaspoon instant espresso or coffee powder

4 ounces (1 stick) unsalted butter

1 teaspoon vanilla extract

1 cup granulated sugar

1 large egg

⅓ cup milk

5 ounces (1 cup) raisins

4 ounces (generous 1 cup) walnut or pecan halves or pieces

GLAZE

¾ cup *sifted* or strained confectioners' sugar

1 tablespoon unsalted butter, melted

½ teaspoon vanilla extract

1 tablespoon milk or light cream

Pinch of salt

Adjust two racks to divide the oven into thirds and preheat oven to 350 degrees. Line two cookie sheets with baking parchment.

Place the chocolate in the top of a small double boiler over hot water on moderate heat. Cover until partly melted. Uncover and stir until completely melted. Remove the top of the double boiler and set aside to cool slightly.

Sift together the flour, baking powder, salt, cocoa, cinnamon, and coffee and set aside.

In the large bowl of an electric mixer, cream the butter. Add the vanilla and then the granulated sugar and beat to mix

well. Then add the egg and the melted chocolate (which may still be slightly warm) and beat well. Beat in the milk. Then, on low speed, add the sifted dry ingredients, scraping the bowl as necessary with a rubber spatula and beating only until mixed. Remove from the mixer and stir in the raisins and nuts.

Use a well-rounded tablespoonful of the dough for each cookie (make these large). Place the mounds at least 1 inch apart (place 12 mounds on each 15½ x 12-inch cookie sheet); they spread only slightly.

Bake for 18 to 20 minutes, reversing the sheets top to bottom and front to back once during baking to ensure even baking.

The cookies are done if they feel slightly firm to the touch and just barely spring back when they are lightly pressed with a fingertip. Do not overbake.

For the glaze:

In a small bowl, stir all the ingredients to mix well. The mixture must be smooth. It should be about the consistency of thin and runny mayonnaise; adjust it with more sugar or milk. Cover the glaze airtight until you are ready to use it.

Just as soon as you take the cookie sheet out of the oven, spoon or brush some of the glaze over the tops of the hot cookies. Do not attempt to cover all over the tops—just spread it on the middle and let it run down the sides a bit. Then, with a wide metal spatula, transfer the cookies to racks to cool.

When the glaze has dried and is no longer sticky, the cookies should be stored airtight. If you package them in a box, put wax paper between the layers. I wrap them, two to a package, bottoms together, in clear cellophane.

CHOCOLATE WHOPPERS

Makes 15 tremendous cookies We were at the Soho Charcuterie, one of my favorite restaurants in New York City. They brought us a dish of huge, gorgeous, dark chocolate cookies that we had not ordered. They smiled secretively and knowingly and watched me. I tasted one, it was wonderful. I was just about to ask for the recipe when they said, "These are yours." I soon learned that they meant it both ways: The cookies were mine to eat or take with me, and also, the recipe was from my first book. They had increased the size of the cookies and made a few other little changes and they called them Chocolate Gobs. They told me that they couldn't make them fast enough. This recipe is based on their adaptation.

At Sonrisa Bakery, in beautiful Rancho Santa Fe in southern California, these were called Charlie's Cookies, in memory of a friend of ours who was a great World War II naval pilot. His name was Charles Stimpson, and he shot down 17 enemy planes. These were Charlie's favorites.

2 ounces unsweetened chocolate

6 ounces semisweet chocolate

3 ounces (¾ stick) unsalted butter

¼ cup *sifted* unbleached all-purpose flour

¼ teaspoon baking powder

½ teaspoon salt

2 large eggs

¾ cup sugar

2 teaspoons instant espresso or coffee powder

2 teaspoons vanilla extract

6 ounces (1 cup) semisweet chocolate morsels (see Notes)

4 ounces (generous 1 cup) walnuts, chopped or broken into large pieces

4 ounces (generous 1 cup) toasted pecans, chopped or broken into large pieces (see Notes)

NOTES

If you wish, in place of semisweet morsels, use 6 ounces semisweet chocolate, cut into ½-inch chunks.

To toast pecans, place them in a shallow pan in the middle of a pre-heated 350-degree oven for 12 to 15 minutes.

Adjust two racks to divide the oven into thirds and preheat oven to 350 degrees. If you are baking only one sheet, adjust a rack to the middle of the oven. Line cookie sheets with baking parchment or foil.

Place the unsweetened chocolate, semisweet chocolate, and butter in the top of a small double boiler over hot water on moderate heat. Cook, covered, for a few minutes. Then stir occasionally until melted and smooth. Remove the top of the double boiler and set aside, uncovered, to cool slightly.

Sift together the flour, baking powder, and salt, and set aside.

In the small bowl of an electric mixer, beat the eggs, sugar, coffee or espresso, and vanilla at high speed for a minute or two.

Beat in the melted chocolate and butter (which may still be quite warm) on low speed just to mix. Add the sifted dry ingredients and again beat on low speed just to mix, scraping the sides of the bowl as necessary with a rubber spatula to incorporate the ingredients. Remove from the mixer and transfer to a larger bowl.

Stir in the chocolate morsels, walnuts, and pecans.

Use a ⅓-cup metal measuring cup to measure the amount of batter for each cookie. Use a rubber spatula to push the mixture into the measuring cup and then to scoop it out onto the lined sheet (the dough is gooey). Put 5 cookies on each cookie sheet, one in the middle and one toward each corner. Do not flatten the tops.

Bake two sheets at a time, reversing the sheets top to bottom and front to back once during baking to ensure even baking. Bake for 16 to 17 minutes — no longer. The surface of the cookies will be dry but the insides will still be soft. There is really no way to test these; just use a portable oven thermometer before baking to be sure your oven is right, and then watch the clock.

If the sheets have four rims the cookies and papers or foil will have to wait on the sheets until cool. If you have used cookie sheets with only one or two raised rims, you can slide the papers off the sheets and let the cookies stand until cool. (It is not necessary to let the sheet cool before sliding it under another paper with unbaked cookies on it.)

When the cookies have cooled, use a wide metal spatula to release them and turn them over to air the bottoms a bit.

I wrap these individually in clear cellophane.

MARJORIE KINNAN RAWLINGS'S CHOCOLATE COOKIES

Makes 25 large cookies Shortly after I finished work on my chocolate book, we were driving through central Florida and stopped for gas in the town of Cross Creek. I was delighted to see a little sign in the garage office that announced "Homemade Brownies 4 Sale." The garage man told me his wife baked them fresh every day and the delivery for that day was expected in an hour. We paid for a dozen brownies and told him we would be back. After an hour of driving around in circles, we returned just as the brownies were being delivered. They were drop cookies, not bar cookies. They were unusually good, and certainly worth waiting for. When I asked for the recipe I was told that his wife would not part with it, but his mother-in-law had worked for Marjorie Kinnan Rawlings and this had been Mrs. Rawlings's recipe. I couldn't wait to get home to see if it was in *Cross Creek Cookery* (Mrs. Rawlings's cookbook). It was. The garage man's wife had made a change (she added the chocolate morsels), and I added the coffee and omitted the baking powder.

They taste like brownies should: chewy, chocolatey, wonderful. Best of all, they are quick and easy to make, and keep well too.

---

1 cup *sifted* unbleached all-purpose flour

¼ teaspoon salt

Scant 2 teaspoons instant espresso or coffee powder

¼ cup boiling water

2 ounces unsweetened chocolate, coarsely chopped

3 ounces (¾ stick) unsalted butter

½ teaspoon vanilla extract

1 cup sugar

2 large eggs

2½ ounces (½ cup) raisins

8 ounces (2 cups) walnuts, chopped or broken into large pieces

6 ounces (1 cup) semisweet chocolate morsels

Adjust two racks to divide the oven into thirds and preheat oven to 350 degrees. Cut baking parchment to fit cookie sheets. Sift together the flour and salt and set aside.

In a small saucepan, dissolve the coffee in the water, add the chocolate, place over low heat, and stir with a rubber spatula until smooth; it will be a thick mixture. Set aside.

continues ↘

Chocolate Hermits
(page 134)

Marjorie
Kinnan
Rawlings's
Chocolate
Cookies

Chocolate
Ladyfingers
(page 141)

Chocolate
Whoppers (page 136)

In the large bowl of an electric mixer, beat the butter until it is soft. Add the vanilla and then the sugar and beat until mixed. Add the chocolate mixture (which may still be warm) and beat until smooth and thoroughly mixed. Then add the eggs one at a time, beating well after each addition. On low speed add the sifted dry ingredients, scraping the bowl with a rubber spatula and beating only until mixed. Remove from the mixer.

Stir in the raisins, nuts, and chocolate morsels.

Use a heaping teaspoonful of the mixture for each cookie. Place them on the parchment, 2 inches apart; 8 cookies will fit on a 15½ x 12-inch sheet. Slide a cookie sheet under the parchment.

Bake for 13 to 15 minutes, reversing the sheets top to bottom and front to back once during baking to ensure even baking. (If you bake only one sheet at a time, bake on the higher rack.) The cookies are done if they just barely spring back (but just barely — do not overbake) when lightly pressed with a fingertip.

With a wide metal spatula, carefully transfer the cookies to rack to cool.

Store in an airtight container.

CHOCOLATE LADYFINGERS

Makes about 25 (5-inch) or 32 (4-inch) ladyfingers

While not a stand-alone dessert, Chocolate Ladyfingers serve as the foundation for many spectacular inspirations, Tiramisu (page 256) being the obvious. Fresh berry trifle is another. Or split one lengthwise and fill with ice cream. Kids love it!

NOTE

⬇

If you do not have superfine sugar, place plain granulated sugar in the bowl of a food processor fitted with the metal chopping blade and process for 30 seconds.

- ⅔ cup plus 2 tablespoons *sifted* unbleached all-purpose flour
- ¼ cup unsweetened cocoa powder (preferably Dutch-process)
- OPTIONAL: 1 tablespoon instant espresso or coffee powder

- 4 large eggs, separated
- 1¼ teaspoons vanilla extract
- ¼ teaspoon salt
- ⅛ teaspoon cream of tartar

- ½ cup plus 3 tablespoons superfine sugar (see Note)
- Confectioners' sugar (for sifting over the tops before baking)

Adjust two racks to divide the oven into thirds and preheat the oven to 325 degrees. Lightly butter two cookie sheets, dust them with flour through a sifter, and shake off excess over the sink. Set aside.

Have ready a 15-inch pastry bag fitted with a plain round tube that has a ⅝-inch opening (#8): Fold down a cuff about 2 inches wide on the outside of the bag. Twist the tube end of the bag and push it up a bit into the bag to prevent the batter from leaking out. Place the bag in a tall glass or jar to support it while you fill it. Set aside.

Sift together the flour, cocoa, and optional espresso or coffee powder until the color is even.

In a small bowl, beat the yolks and vanilla with an eggbeater to mix well. Set aside.

Place the egg whites and salt in a clean small bowl of an electric mixer and, with clean beaters, beat on medium speed until foamy. Add the cream of tartar and beat on high speed until the whites hold a straight point when the beaters are raised. On moderate speed, add the superfine sugar 1 rounded teaspoonful at a time. Then beat on high speed again until the whites are stiff but not dry. Remove the bowl from the mixer.

Add the beaten yolks all at once to the whites and fold together without being thorough about it. Turn into a large mixing bowl. In three additions, sift the flour mixture over the top and fold it in

continues ⬎

with a rubber spatula. At first do not be completely thorough with the folding, and even at the end, fold only until you do not see any dry ingredients. Even if the mixture looks lumpy and not smooth, do not fold any more.

Turn the mixture into the pastry bag. Unfold the cuff, gather the top of the bag closed, untwist the tube end, and press out ladyfingers onto the prepared sheets. Form about 1-inch-wide ladyfingers that are 4 to 5 inches long (unless they are to be used for lining a pan or bowl, in which case make them only as long as necessary to fit the pan or bowl). Allow ½ to ¾ inch of space between ladyfingers. At the end of each ladyfinger, lift the pastry bag slowly toward the other end of the ladyfinger to prevent leaving a tail of the batter.

Through a fine strainer, quickly strain confectioners' sugar generously onto the ladyfingers and bake immediately.

Bake for 15 to 18 minutes, reversing the sheets once, top to bottom and front to back, to ensure even baking. Bake until the ladyfingers are lightly colored and feel dry and springy when gently pressed with a fingertip. Then remove them with a wide metal spatula.

Store the ladyfingers airtight, flat sides together. These are delicious either fresh and soft or after they have become dry and crisp. But for lining a container (as for an ice-box cake) they should be very fresh. They can be frozen.

PENNIES FROM HEAVEN

Makes about 70 small cookie sandwiches Tiny cookie sandwiches, delicate and dainty, with a dough that is a delicious classic shortbread. It is baked in rounds not much larger than quarters, and they are sandwiched together with just a bit of buttercream. Make these for a tea party. Or serve them alongside a fruit or ice cream dessert.

The recipe is from Chris Gargone, the executive pastry chef at Remi, which Gael Greene called the best Italian restaurant in New York City. At Remi they served these on a plate of assorted cookies. However I serve them, I don't have enough. They are too good.

½ cup old-fashioned rolled oats (to use when shaping the dough into long, thin rolls)

1 cup plus 1 tablespoon *sifted* unbleached all-purpose flour

1 cup plus 1 tablespoon strained cornstarch

1 cup plus 1 tablespoon confectioners' sugar

8 ounces (2 sticks) unsalted butter

Pinch of salt

1 teaspoon vanilla extract

FILLING

3 ounces (¾ stick) unsalted butter

¼ teaspoon vanilla extract

¼ teaspoon dark rum

2 teaspoons heavy cream

½ cup confectioners' sugar

NOTE
↓

I want to thank my good friends Nick Malgieri and the late Richard Sax. Without their help, I couldn't have gotten this recipe.

Place the oatmeal in the bowl of a food processor fitted with the metal chopping blade. Pulse the machine several times, until the oatmeal is powdery. Remove from the processor; set aside.

It is not necessary to wash and dry the processor bowl and blade now.

Place the flour, cornstarch, and sugar in the bowl of the food processor fitted with the metal chopping blade. Pulse once or twice to mix. Cut the butter into ½-inch pieces and add to the flour mixture, along with the salt and vanilla. Process only until the ingredients form a ball and hold together.

Work with half the dough at a time.

Spread the processed oatmeal on a large board or work surface. Place the dough on the oatmeal. With your hands, form the dough into a tube shape. Roll gently, back and forth, using both hands. Start at the center and work your hands outward — as

continues ↘

you roll — to the ends. Roll until the dough is 11 inches long, about 1½ inches in diameter, and evenly shaped. Set aside; roll the remaining half of the dough to the same size and shape.

Place the rolls on a cookie sheet (you can just roll them onto it) and refrigerate for about an hour (or longer if you wish).

To bake, adjust a rack in the center of the oven and preheat oven to 325 degrees. Line cookie sheets with baking parchment or aluminum foil, shiny side up.

Use a knife with a very sharp and very thin blade. Cut the dough into slices about ⅛ inch thick or a little thicker. Place the slices 1 inch apart on the lined sheets.

Bake one sheet at a time for 14 to 16 minutes, until the cookies are sandy-colored around the edges (they can still be pale in the centers). Reverse the sheet front to back once during baking to ensure even browning. (If some are done before others, remove them individually.)

Transfer the cookies to a rack to cool or slide the paper or foil off the sheet and let stand until the cookies are cool. You can slice and bake both rolls now or, if you wish, you can wrap and freeze one to bake at some other time.

For the filling:

In the small bowl of an electric mixer, beat the butter until soft. Beat in the vanilla, rum, and cream. Then beat in the sugar.

When well mixed, transfer to a small bowl for ease in handling. Place a small dab (a scant teaspoon) of the filling on the bottom of one cookie. Place another cookie over it, bottoms together, and press gently all around to spread out the filling. There should not be enough to show; it should really just be enough to hold the two cookies together. Continue sandwiching all the cookies.

Place them in the refrigerator briefly, only long enough to harden the filling.

You will probably have leftover filling. It can be saved in the freezer for the next time you make these.

Store the cookie sandwiches in an airtight container.

COCONUT COOKIES

Makes about 36 cookies These are plain, old-fashioned, thin, extra-crisp, perfectly wonderful refrigerator cookies. They are a homemade version of a famous coconut cookie that used to be sold in Havana. My Cuban friends tell me these are better. Note that the dough must be refrigerated overnight or longer before baking.

3½ ounces (1 to 1⅓ cups) sweetened shredded coconut

2 cups *sifted* unbleached all-purpose flour

½ teaspoon baking powder

¼ teaspoon salt

6 ounces (1½ sticks) unsalted butter

1 teaspoon vanilla extract

¼ teaspoon almond extract

1 cup firmly packed light or dark brown sugar

1 large egg

Place the coconut in a shallow baking pan in the center of a preheated 350-degree oven. Stir it occasionally until it is toasted to a golden color. Set aside.

Sift together the flour, baking powder, and salt, and set aside.

In the large bowl of an electric mixer, cream the butter. Add the vanilla and

almond extracts, then the sugar, and beat to mix. Add the egg and beat to mix. On low speed, gradually add the sifted dry ingredients, beating only to mix. Remove from the mixer and stir in the coconut.

Place the mixture in the refrigerator for 20 to 30 minutes to chill a bit. Then flour your hands and a work surface. Turn the dough out onto the floured surface, press it together, and shape it into a cylinder about 6 inches long and 2 to 2½ inches in diameter. Wrap in plastic wrap. Refrigerate overnight. (If this is frozen it becomes difficult to slice thin enough without cracking, but it can be refrigerated for a few days if you wish.)

When you are ready to bake, adjust two racks high in the oven, or adjust them to divide the oven into thirds. If your oven has enough adjustments, higher is better. Preheat the oven to 325 degrees.

With a very sharp knife, cut extra-thin cookies; they should be less than ¼ inch thick. Place the cookies 1 inch apart on unbuttered cookie sheets.

Bake for about 16 minutes, reversing the sheets top to bottom and front to back once during baking to ensure even baking. Watch carefully; if the cookies appear to be browning too much on the bottom, be prepared to slide an additional cookie sheet under them. Do not underbake. Bake until the cookies are lightly browned. You won't believe how wonderfully crisp these are, but only if they are baked enough. (And then they will only stay that way if they are stored airtight.)

With a wide metal offset spatula, gently transfer the cookies to a rack to cool. As soon as they are cool, package them airtight.

CHINESE FORTUNE COOKIES

Makes about 15 fortune cookies These are quick and easy to mix and bake, but — unless you have someone to help you shape them — you can bake and shape only one at a time. (With someone to help, you can bake two on a cookie sheet.) Before you start to make the cookies, write or type the fortunes or greetings on strips of paper about 4 inches long and ½ inch wide.

1 large egg white

⅛ teaspoon vanilla extract

¼ cup *sifted* unbleached all-purpose flour

⅛ teaspoon salt

¼ cup sugar

Adjust a rack one-third up from the bottom of the oven and preheat oven to 400 degrees. Butter a circle about 5 inches in diameter on the middle of a cookie sheet. You will need something to shape the cookies on after they are folded in half; I use the rim of a Pyrex measuring cup.

In a small bowl, beat the egg white and vanilla until foamy. Add the flour, salt, and sugar and beat until smooth. Transfer to a small, shallow cup for ease in handling.

Place a teaspoonful (use a regular teaspoon, not a measuring spoon) of the batter in the middle of the buttered section. Tilt the sheet on a sharp angle in all directions to encourage the batter to run out into a round shape about 3 inches in diameter. Keep the shape as round as possibie, take your time, be patient. Use the tip of a small paring knife to guide the batter. If one area is thicker than the rest, level it by tilting the cookie sheet.

Bake for about 5 minutes, until the cookie has a golden rim almost ½ inch wide; the cookie will remain pale in the center.

As soon as it is baked, you have to work quickly. Place the cookie sheet on a large board (or next to a board). With a wide metal offset spatula, quickly remove the baked cookie and turn it upside down on the board. Quickly place the fortune on the cookie close to the middle, then immediately fold the cookie in half (the fortune goes along the length of the fold on one side of the fold) and quickly place the folded edge of the cookie across the rim of a measuring cup, pulling the pointed ends down, one on the inside and one on the outside of the cup. Hold it there for a few seconds until it becomes crisp.

(About now you might be saying, "Ow — that's hot!" If you wish, wear thin gloves.)

If you work with two cookie sheets, you can be shaping the next cookie while the first is baking. Each cookie sheet has to be washed, dried, and buttered each time. (I tried a nonstick sheet and the cookie didn't hold its shape.)

Continue to bake and shape the cookies. Any time you want to stop, just cover the batter and let it wait at room temperature for a few hours or up to overnight.

Store these in an airtight container.

Chocolate Chip and Almond Biscotti

Gingerful Biscotti (page 153)

Macadamia and Milk Chocolate Biscotti (page 155)

Bittersweet Chocolate Biscotti (page 157)

CHOCOLATE CHIP AND ALMOND BISCOTTI

Makes about 40 biscotti Irresistible. Awesome. With a huge, tremendous amount of chocolate chips. Chocolate chips never had it so good.

- 6 ounces (1¼ cups) blanched (skinned) whole almonds
- 2 cups *sifted* unbleached all-purpose flour
- ½ teaspoon baking soda
- ½ teaspoon baking powder
- ⅛ teaspoon salt
- 1 cup minus 2 tablespoons sugar
- 12 ounces (2 cups) semisweet chocolate morsels
- 2 large eggs
- 1 teaspoon vanilla extract
- 2 tablespoons whiskey or brandy

First toast the almonds in a single layer in a shallow pan in a preheated 350-degree oven for 12 to 15 minutes, shaking the pan a few times, until the almonds are lightly colored and have a delicious smell of toasted almonds when you open the oven door. Set aside to cool.

Adjust two racks to divide the oven into thirds and preheat oven to 375 degrees. If possible, use cookie sheets with two or three flat edges; otherwise use any sheets upside down. Line the sheets with baking parchment and set aside.

Into a large bowl (preferably one with flared rather than straight sides), sift together the flour, baking soda, baking powder, and salt. Add the sugar and stir to mix.

Place about ½ cup of the sifted dry ingredients in the bowl of a food processor fitted with the metal chopping blade. Add about ½ cup of the toasted almonds and process for about 30 seconds, until the nuts are fine and powdery.

Add the processed mixture to the sifted ingredients in the large bowl. Add the remaining toasted almonds and the chocolate morsels; stir to mix.

In a small bowl, beat the eggs with the vanilla and whiskey or brandy, just to mix.

Add the egg mixture to the dry ingredients and stir until the dry ingredients are moistened (I stir with a large rubber spatula). Be patient.

Place a length of baking parchment or wax paper on the counter next to the sink. Turn the dough out onto the parchment or wax paper. Wet your hands with cold water — do not dry them — and press the dough into a round mound.

With a long, heavy, sharp knife, cut the dough into equal quarters.

Continue to wet your hands as you form each piece of dough into a strip about 9 inches long, 2 to 2½ inches wide, and about ½ inch high (you will press, not roll,

continues ⌄

the dough into shape). The ends of the strips should be rounded rather than squared.

Place two strips crosswise on each of the lined sheets.

Bake for 25 minutes, reversing the sheets top to bottom and front to back once during baking.

Remove the sheets from the oven and slide the parchment off the sheets. With a wide metal spatula, transfer the baked strips to a large cutting board and let them cool for 20 minutes.

Reduce the oven temperature to 275 degrees.

With a serrated French bread knife, carefully cut on a sharp angle into slices about ½ inch wide. This is tricky. Cut slowly with a sawing motion.

Place the slices, cut side down, on the two unlined sheets.

Bake the two sheets, turning the slices over (ouch — they're hot) and reversing the sheets top to bottom and front to back once during baking. Bake for 25 to 30 minutes (depending on the thickness of the biscotti).

Turn the oven heat off, open the oven door, and let the biscotti cool in the oven.

When cool, store in an airtight container.

GINGERFUL BISCOTTI

Makes 60 to 70 biscotti Wolfgang Puck shared this vivid memory with me: We and our spouses took a shared holiday to the Kentucky Derby. While there, we were invited to sample rare bourbons at Brookside Distillery. I brought these biscotti. The combination was nirvana.

NOTE

↓

This is a lot of ginger. It's the way I like it — I love it. But use less if you prefer.

- 4 ounces (1 loosely packed cup) crystallized ginger (see Note)
- 6 ounces (1¼ cups) blanched (skinned) or unblanched whole almonds
- 3 cups *sifted* unbleached all-purpose flour
- ¾ teaspoon baking soda
- ¾ teaspoon baking powder
- ¼ teaspoon salt
- 1¼ teaspoons finely ground white pepper (preferably freshly ground)
- 1 teaspoon ground ginger
- ½ teaspoon ground cinnamon
- ½ teaspoon ground mustard powder
- ¼ teaspoon ground cloves
- ½ cup sugar
- 3 large eggs
- ½ cup mild honey

I find it easier to cut crystallized ginger with scissors. Cut it into thin slices and then crosswise to make pieces about the size of small green peas; set aside. (Yes, cutting ginger is boring.)

Toast the almonds in a shallow pan in a preheated 350-degree oven for 12 to 15 minutes, until lightly colored, stirring once during toasting. Set aside to cool.

Into a large bowl, strain or sift together — just to mix — the flour, baking soda, baking powder, salt, pepper, ground ginger, cinnamon, mustard, cloves, and sugar. Stir in the crystallized ginger, then the nuts. In a small bowl beat the eggs and honey to mix and add to the dry ingredients. Stir (preferably with a large rubber spatula) until the dry ingredients are completely moistened.

Place two 18- to 20-inch lengths of plastic wrap on a work surface. You will form two strips of the dough, one on each piece of plastic wrap. Spoon half of the dough by heaping tablespoonfuls in the middle — down the length — of each piece of plastic wrap, to form strips about 13 inches long. Flatten the tops slightly by dipping a large spoon into water and pressing down on the dough with the wet spoon. Rewet the spoon often.

Lift the two long sides of one piece of plastic wrap, bring the sides together on top of the dough, and, with your hands, press on the plastic wrap to smooth the dough and shape it into an even strip 13 to 14 inches long, 2½ to 3½ inches wide, and

continues ↘

about ¾ inch thick (no thicker). Shape both strips and place them on a cookie sheet.

(If there is an air bubble on the dough, pierce a small hole in the plastic wrap with the tip of a sharp knife to allow the air to escape. Then press on the plastic wrap to spread the dough into that space.)

Place the cookie sheet with the strips of dough in the freezer for at least an hour, or until firm enough to unwrap (or as much longer as you wish).

To bake, adjust two racks to divide the oven into thirds and preheat oven to 300 degrees. Line two large cookie sheets with baking parchment or aluminum foil, shiny side up.

To transfer the strips of dough to the sheets, open the two long sides of plastic wrap on top of one strip of dough and turn the dough upside down onto the lined cookie sheet, placing it diagonally on the sheet. Slowly peel off the plastic wrap. Repeat with the second strip of dough and the second cookie sheet.

Bake for 50 minutes, reversing the sheets top to bottom and front to back once during baking to ensure even baking. These will turn quite dark during baking.

Then reduce the temperature to 275 degrees and remove the sheets from the oven. Immediately — carefully and gently — peel the parchment or foil away from the backs of the strips and place them on a large cutting board. Slice the strips while they are still very hot. Use a pot holder or a folded towel to hold a strip in place. Use a serrated French bread knife. Slice on an angle; the sharper the angle, the longer the cookies, and the more difficult it will be to slice them very thin — but you can do it, and they will be gorgeous. Cut them about ¼ to ⅓ inch wide.

Place the slices on a cut side, touching each other, on the cookie sheets. Bake at 275 degrees for about 25 minutes, just until dry. (You have to cool one to know if it is crisp.) Do not overbake. Reverse the sheets top to bottom and front to back once during baking.

(If you bake one sheet alone they will bake in a bit less time. This is true of all cookies, but seems especially noticeable with these.)

Because these are so thin it is not necessary to turn them over during this second baking; they bake evenly without it.

When done, cool and then store them in an airtight container.

To serve, these are especially attractive standing upright in a wide, clear glass.

MACADAMIA AND MILK CHOCOLATE BISCOTTI

Makes about 24 large biscotti These are very large and divinely and deliciously crisp-crunchy. They are loaded with whole, voluptuous macadamias and extra-large chunks of creamy and dreamy milk chocolate. The flavor has a hint of toasted almonds. They involve a little more work — and a little more expense — than most other biscotti. And they are worth it all. Fantabulous! Get the best milk chocolate you can find.

1½ ounces (⅓ cup) blanched (skinned) whole almonds

12 ounces milk chocolate

2 cups *sifted* unbleached all-purpose flour

½ teaspoon baking powder

½ teaspoon baking soda

¼ teaspoon salt

1 cup sugar

7 ounces (1½ cups) roasted and salted whole macadamia nuts (I use Mauna Loa brand)

2 large eggs

1 teaspoon vanilla extract

¼ teaspoon almond extract

2 tablespoons whiskey or brandy

First toast the almonds in a shallow pan in a preheated 350-degree oven for 12 to 15 minutes, shaking the pan a few times, until the nuts are lightly colored and have a delicious smell of toasted almonds when you open the oven door. Set aside to cool.

Adjust a rack to the middle of the oven and preheat the oven to 375 degrees. Line a large, flat cookie sheet (preferably 17 x 14 inches) with heavy-duty aluminum foil. Set the sheet aside.

To cut the chocolate into chunks, I use an ice pick. However you do it, cut the chocolate into uneven pieces no more than about ½ inch in any direction. Set aside.

Into a large bowl (preferably one with flared rather than straight sides), sift together the flour, baking powder, baking soda, salt, and sugar.

Place about ⅓ cup of the sifted dry ingredients in the bowl of a food processor fitted with the metal chopping blade. Add the toasted almonds. Process for about 45 seconds, until the nuts are very fine and powdery.

Add the processed mixture to the sifted ingredients in the large bowl. Add the macadamia nuts and the cut-up chocolate. Stir to mix.

In a small bowl, beat the eggs, vanilla and almond extracts, and the whiskey or brandy, beating until well mixed.

Add the egg mixture to the dry ingredients and stir — and stir — until the dry ingredients are all moistened (I stir with a large rubber spatula — and a lot of patience). You will think there are not enough liquids; just

continues ⌎

keep on stirring. (Actually, stir and then turn the ingredients over and over and press down on them firmly with the spatula until the dry ingredients are incorporated.)

Generously spray the lined cookie sheet with nonstick cooking oil spray.

Turn the dough out onto the lined sheet. Wet your hands with cold water — do not dry them — and with your wet hands press the dough together to form a mound. Then shape it into an oval and flatten it a bit. With a dough scraper or with a large, metal spatula, cut the dough lengthwise into equal halves. Continue to wet your hands and shape into two strips, each one about 12 inches long, about 3 inches wide, and about 1 inch thick, with rounded ends. There should be 2 or 3 inches of space between the two strips, and the strips should be pressed firmly so that they are compact.

Bake for 28 minutes, reversing the sheet front to back once during baking.

Remove the sheet from the oven, slide the foil off the sheet onto a large cutting board, and let stand for 20 minutes.

Reduce the oven temperature to 275 degrees and adjust two racks to divide the oven into thirds.

With a wide metal spatula, transfer the baked strips to the cutting board.

Now, to cut these into biscotti, you must be careful. Use a serrated bread knife and cut with a sawing motion. (Actually, I find it is best to cut through the top crust with a serrated knife, and then finish the cut with a very sharp, straight-bladed knife. Or, you might use only one knife — try different knives.) Cut on an angle; the sharper the angle, the larger the biscotti will be. Unless you want very large biscotti, do not cut at too sharp an angle. Cut the biscotti about a scant ¾ inch wide.

At this stage, the biscotti are very fragile; use a large metal spatula or pancake turner to carefully transfer them to two unlined cookie sheets, placing them cut side down. Bake the two sheets for 35 minutes. Once during baking, turn the slices over and reverse the sheets top to bottom and front to back.

When finished, turn the oven off, open the oven door, and let the biscotti cool in the oven.

When they are cool, the chunks of chocolate might still be soft. If so, let the biscotti stand for about an hour, and then store them airtight.

BITTERSWEET CHOCOLATE BISCOTTI

Makes about 36 biscotti Extra hard and crunchy — thicker than most — and especially dark and delicious, made with chocolate and cocoa.

After you mix and shape the dough, it will have to spend 45 minutes in the freezer before it is baked. It will then be baked twice for a total of 1 hour and 45 minutes.

- 9 ounces (generous 2 cups) blanched (skinned) whole almonds
- 6 ounces semisweet chocolate
- 1¾ cups *sifted* unbleached all-purpose flour
- 1 teaspoon baking soda
- ⅛ teaspoon salt
- ⅓ cup unsweetened cocoa powder (preferably Dutch-process)
- 1 tablespoon instant espresso or coffee powder
- 1 cup granulated sugar
- 3 large eggs plus 1 large egg white
- ½ cup firmly packed light brown sugar
- 1 teaspoon vanilla extract
- Scant ½ teaspoon almond extract or ¼ teaspoon bitter almond extract

First toast the almonds in a wide, shallow pan in the center of a preheated 375-degree oven, stirring once or twice, for 12 to 13 minutes, until very lightly colored. Set aside to cool.

Chop or break the chocolate into small pieces and place in the bowl of a food processor fitted with the metal chopping blade. Let stand.

Into a large bowl, sift together the flour, baking soda, salt, cocoa, espresso, and granulated sugar.

Add about ½ cup of the sifted dry ingredients and about ½ cup of the almonds to the chocolate. Process for about 30 seconds, until the chocolate and nuts are fine and powdery.

Add the processed ingredients to the remaining sifted dry ingredients and stir to mix. Stir in the remaining almonds; set aside.

In a small bowl, beat the eggs and egg white, brown sugar, and vanilla and almond extracts until mixed.

Stir the egg mixture into the dry ingredients (you will think there's not enough liquid, but it will be OK). I use a large rubber spatula and push the ingredients together.

Now place two 15- to 20-inch lengths of plastic wrap on the work surface.

The dough will be thick and sticky. You will form a strip of it on each piece of the plastic wrap. Spoon half the dough in the middle — down the length — of one piece of plastic wrap to form a strip 12 inches long.

continues ⌄

Lift the two long sides of the plastic wrap, bring them together on top of the dough, and, with your hands, press on the plastic wrap to smooth the dough and shape it into an even strip 12 inches long, 3 inches wide, and ¾ inch high, with squared ends.

Repeat to form the second strip.

Place the strips on a cookie sheet and put in the freezer for about 45 minutes or until firm.

To bake, adjust two racks to divide the oven into thirds, and preheat oven to 300 degrees. Line two cookie sheets with baking parchment.

Open the two long sides of the plastic wrap on one strip of dough and turn the dough upside down on a lined sheet, placing it diagonally on the sheet; slowly peel off the plastic wrap. Repeat with the second strip and the second cookie sheet.

Bake for 1 hour, reversing the sheets top to bottom and front to back once during baking to ensure even baking.

After one hour, reduce the temperature to 275 degrees and remove the sheets from the oven. Immediately, while very hot, peel the parchment away from the back of a strip and place it right side up on a cutting board.

Use a pot holder or folded kitchen towel to hold the hot strip, and use a serrated French bread knife to cut. Cut across the strip, either straight across or on an angle (straight across is easier), cutting slices about ¾ inch wide.

Place the slices, standing upright, on a cookie sheet.

Repeat with the second strip.

Bake at 275 degrees for about 45 minutes, until completely dry. Reverse the sheets top to bottom and front to back once during baking.

Cool and store in an airtight container.

PEANUT BUTTER PILLOWS

Makes 16 to 20 filled cookies Peanut butter is sandwiched between two peanut butter icebox cookies and then the cookies are baked. They are crisp; the filling is soft.

- 1½ cups *sifted* unbleached all-purpose flour
- ½ teaspoon baking soda
- ¼ teaspoon salt
- 4 ounces (1 stick) unsalted butter
- ½ cup smooth (not chunky) peanut butter, plus more for filling (a scant ½ cup)
- ½ cup sugar
- ¼ cup light corn syrup (e.g., Karo)
- 1 tablespoon milk

NOTE

This dough may be mixed without a mixer. Simply place the sifted *dry ingredients and the sugar in a mixing bowl. With a pastry blender, cut in the butter and the peanut butter until the mixture resembles coarse meal. Stir in the syrup and milk. Then, on a board or a smooth work surface, knead the dough briefly with the heel of your hand until it is smooth.*

Sift together the flour, baking soda, and salt and set aside. In the small bowl of an electric mixer (or see Note), cream the butter. Add the peanut butter and sugar and beat until thoroughly mixed. Beat in the corn syrup and milk. On low speed, add the sifted dry ingredients, scraping the bowl as necessary with a rubber spatula and beating only until smooth.

Turn the dough out onto a large board or a smooth work surface. Knead it briefly and then, with your hands, form it into an even roll or oblong about 7 inches long and 2¼ to 2½ inches in diameter. Wrap the dough in wax paper. Slide cookie sheets under the paper and transfer the dough to the refrigerator and chill for several hours, or longer if you wish.

Adjust two racks to divide the oven into thirds and preheat oven to 350 degrees. Line cookie sheets with parchment.

With a sharp knife, cut half of the roll of dough into slices ⅛ to ¼ inch thick and, as you cut the slices, place them 2 inches apart on the cookie sheets.

Place 1 level measuring teaspoonful of the additional peanut butter in the center of each cookie. Then spread the peanut butter only slightly to flatten it, leaving a ½- to ¾-inch border.

Slice the remaining half of the roll of dough (same thickness) and, as you cut each slice, place it over one of the peanut butter–topped cookies. Let the cookies stand for 2 to 3 minutes for the dough to soften slightly. Then seal the edges by pressing them lightly with the back of the tines of a fork, dipping the fork in flour as necessary to keep it from sticking. (Don't worry about slight cracks in the tops.)

Bake for 12 to 15 minutes, until the cookies are lightly colored, reversing the position of the cookie sheets top to bottom and front to back to ensure even browning. (If you bake only one sheet at a time, bake it high in the oven.)

Let the cookies stand on the sheets for about a minute. Then, with a wide metal spatula, transfer them to racks to cool.

SKINNY PEANUT WAFERS

Makes about 28 wafers These are extremely thin wafers, crisp, crunchy, chewy, divine. They will remind you of peanut brittle. They are easy, fun, and very special. They could be served at the most elegant event, or at the simplest.

4 ounces (1 cup) salted peanuts (preferably honey roasted), plus optional additional peanuts to use as topping

1 cup sugar

2 tablespoons unsalted butter

1 cup *sifted* unbleached all-purpose flour

½ teaspoon baking soda

1 large egg

2 tablespoons milk

Adjust an oven rack to the center of the oven (you will bake only one sheet at a time). Preheat oven to 400 degrees. If you have cookie sheets with only one raised rim, these are best for this recipe; otherwise, turn your cookie sheet upside down. Line cookie sheets with aluminum foil, shiny side up. (Do not use heavy-weight foil—the cookies won't bake well.) Generously spray the foil with nonstick cooking oil spray. Set aside.

Place the peanuts in the bowl of a food processor fitted with a metal chopping blade. Add a few tablespoons of the sugar (reserve remaining sugar). Briefly pulse the machine 10 times to chop the nuts into coarse pieces; some will be powdery, some coarse, some still whole. Set aside.

Melt the butter in a small pan over moderate heat; set aside.

Sift together the flour and baking soda; set aside.

Place the reserved sugar, the melted butter, the egg, and the milk in the large bowl of an electric mixer and beat until mixed. Add the sifted dry ingredients and the chopped peanuts and beat again until mixed. Transfer to a shallow bowl for ease in handling.

Place the dough by slightly rounded tablespoonfuls (not heaping) on a prepared sheet, placing the mounds 3 inches apart (I place six on a 15½ x 12-inch sheet). Try to keep the shapes neat. Top each cookie with a few of the optional peanuts, or with as many as you can fit on the top of each cookie. With your fingers flatten the tops a bit.

Bake one sheet at a time for a total of 7 to 8 minutes. After 5 minutes, reverse the sheet front to back. The cookies will rise up, spread out, and then flatten into very thin wafers with bumpy tops; they will spread out to 3½ to 4½ inches in diameter. The cookies should be barely brown all over—but they will continue to brown a bit after baking just from the heat of the sheet.

Remove from the oven. If the cookies have run into each other, cut them apart immediately, while very hot. Cool on the sheet for a minute or two. Then slide the foil off the sheet. Let the cookies stand until they are firm enough to be removed. Then it will be easy to peel the foil away from the backs.

As soon as they are cool, store in an airtight container.

Chocolate and
Peanut Butter
Ripples (page 162)

Peanut Butter
Pillows (page 159)

Skinny Peanut
Wafers

CHOCOLATE AND PEANUT BUTTER RIPPLES

Makes about 30 cookies A chocolate dough and a peanut butter dough, baked together, make this a rather thin, crisp, candy-like cookie.

CHOCOLATE DOUGH

2 ounces unsweetened chocolate

4 ounces (1 stick) unsalted butter

1 teaspoon vanilla extract

¼ teaspoon salt

¾ cup granulated sugar

1 large egg

1 cup *sifted* unbleached all-purpose flour

PEANUT BUTTER DOUGH

2 tablespoons unsalted butter

¼ cup smooth (not chunky) peanut butter

½ cup firmly packed light brown sugar

2 tablespoons *sifted* unbleached all-purpose flour

Adjust two racks to divide the oven into thirds and preheat oven to 325 degrees. Line cookie sheets with baking parchment.

First, make the chocolate dough: Melt the chocolate in the top of a double boiler over hot water on moderate heat. Set the chocolate aside.

In the large bowl of an electric mixer, cream the butter. Add the vanilla, salt, and granulated sugar and beat well. Beat in the egg and then the melted chocolate, scraping the bowl as necessary with a rubber spatula. On low speed, gradually add the flour and mix only until smooth. Transfer the dough to a small shallow bowl for ease in handling. Set it aside.

Then make the peanut butter dough. In the small bowl of the electric mixer, cream the butter with the peanut butter. Beat in the brown sugar until well mixed. Add the flour and beat to mix. Transfer to a small shallow bowl for ease in handling.

Now shape the cookies: Divide the chocolate dough in half and set one half aside. By level or barely rounded teaspoonfuls, drop the remaining half on the cookie sheets, placing the mounds 2 inches apart. You will need two to three cookie sheets and will end up with 30 mounds of the dough.

Top each mound with a scant teaspoon of peanut butter dough. And then top each cookie with another teaspoonful of the chocolate dough. Don't worry about the doughs being exactly on top of each other. Flatten the cookies slightly with a fork, dipping the fork in granulated sugar as necessary to keep it from sticking.

Bake for 15 minutes, reversing the cookie sheets top to bottom and front to back once to ensure even baking. (If you bake only one sheet at a time, use the higher rack.) Do not overbake. These cookies will become crisp as they cool.

Let the cookies cool briefly on the sheets, only until they are firm enough to transfer with a wide metal spatula to racks. When cool, handle with care. Store in an airtight container.

HAMANTASCHEN

Makes 27 hamantaschen The word *hamantaschen* means "Haman's hats." In the Bible, Haman was a wicked man who wanted to destroy the Jewish people, but Queen Esther did him in fast. Haman wore a triangular hat (like Napoleon's), and these cookies are made to resemble that shape. They are traditionally served during the Jewish holiday of Purim, the Feast of Esther, which is the most joyous day of the Hebrew year. Traditionally they are filled with prune jam, called *lekvar,* or with a poppy seed and honey mixture. This version is slightly different. (The pastry must be refrigerated overnight.)

NOTES

↓

These are better with a mild clover honey than a strongly flavored one.

↓

There may be a little filling left over. If so, it makes a wonderful conserve to serve with crackers, toast, or biscuits—along with, if you wish, butter or cottage cheese. You might like it so much that you decide to make it especially for that purpose. If you do, don't allow it to get as dry as you want it to be for the Hamantaschen. If it becomes too dry from standing, stir in a bit more orange juice, prune juice, or apricot juice.

PASTRY

- 2 cups *sifted* unbleached all-purpose flour
- 2 teaspoons baking powder
- ¼ teaspoon salt
- ¾ cup sugar
- 4 ounces (1 stick) unsalted butter, cold and firm
- 1 large egg
- Finely grated zest of 1 bright-colored orange
- 1½ tablespoons orange juice

FILLING

- 12 ounces unsweetened dried pitted prunes (about 2 cups, lightly packed)
- 6 ounces unsweetened dried apricots (about 1 cup, lightly packed)
- 1 cup water
- 1 tablespoon lemon juice
- ½ cup honey (see Notes)
- 2½ ounces (¾ cup) walnuts, chopped into medium-size pieces

For the pastry:

Into a large mixing bowl, sift together the flour, baking powder, salt, and sugar. Cut the butter into ½-inch slices and, with a pastry blender, cut into the dry ingredients until the particles are fine and the mixture resembles coarse meal. Beat the egg lightly just to mix. Stir the egg, orange zest, and juice into the dough. Mix thoroughly and then stir well, until the dough is completely moistened and smooth. Wrap in wax paper or plastic wrap, flatten the dough slightly, and refrigerate overnight.

continues ↘

Hamantaschen

Rugelach (page 166)

For the filling:

The filling may be made the next day, or it may be made ahead of time and kept at room temperature for a day or two, or refrigerated for a longer time.

Cut the prunes and apricots into small pieces. Place them in a saucepan with the water. Bring to a boil, cover, and lower the heat so that they just simmer for 10 to 15 minutes, until very soft. (Some fruits are drier than others — if the water evaporates before the fruit is soft, add another spoonful or two of water and cook a bit longer.) Add the lemon juice and honey. Cook, stirring almost constantly, for about 5 minutes (it should not get too thick; it will thicken more while cooling). Stir in the nuts and set aside to cool.

When you are ready to bake, adjust two racks to divide the oven into thirds and preheat oven to 400 degrees. Line cookie sheets with baking parchment or foil.

Work with half of the pastry at a time; keep the other half refrigerated. Work quickly or the dough will become sticky. On a floured pastry cloth with a floured rolling pin, roll out the dough, turning it over occasionally to keep both sides floured. Roll it to an even ⅛-inch thickness (that is thin, but be careful — if you roll the dough too thin it will be hard to handle). With a plain round 3-inch cookie cutter, cut the dough into rounds. (Reserve the scraps of dough, press them together, and rechill until firm enough to reroll.)

Hold one round in your hand. Place a rounded teaspoonful of the filling in the center, mounding it rather high — it will not run out in baking. Fold up two sides of the dough — each side should be a third of the circle — and pinch them together where they meet. Now fold up the third side and pinch together at both sides, forming a triangle and leaving a generous opening at the top. The filling should extend above the top of the pastry. (If the rounds of pastry become soft or sticky before you shape them, transfer them with a wide metal spatula to a tray or cookie sheet and chill briefly in the freezer or refrigerator, only until they are firm enough to handle.)

Place the Hamantaschen 1½ to 2 inches apart on the lined cookie sheets. Bake for 12 to 15 minutes, until the cookies are barely colored on the sides, slightly darker on the edges. (If you bake only one sheet at a time, use the higher rack.) Reverse the sheets top to bottom and front to back to ensure even browning.

With a wide metal spatula, transfer the Hamantaschen to racks to cool, or serve them warm. If anyone is in the kitchen with me when I bake these, very few if any actually have a chance to cool.

Store in an airtight container.

RUGELACH (WALNUT HORNS)

Makes about 48 cookies This is a traditional Jewish recipe that my grandmother used to make. Like all pastry, Rugelach are best when very fresh, but they freeze perfectly. The dough must be refrigerated overnight. This is one of the most popular recipes I ever wrote.

CREAM CHEESE PASTRY

- 8 ounces (2 sticks) unsalted butter
- 8 ounces Philadelphia brand cream cheese
- ½ teaspoon salt
- 2 cups *sifted* unbleached all-purpose flour

FILLING

- ½ cup plus 2 tablespoons sugar
- 1 tablespoon ground cinnamon
- 3 tablespoons unsalted butter, melted
- ¾ cup currants
- 5 ounces (1¼ cups) walnuts, finely chopped

GLAZE

- 1 large egg yolk
- 1 teaspoon water
- OPTIONAL: crystal sugar

For the pastry:

In the large bowl of an electric mixer, cream the butter and cream cheese together until completely blended and smooth. Beat in the salt and, on low speed, gradually add the flour. While beating in the flour, the dough might start to run up on the beaters toward the end. If so, the last of it may be stirred in by hand. When the dough is smooth, flour your hands lightly and, with your hands, form it into a short, fat roll. Cut the roll into three equal pieces. Form each piece into a round ball, flatten slightly, and wrap each individually in plastic wrap or wax paper. Refrigerate the balls of dough overnight or for at least 5 to 6 hours.

When you are ready to bake, adjust two racks to divide the oven into thirds. Preheat the oven to 350 degrees. Line cookie sheets with baking parchment.

To fill the pastry:

Stir the sugar and cinnamon together and set aside. (Do not mix the remaining ingredients.)

Place one ball of dough on a floured pastry cloth. With a floured rolling pin, pound the dough firmly to soften it slightly. On the floured cloth with the floured rolling pin, roll out the dough (turn it over occasionally) into a 12-inch circle — don't worry about slightly uneven edges.

With a pastry brush, brush the dough with 1 tablespoon of the melted butter and, quickly before the cold dough hardens the butter, sprinkle with one-third of the sugar-cinnamon mixture. Then sprinkle with one-third of the currants and one-third of the nuts. With the rolling pin, roll over the filling to press the topping slightly into the dough.

With a long, sharp knife, cut the dough into roughly 16 pie-shaped wedges. Roll each wedge jelly-roll fashion, rolling from the outside toward the point. Then place the little rolls, with the point down, 1 inch apart on a lined sheet.

Repeat with the remaining dough and filling. Since some of the filling will fall out while you are rolling up the horns, after preparing each third of the dough it will be necessary to clean the pastry cloth; either shake it out or scrape it with a dough scraper or a wide metal spatula and then reflour it.

For the glaze:

In a small cup with a fork, stir the yolk and water just to mix. With a pastry brush, brush the glaze over the tops of the horns. Sprinkle generously with the optional sugar.

Bake the Rugelach:

Bake two sheets at a time for about 30 minutes, until the horns are golden brown. (If you bake one sheet at a time, use the higher rack.) Reverse the sheets top to bottom and front to back once to ensure even browning.

With a wide metal spatula, immediately transfer the horns to racks to cool.

Store in an airtight container.

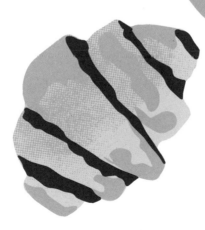

OATMEAL MOLASSES COOKIES

Makes 72 cookies These are crunchy and chewy, and you will definitely taste the molasses in them. Unless you love the flavor of strong, dark molasses, use a light mild-flavored kind.

3 cups *sifted* unbleached all-purpose flour

2 teaspoons baking soda

1 teaspoon salt

1 teaspoon ground cinnamon

¾ teaspoon ground ginger

8 ounces (2 sticks) unsalted butter

1½ teaspoons vanilla extract

2 cups sugar

½ cup molasses

2 large eggs

2 cups old-fashioned or quick-cooking rolled oats

3½ ounces (1 cup, firmly packed) shredded coconut

4 ounces (generous 1 cup) walnuts or pecans, chopped or broken into medium-size pieces

Adjust two racks to divide the oven into thirds and preheat oven to 375 degrees. Line cookie sheets with baking parchment.

Sift together the flour, baking soda, salt, cinnamon, and ginger and set aside. In the large bowl of an electric mixer, cream the butter. Beat in the vanilla and then add the sugar and beat well. Add the molasses and beat to mix. Add the eggs one at a time, scraping the bowl with a rubber spatula and beating well after each addition. On low speed, gradually add the sifted dry ingredients, continuing to scrape the bowl and beating only until mixed. Then add the rolled oats, coconut, and nuts, stirring only until mixed.

Use a well-rounded (but not heaping) teaspoonful of the dough for each cookie. Place them 2 inches apart on the lined cookie sheets.

Bake for about 15 minutes, reversing the cookie sheets top to bottom and front to back as necessary during baking, until the cookies are lightly colored. The cookies will still feel slightly soft and underdone, but do not overbake. If you bake only one sheet at a time, use the upper rack (it will take less time to bake than two sheets).

Remove from the oven and let the cookies stand on the sheets for a minute or so and then, with a wide metal spatula, transfer them to racks to cool.

ALMOND SUGAR COOKIES

Makes 10 very large cookies These are Swedish; quick and easy, fancy and elegant. Crisp, rich, crumbly, not too sweet. A plain sugar-and-butter dough made with egg yolks and ground almonds is rolled with a rolling pin, cut with a scalloped cookie cutter, decorated with lines made with a fork, and topped with more almonds and sugar. Although these are a snap to make, they are for a fancy tea party or a swank dinner. They keep well, they may be frozen, and the recipe may be multiplied to make more if you wish.

DOUGH

2½ ounces (generous ½ cup) blanched (skinned) whole almonds

1 cup *sifted* unbleached all-purpose flour

¼ teaspoon salt

2 ounces (½ stick) unsalted butter

¼ cup sugar

2 large egg yolks

½ teaspoon vanilla extract

¼ teaspoon almond extract

TOPPING

1 large egg yolk

1 teaspoon water

About 2 tablespoons coarsely chopped (or sliced or slivered) blanched (skinned) or unblanched almonds

Sugar, for sprinkling

Adjust two racks to divide the oven into thirds and preheat the oven to 375 degrees. Cut aluminum foil to fit cookie sheets.

For the dough:

The almonds must be ground very fine. It can be done in a food processor, a blender, or a nut grinder. If you use a processor or a blender, add a bit of the sugar to keep the nuts from lumping.

Then all of the dough ingredients may be combined in one of three ways: If you have ground the almonds in a processor, the remaining ingredients may all be added and processed until thoroughly mixed. Or they can all be mixed together in an electric mixer. Or they can be stirred together by hand in a mixing bowl.

Once combined, turn the dough out onto a work surface and "break" the dough as follows: First form it into a ball. Then, starting at the side of the ball farthest from you and using the heel of your hand, push off small pieces (about 2 tablespoons), pushing against the work surface and away from you. Continue until all the dough has been pushed off. Repeat "breaking" the dough once or twice until it is smooth.

Do not chill the dough before rolling it out.

Form the dough into a ball, flour it lightly, and flatten it slightly. Place it between two pieces of wax paper. With a rolling pin, roll over the top piece of paper until the dough is a scant ¼ inch thick.

Peel off the top piece of paper just to release it and then replace it. Turn the

continues ↘

dough over with both pieces of paper. Then peel off the other piece of paper but do not replace it.

Use a scalloped, round cookie cutter 3¼ inches in diameter (or any other size, shape, or design that you prefer). Cut the cookies, starting at the outside edge of the dough, and cutting them as close to each other as possible. This dough wants to stick; I find that the best way to transfer the cookies is to lift one carefully with a wide metal spatula, turn it over into the palm of my hand, and then place it, either side up, on the foil.

Press the scraps of dough together and reroll and cut cookies until it is all used.

For the topping:

In a small cup, stir the yolk and water just to mix. With a pastry brush, brush the mixture generously over the tops of the cookies.

Then, to form a plaid design completely covering the tops, hold a four-pronged fork as though you were eating with it. Rest the back of the tines lightly on a cookie and pull it across the cookie from one side to the other side to score the top lightly. Repeat, making additional lines, to cover the top of the cookie completely with lines all going in one direction. Then score again, this time at right angles to the first lines.

Now brush a little more of the egg-yolk mixture on the middle of each cookie. Sprinkle a few of the almonds on the middle of each cookie. With your fingertips, sprinkle sugar over each cookie, sprinkling it heavily in the middle and lightly at the edges.

Slide cookie sheets under the aluminum foil.

Bake for about 15 minutes, reversing the sheets top to bottom and front to back as necessary to ensure even browning. The cookies will have a nice golden color and a shine like varnish.

With a wide metal spatula, transfer to racks to cool.

Store airtight.

MEXICAN WEDDING CAKES

Makes 24 small cookies Someone once asked me what wine I serve with cookies. Champagne, of course — only the best champagne. I am very rigid about that, and won't compromise. These are not cakes, really, but dainty perfect cookies dusted liberally with confectioners' sugar. They go perfectly with a flute of champagne.

- 4 ounces (1 stick) unsalted butter
- 2 tablespoons confectioners' sugar, plus more for topping
- ½ teaspoon vanilla extract
- 1 cup *sifted* unbleached all-purpose flour
- 2½ ounces (¾ cup) walnuts, very finely chopped (but not ground)

Adjust rack one-third down from top of the oven. Preheat oven to 375 degrees.

In small bowl of electric mixer, cream the butter. Add the sugar and vanilla and beat for 1 to 2 minutes. On lowest speed, add the flour and then the walnuts, beating until the dough holds together.

Remove from mixer. Using a scant tablespoon of dough for each cookie, roll into 1-inch balls and place 1 inch apart on unbuttered cookie sheet.

Bake for about 15 minutes, reversing position of sheet during baking, until lightly colored.

With a metal spatula, transfer to a rack to cool. When completely cool, strain confectioners' sugar generously over the tops.

Store in an airtight container.

MORAVIAN WAFERS

NOTE

↓

When cutting the strip of dough into thin slices, use a ruler and the tip of a small, sharp knife to mark the strip in 1-inch lengths. Then slice the strip slowly, carefully, and evenly, counting the slices in each inch. If you get 8 to 10 slices from each inch, you are doing great. Try to cut them the same thinness in order to have them all finish baking at the same time.

Makes 90 to 100 very thin wafers Moravians are members of a Protestant religious group that settled in Winston-Salem, North Carolina, in 1776. Since then they have been making these special paper-thin spice cookies, especially at Christmas time. They are crisp, brittle, and very peppery-sharp-spicy molasses cookies. Although I bought them for years, I hadn't known until more recently how to make them. They are great!

After you mix and shape the dough into a roll, it must be placed in the freezer for a few hours or overnight (or longer) before you slice and bake the cookies.

2 cups *sifted* unbleached all-purpose flour

Scant ½ teaspoon salt

1 teaspoon baking powder

½ teaspoon baking soda

1½ teaspoons ground cinnamon

1 teaspoon ground ginger

½ teaspoon ground cloves

1 teaspoon finely ground white pepper (preferably freshly ground)

½ teaspoon dry mustard powder

4 ounces (1 stick) unsalted butter

1 cup sugar

½ cup mild molasses

1 large egg yolk

Sift together the flour, salt, baking powder, baking soda, cinnamon, ginger, cloves, pepper, and mustard and set aside.

In the large bowl of an electric mixer, beat the butter until soft. Add the sugar and beat until mixed. Beat in the molasses and egg yolk. On low speed, gradually add the sifted dry ingredients and beat until mixed.

Place a piece of plastic wrap about 18 inches long on a work surface. Spoon the dough down the middle, forming a strip 12 inches long. Lift the two long sides of plastic wrap and bring the sides together on top of the dough. With your hands, press on the plastic wrap to smooth the dough into an even strip 12 inches long, 2¾ inches wide, and 1¼ inches high, with squared ends.

Place the wrapped strip of dough on a cookie sheet and place in the freezer for a few hours, until firm, or as much longer as you wish.

continues ↘

To bake, adjust two racks to divide the oven into thirds and preheat oven to 350 degrees. Line two large cookie sheets with baking parchment or aluminum foil, shiny side up.

Unwrap the strip of dough and place it on a large cutting board. Use a long, sharp knife with a thin blade to cut the dough into slices ⅛ to ⅒ inch wide (see Note). That's very thin. Place the cookies 1 inch apart on the lined sheets.

Bake both sheets at the same time, reversing the sheets top to bottom and front to back once during baking to ensure even baking. Bake for 8 to 10 minutes, depending on the thickness of the cookies, until they are lightly colored.

Remove from the oven and let stand for a few minutes until the cookies are cool, then remove from the sheets with a metal spatula.

Store in an airtight container.

VIENNESE LINZER COOKIES

Makes 24 cookies This is the classic Linzertorte, but cut into small bars. It has a bottom crust, a raspberry-preserve filling, and a thin lattice topping of strips of crust—all baked together. The filling keeps the cookies moist and juicy. I make these without an electric mixer.

1½ cups plus 2 tablespoons *sifted* unbleached all-purpose flour

½ teaspoon baking powder

1 teaspoon ground cinnamon

⅛ teaspoon ground cloves

¼ teaspoon salt

¼ cup granulated sugar

½ cup firmly packed dark brown sugar

4 ounces (1 stick) unsalted butter

2½ ounces (½ cup) blanched (skinned) whole almonds

1 large egg

Finely grated zest of 1 large lemon

¾ cup thick red or black raspberry preserves

1 large egg yolk plus 1 teaspoon water, for glazing the tops of the cookies

Adjust an oven rack one-third up from the bottom and preheat oven to 375 degrees. Sift together 1½ cups of the flour (reserve the remaining 2 tablespoons), the baking powder, cinnamon, cloves, salt, and granulated sugar into a large mixing bowl. Add the brown sugar and stir to mix well.

Slice the butter into ½-inch pieces. With a pastry blender, cut the butter into the dry ingredients until the mixture is fine and crumbly.

Grind the almonds to a fine powder in a nut grinder or a food processor. Add the ground almonds to the dry ingredients and butter and stir to mix well.

In a small bowl, stir the egg lightly with a fork just to mix. Add the lemon zest and stir to mix. Then add the egg to the dough and, with a fork, stir well until the dry ingredients are evenly moistened. Remove and reserve ½ cup of the dough.

Place the remaining dough in an unbuttered 9-inch square baking pan and set aside.

Replace the reserved ½ cup of dough in the mixing bowl. Add the reserved 2 tablespoons flour. Stir together until the flour is incorporated. With your hands, form the dough into a flattened square and place it between two large pieces of wax paper. With a rolling pin, roll over the wax paper to roll the dough into a 9-inch square—the same size as the bottom of the pan. (Keep the shape as square as you can, but if the sides are not exact don't worry—a few uneven strips will not really matter.) Slide a cookie sheet under the paper and transfer the dough to the freezer for a few minutes. When the dough is rolled out into about a 9-inch square it will be very thin. You will have to be extremely careful handling it when cutting it into strips.

continues ↘

Meanwhile, flour your fingertips and press the dough that is in the pan to even it out on the bottom of the pan.

In a small bowl, stir the preserves slightly just to soften. Spread them evenly over the layer of dough in the pan, keeping the preserves ¼ to ⅓ inch away from the edges.

Now remove the chilled dough from the freezer. Remove and replace one piece of wax paper just to loosen it. Turn the dough and both pieces of wax paper over. Then remove and do not replace the other piece of paper. With a long knife, cut the dough into ½-inch-wide strips; you will have 18 strips, each ½ inch wide and 9 inches long. Place half of the strips over the preserves, placing them ½ inch apart and parallel. Then place the remaining strips crosswise over the first ones, again placing them ½ inch apart, to form a lattice top. (If the strips become too soft to handle while you are working with them, rechill as necessary.)

To make the glaze, stir the egg yolk and water together lightly just to mix. With a soft brush, brush the glaze over the top of the lattice and the preserves.

Bake for 30 minutes, or until the top is a rich golden brown. If the cake is not dark enough, raise the pan to a higher rack. When the cake is done, you should see the preserves bubbling up in the spaces on top.

Cool the cake completely in the pan. When completely cool, with a small, sharp knife, cut around the cake to release it, then cut it into quarters, cut each quarter in half, and then cut each strip into thirds. With a metal spatula, transfer the bars to a tray or serving plate.

Or cut the cake into quarters in the pan and, with a wide metal spatula, transfer the quarters to a cutting board. Then, with a long, heavy knife, cut into small bars.

If you wish, these may be wrapped individually in clear cellophane or wax paper. Or they may be stored in a covered box with plastic wrap or wax paper between the layers.

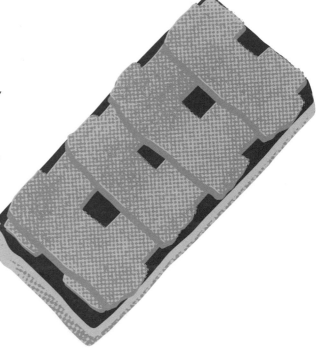

MUSHROOM MERINGUES

Makes 24 rather large or 36 medium mushrooms I did not originally want to include this recipe because I thought it would be too difficult for most people to make. I was stunned when soon after the original publication of this recipe readers started sending me photos of their Mushroom Meringues. They were perfect! I received several letters from people who were making them from this recipe and selling them to department stores (Bloomingdale's, Henri Bendel, and others).

These meringues can last and last. Years ago, I entered an international cooking Olympics. (Incidentally, I won first prize for originality.) A large basket of Mushroom Meringues was part of my entry. The display of food at the Olympics lasted three or four days. Then Burdines, a department store here in Miami, asked if they could use my entry in a window display. And that lasted for two weeks with the sun beating down on the window most of the time. After Burdines, I took my entry home. The meringues were perfect. I put the basket of them on a table in the living room, where it remained for many months. The mushrooms looked the same as the day they were made.

These call for patience, talent with a pastry bag, and a dry atmosphere. Making them is an art.

½ cup egg whites (about 4 large whites), at room temperature	1 cup sugar
	1 teaspoon vanilla extract
Scant ¼ teaspoon salt	Unsweetened cocoa powder (preferably Dutch-process)
¼ teaspoon cream of tartar	Chocolate (see Note)

NOTE
[↓]

Compound chocolate is the easiest to use for these mushrooms. Real chocolate will discolor (unless you temper it), but compound chocolate will not.

Adjust two racks to divide the oven into thirds. Preheat oven to 225 degrees. Cut baking parchment to fit two cookie sheets at least 15 x 12 inches.

In the small bowl of electric mixer at moderately slow speed, beat the egg whites for about half a minute, or until they are just foamy. Add the salt and cream of tartar. Increase the speed to moderate and beat for almost a minute more, until whites hold a soft shape. Continue to beat and start adding the sugar, 1 rounded tablespoonful at a time, beating about half a minute between additions. When half the sugar has been added, add the vanilla and then continue adding the sugar as before. When all the sugar has been added, increase the speed to high and beat for 7 to 8 minutes more, until the meringue is very stiff and the sugar is dissolved — test it by rubbing a bit between your fingers. (Total beating time from start to finish is 15 to 18 minutes, but it depends on the power of your mixer.)

To hold the parchment in place, put a dot of the meringue on each corner of the cookie sheets. Cover with the parchment and press firmly on the corners.

Do not let the meringue stand. Fit a large pastry bag (preferably at least 15 to 16 inches long) with a plain, round tube ½ to ¾ inches in diameter. (I like to use one that is ⅝ inch.) Fold down the top of the bag to form a deep cuff on the outside. Support the bag by holding it under the cuff with one hand (or place in a tall jar). Using a rubber spatula in your other hand, transfer all the meringue into the bag. Lift the cuff up and twist the top closed.

On one piece of the parchment, shape the mushroom stems first: Hold the bag at a right angle and close to the cookie sheet. Press the meringue out gently while slowly raising the bag straight up. The base of the stem should be a bit wider for support. Keep the stem as straight as possible. Hold the bag upright and steady with one hand and, with the other hand, use a small knife to cut the meringue away from the tube. Don't worry if a small point is left on top of the stem; it can be removed later. The stems may be 1 to 1½ inches high (the taller they are, the more difficult), but they may vary as real mushroom stems do. They should be placed ½ to 1 inch apart. (Some of the stems may fall onto their sides, so it is a good idea to make a few extras to be sure you wind up with a stem for each cap.)

Strain cocoa through a fine strainer lightly over the stems to imitate soil and natural mushroom coloring. Place in the oven on the higher rack.

On the other sheet, shape the mushroom caps: Holding the bag straight up and close to the sheet, press out even rounds of the meringue. The caps should be piped about ½ inch apart. The caps may average about 1½ to 1¾ inches in width and ¾ inch in height, but they may also vary as real mushroom caps do. Sharply twist the bag away to avoid leaving a peak on the top. The top should be as smooth as possible. The measurements I have given are approximate. Smaller or larger mushrooms are equally attractive. Even mushroom meringues with crooked stems or a slight point on the cap will look great when finished.

Strain cocoa lightly over the caps. Bake on the lower rack for 1 hour or longer depending on size, until meringues may be lifted easily from the sheet and the bottoms are firm to the touch. The longer they bake, the drier they are — and the better — but they should not be allowed to color (it affects the taste). Turn the heat off, prop the oven door open a little, and let the meringues dry out even more in the turned-off oven until cool. (I have, at times, put the meringues back in a barely warm oven for the night.)

Remove meringues from the sheets. They may be placed on a clean piece of paper, or on a tray. Immediately, while the meringues are very crisp, using a finely serrated knife or a sharp paring knife, gently saw any points off the tops of the stems, cutting parallel with the base.

Now, to glue the tops and stems together, it is best to use compound chocolate (see Note). One ounce of chocolate will be needed for five mushroom caps measuring 1½ to 2 inches in diameter. Using this formula, figure how much chocolate you will need. Cut it coarsely and place in the top of a small double boiler over warm water to melt slowly over low heat. When almost melted, remove from the heat and stir until completely melted and smooth.

Hold a mushroom cap upside down. With a demitasse spoon, spread a layer of chocolate over the bottom of the cap, spreading it just to the edge. It should be thin but not too thin. Place a stem upside down on the chocolate.

Now the mushroom must stand in that position, upside down, until the chocolate hardens. There are several ways to do this. The inverted mushrooms will rest securely in small cordial glasses, small brandy snifters, small egg cups, or in an empty egg carton — it will depend on their size.

Let stand until the chocolate is hard — and then, do not cover airtight. Serve the mushrooms either standing upright on a platter, or tumbled in a basket like real mushrooms, which these will resemble to an unbelievable degree. (Try a napkin-lined basketful as a centerpiece — then pass it around at dessert time.)

The number of mushrooms this recipe yields will depend on their size — approximately 24 rather large or 36 medium. If you want more, prepare and bake one batch, and then repeat; meringue should not stand any longer than necessary before baking.

PIES, TARTS, BROWNIES, BARS, AND MORE

BROWNIES

Makes 24 or 32 brownies These are the Brownies with which I started my reputation as a pastry chef when I was about ten years old. People who barely knew me, knew my Brownies. Since I always wrapped them individually, I usually carried a few to give out. I occasionally run into people I never knew well and haven't seen in many years, and the first thing they say is, "I remember your Brownies." Sometimes they have forgotten my name — but they always remember my Brownies. I have continuously revised the recipe over the years.

5 ounces unsweetened chocolate

6 ounces (1½ sticks) unsalted butter

1 tablespoon instant espresso or coffee powder

4 large eggs

½ teaspoon salt

2 cups sugar

1 teaspoon vanilla extract

¼ teaspoon almond extract

1 cup *sifted* unbleached all-purpose flour

10 ounces (2½ generous cups) walnut halves or pieces

Adjust rack one-third up from bottom of oven and preheat to 450 degrees. Butter a 15½ x 10½ x 1-inch rimmed baking sheet and then line it with aluminum foil as follows: Turn the pan upside down. Center a piece of foil 18 to 19 inches long (12 inches wide) over the pan, shiny side down. Fold down the sides and corners to shape the foil. Remove the foil, turn the pan right side up, place the shaped foil in the pan, and press it carefully into place. Brush the foil all over with melted butter.

Melt the chocolate and butter in a heavy saucepan over low heat or in the top of a large double boiler over hot water on moderate heat. Stir with a small wire whisk to blend. When melted and smooth, add instant coffee and stir to dissolve. Remove from the heat and set aside to cool.

Meanwhile, in small bowl of electric mixer, beat the eggs and salt until slightly fluffy. Gradually add the sugar and continue to beat at medium-high speed for 15 minutes, until the mixture forms a ribbon when the beaters are raised. Transfer to large mixer bowl.

Add the vanilla and almond extracts to the cooled chocolate mixture. On lowest speed, add the chocolate mixture to the eggs, scraping the bowl with a rubber spatula and beating *only enough to blend*. Still using lowest speed and rubber spatula, add the flour, again beating *only enough to blend*. Fold in the nuts, handling the mixture as little as possible.

Pour into prepared pan and spread smooth. Place in oven. *Immediately* reduce oven temperature to 400 degrees. Bake for 21 to 22 minutes. Test with a toothpick. It should just barely come out dry. Do not overbake. Brownies should be slightly moist inside.

continues ↘

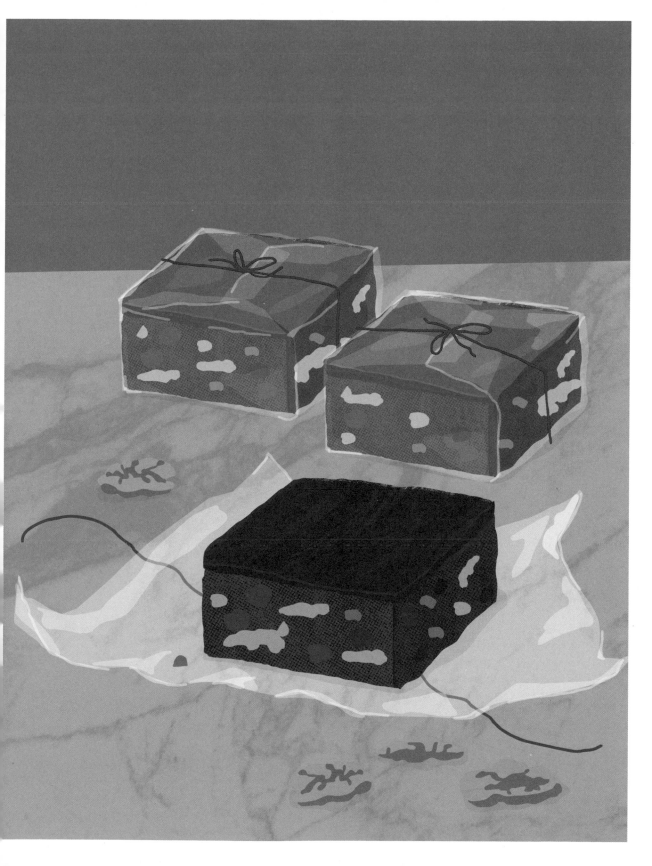

Remove from oven. Immediately cover with a large rack or cookie sheet and invert. Remove pan and foil. Cover with a large rack and invert again. After 10 or 15 minutes, invert once again only for a moment to make sure that the Brownies are not sticking to the rack.

Cool completely and then chill for about 30 minutes or a bit longer in the freezer, or overnight in the refrigerator. Transfer to a large cutting board.

To mark portions evenly, measure with a ruler and mark with toothpicks to get the number and size you desire. Use a long, thin, very sharp knife, or one with serrated edge. Cut with a sawing motion into squares. I wrap these individually in clear cellophane, but you may package them any way that is airtight — do not let them stand around to dry out.

CREAM-CHEESE BROWNIES

Makes 24 brownies Part brownies, part cheesecake — layered and marbled together. These must be stored in the refrigerator or frozen. And they may be eaten directly from the freezer or thawed.

CHOCOLATE MIXTURE

- 1 cup *unsifted* unbleached all-purpose flour
- ½ teaspoon baking powder
- ¼ teaspoon salt
- 4 ounces semisweet chocolate
- 3 tablespoons unsalted butter
- 2 large eggs
- ¾ cup sugar
- 1 teaspoon vanilla extract
- 2½ ounces (¾ cup) walnuts, chopped into medium-size pieces

CHEESE MIXTURE

- 4 ounces cream cheese
- 2 tablespoons unsalted butter
- ½ teaspoon vanilla extract
- ¼ cup sugar
- 1 large egg

Adjust a rack one-third up from the bottom of the oven and preheat oven to 350 degrees. Prepare a 9-inch square pan as follows: Turn it upside down and place a 12-inch square of aluminum foil shiny side down over the inverted pan. Turn down the sides and corners of the foil just to shape it. Remove the foil and turn the pan right side up. Place the foil in the pan. In order not to tear the foil, place a folded towel or a pot holder in the pan and, pressing against the towel or pot holder, press the foil gently into place. Coat the foil with soft or melted butter, spreading it thinly with a pastry brush or crumpled wax paper.

For the chocolate mixture:

Sift together the flour, baking powder, and salt and set aside. Melt the chocolate and the butter in the top of a small double boiler over hot water on moderate heat. Stir until smooth, remove from heat, and set aside to cool slightly.

In the small bowl of an electric mixer, beat the eggs until foamy. Add the sugar and vanilla and beat at high speed for 3 to 4 minutes, until the mixture is slightly lemon-colored and forms a ribbon when beaters are lifted. On low speed, beat in the chocolate mixture and then the sifted dry ingredients, scraping the bowl with a rubber spatula and beating only until the dry ingredients are incorporated.

Remove and set aside ¾ cup of the chocolate mixture. To the remaining batter, add ½ cup of the nuts (reserve ¼ cup for topping) and stir to mix. Spread the chocolate mixture evenly in the pan; it will be a very thin layer.

For the cheese mixture:

In the small bowl of an electric mixer, beat the cream cheese with the butter until soft and smooth. Add the vanilla and sugar, and beat well. Then add the egg and beat again until very smooth.

continues ⌄

To cover the chocolate mixture with a thin layer of the cheese mixture, slowly pour the cheese mixture over the chocolate layer, then smooth with the back of a spoon to the edges of the pan. Place the reserved ¾ cup chocolate mixture by heaping tablespoonfuls onto the cheese layer, letting the cheese show through between mounds — you should have 8 or 9 chocolate mounds. With a small metal spatula or a table knife, cut through the chocolate mounds and the cheese layer. It is best if you don't cut down into the bottom layer. Zigzag the knife to marbleize the batters slightly; don't overdo it. Sprinkle with reserved ¼ cup nuts. Bake for 35 minutes.

Let stand at room temperature for a few hours. Then cover the pan with a sheet or board. Turn upside down. Remove the pan and foil. Cover with another sheet or board. Turn upside down again. Cut the cake into quarters. Cut each quarter into 6 bars.

Transfer the bars to a serving plate, cover airtight with plastic wrap, and refrigerate. Or pack them in a freezer box and freeze. Or they may be wrapped individually in clear cellophane or wax paper and then placed in the refrigerator or freezer.

PALM BEACH BROWNIES WITH CHOCOLATE-COVERED MINTS

Makes 32 brownies This recipe is one of the two or three most popular recipes in all of my books. These are the thickest, gooiest, chewiest, darkest, sweetest, mostest-of-the-most chocolate bars with an almost wet middle and a crisp, crunchy top. A layer of chocolate-covered mints in the middle stays whole (the mints don't melt), and they look and taste gorgeous.

The baked cake should be refrigerated for at least a few hours, or overnight, or frozen for an hour or two before it is cut into bars.

NOTE

↓

When you remove the cake from the pan you might see burned and caramelized edges. (You might not — it depends on the pan.) If you do, you can leave them or cut them off. I have friends who say that this is the best part. I cut them off, but then I can't resist eating them.

- 8 ounces unsweetened chocolate
- 8 ounces (2 sticks) unsalted butter
- 8 ounces (2 generous cups) walnut halves or pieces
- 5 large eggs (1 cup)
- 2 teaspoons vanilla extract
- ½ teaspoon almond extract
- ¼ teaspoon salt
- 1 tablespoon plus 1 teaspoon instant espresso or coffee powder
- 3¾ cups sugar
- 1⅔ cups sifted unbleached all-purpose flour
- 2½ (12-ounce) bags York chocolate-covered Peppermint Patties (Miniature Classics), unwrapped

Adjust an oven rack one-third up from the bottom and preheat oven to 425 degrees. Line a 13 x 9 x 2-inch pan as follows: Invert the pan and center a 17-inch length of nonstick aluminum foil, shiny side down, over the pan. With your hands, press down the sides and corners of the foil in the pan and very carefully press it into place in the pan. Now, to butter the foil, place a piece of butter (additional to that in ingredients) in the pan, and put the pan in the oven.

When the butter is melted, use a pastry brush or a piece of crumpled plastic wrap to spread the butter all over the foil. Set the prepared pan aside.

Place the chocolate and butter in the top of a large double boiler over hot water on moderate heat, or in a 4- to 6-cup heavy saucepan over low heat. Stir occasionally, until the chocolate and butter are melted. Stir to mix. Remove from the heat and set

continues ↘

aside. (Or you may wish to zap this in a microwave one minute at a time at 50 percent power until melted.)

Break any walnut halves into large pieces; set aside.

In the large bowl of an electric mixer, beat the eggs with the vanilla and almond extracts, salt, espresso, and sugar at high speed for 10 minutes. On low speed, add the chocolate mixture (which may still be warm) and beat only until mixed. Then add the flour and again beat on low speed only until mixed. Remove the bowl from the mixer.

Stir in the nuts.

Spoon half the mixture (about 3½ cups) into the prepared pan and smooth the top.

Place a layer of the mints, touching each other and the edges of the pan, all over the chocolate layer. (You will not use all the mints; there will be some left over.)

Spoon the remaining chocolate mixture all over the mints and smooth the top.

Bake for 35 minutes, reversing the pan front to back once during baking to ensure even baking. At the end of 35 minutes the cake will have a firm crust on top, but if you insert a toothpick in the middle it will come out wet and covered with chocolate. Nevertheless, it is done. Do not bake any longer.

Remove the pan from the oven; let stand until cool. Cover the pan with a cookie sheet and invert the pan and the sheet. Remove the pan and foil lining.

Cover the cake with a length of wax paper and another cookie sheet and invert again, leaving the cake right side up.

Now the cake must be refrigerated for a few hours or overnight before it is cut into bars.

When you are ready to cut the cake, use a long, heavy knife with a sharp blade, either serrated or straight — try both. Cut the cake into quarters. Cut each quarter in half, cutting through the long sides. Finally, cut each piece into 4 bars, cutting through the long sides. (I think these are better in narrow bar shapes than in squares.)

Pack in an airtight box, or wrap individually in clear cellophane, wax paper, or foil.

These freeze perfectly and can be served very cold or at room temperature.

FLORIDA LEMON SQUARES

Makes 24 or 32 squares These are rich layered bars with a baked-in tart lemon filling. They should be refrigerated until serving time.

1½ cups *sifted* unbleached all-purpose flour

1 teaspoon baking powder

½ teaspoon salt

1 (14- or 15-ounce) can unsweetened condensed milk

Finely grated zest of 1 large lemon

½ cup lemon juice

5⅓ ounces (1¼ sticks plus 2 teaspoons) unsalted butter

1 cup firmly packed dark brown sugar

1 cup old-fashioned or quick-cooking rolled oats

OPTIONAL: confectioners' sugar

Adjust a rack one-third up from the bottom of the oven and preheat oven to 350 degrees. Butter a 13 x 9 x 2-inch pan.

Sift together the flour, baking powder, and salt and set aside. Pour the condensed milk into a medium mixing bowl. Add the grated lemon zest and then, gradually, add the lemon juice, stirring with a small wire whisk to keep the mixture smooth. (The lemon will thicken the milk.) Set the mixture aside.

In the large bowl of an electric mixer, cream the butter. Add the brown sugar and beat well. On lowest speed, gradually add the sifted dry ingredients, scraping the bowl with a rubber spatula and beating only until thoroughly mixed. Mix in the rolled oats. The mixture will be crumbly — it will not hold together.

Sprinkle a bit more than half of the oatmeal mixture (2 generous cups) evenly over the bottom of the prepared pan. Pat the crumbs firmly with your fingertips to make a smooth, compact layer. Drizzle or spoon the lemon mixture evenly over the crumb layer and spread it to make a thin smooth layer. Sprinkle the remaining crumbly oat mixture evenly over the lemon layer. Pat the crumbs gently with the palm of your hand to smooth them — it is OK if a bit of the lemon layer shows through in small spots.

Bake for 30 to 35 minutes, until the cake is lightly colored.

Cool the cake completely in the pan. Then refrigerate it for about 1 hour (or more).

With a small, sharp knife, cut around the sides of the cake to release it. Cut it into small squares. With a wide metal spatula, remove the squares from the pan; transfer them to a serving plate, cover with plastic wrap, and refrigerate.

If you like, just before serving, the squares may be topped with confectioners' sugar. Use your fingertips to press the sugar through a fine strainer held over the squares. (It is best to have the squares on wax paper while coating them with sugar.)

PECAN SQUARES AMERICANA

Makes 32 to 48 (or more) squares Many years ago a Miami newspaper published a letter to the food editor from the wife of Governor Collins of Florida. She raved about the pecan cookies she had eaten at the Americana Hotel in Miami Beach. She went on to say that she had requested the recipe from the hotel, that they had given it to her, but it did not work for her. The letter included the recipe as she had received it. I ran to the kitchen to try it. The recipe did not work for me either. I called the hotel and asked to speak to the pastry chef. His name was Jacques Kranzlin; he could not have been more gracious or charming, and he invited me to his kitchen to watch him work. It was a treat.

When I got home I was able to make the Pecan Squares. I made them again and again and again. I wrote the recipe. I taught it in my dessert classes. It was unanimously the best! I included the recipe in my first dessert book. And when I taught classes around the country, it was one of my favorite recipes to teach because I knew how people would rave about them.

During a class in Ohio, as I started to make the recipe, I explained that there was one hitch: The filling sometimes ran through the bottom crust and stuck to the pan, making it difficult to remove the cookies. A nice lady in the class said, "Since you use so much foil to line so many pans, why not line this one?"

I had not thought of it. I tried it right then and it was great! It was terrific! The cookies simply cannot stick to the pan this way. I have always worried about the people who are making this without the foil.

PASTRY SHELL

- 8 ounces (2 sticks) unsalted butter
- ½ cup granulated sugar
- 1 large egg
- ¼ teaspoon salt
- Finely grated zest of 1 large lemon
- 3 cups sifted unbleached all-purpose flour

PECAN TOPPING

- 8 ounces (2 sticks) unsalted butter
- ½ cup honey
- ¼ cup granulated sugar
- 1 cup plus 2 tablespoons firmly packed dark brown sugar
- ¼ cup heavy cream
- 20 ounces (5 cups) pecan halves or large pieces

For the pastry:

Butter a 15½ x 10½ x 1-inch rimmed baking sheet and then line it with aluminum foil as follows: Turn the pan upside down. Center a piece of foil 18 to 19 inches long (and 12 inches wide) shiny side down over the pan; check the long sides to be sure there is the same amount of overhang on each

continues ↘

side. Fold down the sides and the corners to shape the foil. Remove the foil, turn the pan right side up, place the shaped foil in the pan, and press it carefully into place. Do not butter the foil. Place the prepared pan in the freezer (it is easier to spread this dough on a cold pan — the coldness will make the dough cling to the pan).

In the large bowl of an electric mixer, beat the butter until it is softened, add the granulated sugar and beat to mix well. Beat in the egg, salt, and lemon zest. Gradually add the flour and beat, scraping the bowl with a rubber spatula, until the mixture holds together.

Now you are going to line the pan with the dough; it is important that you have enough dough on the sides of the pan to reach generously to the top of the pan. It will work best and be easiest if you place the dough, one rounded teaspoonful at a time, around the sides of the pan, just pressing against the raised sides. (I don't actually use teaspoons for this. It is easiest to lift a generous mound of the dough, hold it in one hand, and use the fingers of your other hand to break off teaspoon-size pieces.) Place the pieces about ½ to 1 inch apart. Then place the remaining dough the same way all over the rest of the bottom of the pan. Flour your fingertips (if necessary) and start to press the mounds of dough, working up the sides first and then on the bottom, until you have formed a smooth layer all over the sides and bottom. There must not be any thin spots on the bottom or any low spots on the sides (it is best if it comes slightly above the top). Take your time; it is important for this shell to be right. Patience is the name of the game.

With a fork, carefully prick the bottom at about ½-inch intervals. Chill in the refrigerator for about 15 minutes.

Adjust a rack one-third up from the bottom of the oven and preheat oven to 375 degrees.

Bake for 20 minutes. Watch it constantly. If the dough on the sides starts to slip down a bit, reach into the oven and press it with your fingertips or the back of a spoon to put it back into place (although this does not seem to happen since I stopped buttering the foil). If the dough starts to puff up, prick it gently with a cake tester to release trapped air and flatten the dough. (There have been times when it insisted on puffing up, and it was a question of which one of us would win. I did. Here's how: Place one or more pot holders on the puffed-up part for a few minutes. The puffed-up dough will get the message and will know you mean business, and it will lie down flat.) After 20 minutes, the edges of the dough will be lightly colored; the bottom will be pale but dry. Remove from the oven but do not turn off the heat.

For the topping:

In a heavy 3-quart saucepan over moderately high heat, cook the butter and honey, stirring occasionally, until the butter is melted. Add both sugars, stir to dissolve, bring to a boil, and let boil without stirring for exactly 2 minutes.

Without waiting, remove from the heat and stir in the heavy cream, then the pecans. Wait 5 minutes. (Although the original recipe says to do the next step immediately, I have recently decided it is better to wait a bit.) Then, with a large slotted spoon, place most of the pecans evenly over the crust. Then drizzle the remaining mixture over the pecans so it is distributed evenly — watch the corners. Use a fork or a spoon to move around any nuts that are piled too high and place them in any empty or thin spots. (It will look like there is not enough of the thin syrupy mixture, but it is OK.)

Bake at 375 degrees with the rack one-third up from the bottom for 25 minutes. (Now you will see that the syrupy mixture has spread out and boiled up and filled in any hollows.)

Cool to room temperature — do not chill.

Cover with a large rack or a cookie sheet, hold them firmly together, turn the pan and rack or sheet over, and remove the pan and the foil. If the bottom of the dough looks very buttery, you may pat it with a paper towel if you wish, but it is not really necessary; the dough absorbs it as it stands. Cover with a rack or sheet and turn over again, leaving the cake right side up. It is easiest to cut the cake into neat pieces if it is chilled first; chill it briefly in the refrigerator. Then transfer it to a large cutting board. Use a ruler and toothpicks to mark the cake into quarters. Use a long and heavy, sharp knife, and cut straight down (not back and forth). These are very rich, and although most people like them cut into 48 bars, I know several caterers who make them almost as small as lump sugar. And I have made them larger because I wrap them individually in clear cellophane and it is more fun to wrap cookies that are not too small.

GEORGIA PECAN BARS

Makes 32 bars The taste and texture of these will remind you of pecan pie.

CRUST

- 1½ cups *sifted* unbleached all-purpose flour
- ½ teaspoon baking powder
- ½ cup firmly packed dark brown sugar
- 4 ounces (1 stick) unsalted butter, cut into ½- to 1-inch slices

TOPPING

- 2 large eggs
- 1 teaspoon vanilla extract
- ¼ cup firmly packed dark brown sugar
- ¾ cup dark corn syrup
- 3 tablespoons *sifted* unbleached all-purpose flour
- 7 ounces (2 cups) pecan halves or large pieces

Adjust a rack one-third up from the bottom of the oven and preheat oven to 350 degrees. Butter a 13 x 9 x 2-inch square cake pan as follows: Turn it upside down and place a 17-inch length of aluminum foil shiny side down over the inverted pan. Turn down the sides and corners of the foil just to shape it. Remove the foil and turn the pan right side up. Place the foil in the pan. In order not to tear the foil, place a folded towel or a pot holder in the pan and, pressing against the towel or pot holder, press the foil gently into place. Coat the foil with soft or melted butter, spreading it thinly with a pastry brush or crumpled wax paper.

For the crust:

Sift the flour and baking powder together into a bowl. Stir in the sugar. Add the pieces of butter to the bowl with the dry ingredients. With a pastry blender, cut in the butter until the mixture resembles fine meal.

Turn the crust mixture into the buttered pan. With your fingertips and with the palm of your hand, press down on the crust to make a smooth, firm layer. Set aside and prepare the topping.

For the topping:

In a bowl, beat the eggs lightly just to mix. Add the vanilla, sugar, corn syrup, and flour, and beat until smooth.

Pour the topping over the crust and tilt the pan gently to form an even layer. If the pecan halves are large they may be placed evenly, rounded side up, to cover the topping completely. But if the halves are small or if you use pieces, sprinkle them over the topping.

Bake for 35 to 40 minutes, until the top is golden, reversing the position of the pan once during baking to ensure even browning. If the cake puffs up during baking, pierce it gently with a cake tester or a small, sharp knife to release the trapped air.

continues ↘

Do not overbake, the bars should remain slightly soft in the center.

Cool the cake in the pan for 15 to 20 minutes. Then cover the cake pan with a cookie sheet and invert. Remove the pan and foil. Cover the cake with a rack and invert again to finish cooling right side up.

When the cake is completely cool, transfer to the freezer for about 20 minutes or to the refrigerator for about an hour, until firm enough to cut.

If the cookies are cut with a plain, straight knife they will squash and look messy. Use a serrated bread knife and cut with a back-and-forth, sawing motion — they will cut perfectly. Cut into bars.

They may be placed on a serving tray and covered with plastic wrap or they may be wrapped individually in clear cellophane or wax paper. Or go ahead and freeze them.

APPLE PIE, U.S.A.

Makes 6 portions This is the traditional, old-fashioned, "American as apple pie" apple pie. Once you have made it, you will glory in the spotlight, be thrilled with pride, and be in apple-pie-in-the-sky heaven.

It is best to put together the pie dough at least an hour before using it, or the day before. (It will be easier to handle cold, and letting the dough rest allows for the water to be absorbed more equally.)

Choose the apples carefully. Some are too watery (McIntosh), some are too dry, some have more flavor than others. But there are many varieties that are just right. Choose Granny Smith apples for a firmer bite, or Golden Delicious for a softer result.

NOTE

↓

The amount of flour in the filling depends on how juicy the apples are and on how juicy you like your pie. I use 3 tablespoons of flour on average. Many people—especially country and farm people, who have probably eaten more pie than most of us—think that any thickening at all is un-American; to those people a good pie has to be eaten from a wide soup bowl with a spoon.

Double recipe Pie Pastry (for a 9-inch pie, page 205)

1 teaspoon unbleached all-purpose flour

FILLING

3 tablespoons *unsifted* unbleached all-purpose flour

¾ cup sugar, plus more for sprinkling

1 teaspoon ground cinnamon

¼ teaspoon ground nutmeg

¼ teaspoon salt

About 3 pounds apples (to make 8 to 9 cups sliced)

2 tablespoons unsalted butter, cut into small pieces (it is best to cut the butter ahead of time and refrigerate it)

Milk, for brushing

Prepare the double amount of Pie Pastry for a 9-inch pie, divide it in half, and shape each half into a ball. Flour each lightly, flatten slightly, wrap in plastic wrap, and refrigerate for an hour or longer.

If the pastry was refrigerated overnight, let it stand at room temperature for 10 to 15 minutes before rolling it out. Place 1 ball of dough on a lightly floured pastry cloth. Pound it lightly with a floured rolling pin. With the rolling pin, roll out the dough,

keeping the pin, the cloth, and the top of the dough very lightly floured. Roll from the center of the dough out toward the edges. As you start to roll out the dough, watch the edges; if cracks form, pinch them together before they become deep. Keep the shape round and the thickness even. Roll out until you have a circle about 12 inches in diameter.

continues ↘

There are two ways to transfer the circle of dough to the pie plate. One is to fold it in half and place it in the plate. Then unfold it and ease it gently into place in the pan. The other is to roll it up loosely around the rolling pin and unroll it over the plate and then ease it gently into place in the pan. (I think the choice of method depends on your fingernails; if they are long you will probably prefer rolling the dough on the pin to transfer it.)

If you have a cake-decorating turntable, place the pie plate on it. Trim the edges of the dough with scissors, leaving enough for the dough to lie down flat on the rim of the plate and extend only a scant ¼ inch beyond the outside of the rim.

Place the 1 teaspoon flour in the crust and, with a dry pastry brush, spread it over the bottom.

Refrigerate the pie plate with the bottom crust in place.

Lightly re-flour the pastry cloth and roll out the second piece of dough until it is about 12 inches wide (the same as the bottom crust). Slide a flat-rimmed cookie sheet (or anything else that will work) under the pastry cloth and transfer the cloth and dough to the refrigerator.

Adjust a rack one-third up from the bottom of the oven. Preheat the oven to 450 degrees.

For the filling:

In a small bowl mix together the 3 tablespoons flour with the sugar, cinnamon, nutmeg, and salt and set aside.

With a vegetable peeler, peel the apples, then cut them into quarters, remove the cores, and slice them lengthwise. (Each quarter of a small apple should be cut into 3 slices; each quarter of a large apple should be cut into 4 slices.)

Measure 8 to 9 cups of the apples and place in a large bowl. Add the sugar-flour mixture and toss with your hands to mix thoroughly.

Turn the mixture into the floured bottom crust. Use your fingers to move things around and make an even mound, but do not press down on the apples or you will punch a hole in the crust. Scatter the pieces of butter over the top.

Place a little cup of cold water next to you. With a soft brush or your fingers, wet the top of the rim of the bottom crust.

Transfer the top crust (using the same procedure you used for the bottom crust) over the apples, centering it carefully.

Flour your fingertips and press the rim of the top crust against the wet top rim of the bottom crust. Then, with scissors, trim the top crust, allowing it to extend about ¼ to ½ inch beyond the bottom crust. With your fingertips and a bit of cold water, wet the bottom (the underside) of the rim. Fold the edge of the top crust over and then under the rim of the bottom crust (like tucking in

continues ◢

a sheet around a mattress). Press together firmly. Now raise the rim so it stands upright and with your fingers flute a simple zigzag design on the rim (see To Form an Extra-Deep Pie Shell, page 208). Be very careful that the crust does not extend out over the rim of the pan, or it might droop and sag and fall off when the pie is baked.

With a small, sharp knife, cut eight 1-inch slits in the top to allow steam and/or juices to escape.

With a pastry brush, brush milk over the top of the crust (except the rim), being careful not to use so much that it runs down in puddles against the rim; if it does, sponge it up with a small piece of paper towel. Sprinkle generously with sugar.

Be prepared to slide a cookie sheet or foil on a rack below to catch juices that might bubble over. If you do not have a

rack below you might want to put foil on the floor of the oven, but wait until the pie is almost baked and might start to bubble over (which depends on how juicy the apples are) because the cookie sheet or foil might interfere with the baking.

Bake at 450 degrees for 15 minutes. Then open the oven and quickly reach in to cover the rim with an aluminum foil frame (see page 209), folding the points down as quickly as possible.

Lower the oven temperature to 425 degrees and bake for about 45 minutes more (total time is about 1 hour), until the crust is nicely browned and the apples are tender (you can test them with a toothpick through the slits on top).

Cool on a rack. Serve when barely cooled or at room temperature.

PIE PASTRY

Makes 1 (9-inch) crust (see Notes) I recommend using an ovenproof glass pie plate.

1 cup *sifted* unbleached all-purpose flour

Scant ½ teaspoon salt

3 tablespoons vegetable shortening (e.g., Crisco), cold and firm

3 tablespoons unsalted butter, cold and firm, cut into very small squares

About 3 tablespoons ice water

If the room is warm, it is a good idea to chill the mixing bowl and even the flour beforehand. Some pie pros store their flour in the freezer or refrigerator, so it will be cold and ready.

Place the flour and salt in a large, wide mixing bowl. Add the shortening and butter. With a pastry blender, cut them in until the mixture resembles coarse crumbs. It is all right to leave a few pieces about the size of tiny peas.

Sprinkle 1 tablespoon of the ice water by small drops all over the surface. Stir/mix/toss with a fork. Continue adding the water only until the flour is barely moistened. (Too much water makes the pastry sticky/soggy/tough. Too little makes it hard to roll out without cracks and breaks in the dough.) Do not ever dump a lot of water in any one spot. If you add the water too quickly — if you don't stir/mix/toss enough while you are adding it — you might be convinced that you need more water. But maybe you don't; maybe you just need to add the water more slowly and stir/mix more. When adequate water has been added, the mixture will still be lumpy and will not hold together, but with practice you will know by the look of it that it will form a ball when

pressed together. I have occasionally had to add a little more water, but very little — 1 to 2 teaspoons at the most.

The shortening and butter must not melt (they should remain in little flour-coated flakes), so do not handle now any more than necessary. Turn the mixture out onto a large work surface and, with your hands, just push the mixture together to form a ball. (My mother never touched the dough

continues ↘

NOTES

The ingredients for the crust may easily be doubled for two shells or for a pie with both a bottom and a top crust.

For a 10-inch crust, increase the amounts to 1¼ cups flour, generous ½ teaspoon salt, 3¾ tablespoons vegetable shortening, 3¾ tablespoons butter, and 3¾ tablespoons ice water.

It is a great luxury to have an unbaked pie shell in the freezer. I try to keep one, frozen in the pie plate, all ready for the oven. I first freeze it, uncovered, then wrap it in plastic wrap or put it in a freezer bag. Then I have only to line it with foil and fill it with beans or weights when I am ready to bake. (I think a pie shell freezes better unbaked than when already baked.)

with her hands at this stage — she turned it out onto a piece of plastic wrap, brought up the sides and corners of the plastic, and squeezed them firmly together at the top, letting the mixture form a ball without touching it. Then she flattened it slightly. Now I do it this way too.)

If the dough is too dry to hold together, do not knead it (don't even think about kneading it), but replace it in the bowl, cut it into small pieces with a knife, add a few more drops of water, and then stir again.

However you do it, form the dough into a ball quickly, flatten it slightly, smooth the edges, wrap in plastic wrap, and refrigerate for at least an hour, but preferably overnight. Chilling the dough not only makes it firmer, less sticky, and easier to handle, but also allows time for the water to moisten the flour more evenly. If it has been refrigerated overnight, let it stand at room temperature 10 to 15 minutes before rolling it out.

To roll out the dough:

Rolling out the dough is easiest if you work on a pastry cloth. Flour the cloth by rubbing in as much flour as the cloth will absorb, then lightly wipe off any loose excess flour. Rub flour on the rolling pin.

Place the flattened ball of dough on the cloth. If the dough is very firm, pound/whack it sharply — but not too sharply — in all directions with the rolling pin to flatten it into a circle about 7 inches in diameter. (Don't pound the dough so hard that it forms deep cracks on the rim.) With your fingers, smooth and pinch together any small cracks at the edges.

Now start to roll, preferably from the center out rather than back and forth, and do not turn the dough upside down (it absorbs too much flour and becomes tough). Roll first in one direction and then another, trying to keep the shape round. If the edges crack slightly, pinch them together before the cracks become deep. If the dough cracks anywhere other than on the edges, or if the circle is terribly uneven, do not reroll the dough; simply cut off uneven edges and use the scraps as patches. Moisten the edges of each patch with water, turn the patch upside down, and press it firmly into place.

Re-flour the rolling pin as necessary. It should not be necessary to re-flour the cloth, but if there is any hint that the dough might stick, reflour it lightly.

Roll the dough into a 12-inch circle for a 9-inch crust or a 13-inch circle for a 10-inch crust. It is important that the rolled-out dough be the same thickness all over (a scant ⅛ inch thick) so it will bake evenly.

To transfer the dough to the pie plate, drape it over the rolling pin as follows: Hold the pin over the left side of the dough, raise the left side of the pastry cloth to turn the dough over the rolling pin, roll it up loosely, then move it to the right side of the pie plate and unroll it, centering it evenly. Or fold it in half and lift it over the plate. With your fingers, ease the sides down into the plate. Do not stretch the dough or it will shrink during baking.

If you have a cake-decorating turntable, place the pie plate on it.

Press the dough into place all over. If your fingernails are in the way, cut a small portion of the dough from an uneven edge, form it into a small ball, flour it lightly, and use it as a tamping tool to press the dough.

With scissors, cut the edge of the crust, leaving an even ½- to ¾-inch overhang beyond the outside edge of the pie plate.

Now, to form a hem. I had always believed it was correct to turn the edge of the dough toward the outside and under — back onto itself. Recently I have been turning it toward the inside, and back onto itself. I like it better. So, with floured fingertips, fold the edge to make a hem that extends about ½ inch higher than the rim. Press the hem lightly together between your floured fingertips, pressing it a bit thinner, and making it stand upright.

There are many ways of forming a decorative edge. Here's one: Flour your fingertips. You will be working clockwise around the rim, starting at three o'clock. Place your left forefinger at a right angle across the rim of the dough. (Your left hand will be over the inside of the plate with your finger sticking over to the outside.) With your right hand, grip the dough rim, using the thumb and bent-under forefinger. Grip slightly ahead (clockwise) of your left finger and twist the dough edge toward the center of the plate. Remove both hands and then replace your left forefinger just ahead (clockwise again) of the twist you have just formed. This will be at about four o'clock on the rim. Repeat the twists all around. Check and reshape any uneven spots.

To Prebake a Pie Shell

Prick fork holes in the bottom of the pastry ¼ inch apart when baking an empty pie shell.

Place the shell in the freezer for 15 minutes or more, until it is frozen firm (this helps prevent shrinking). Wrapped airtight (after it is firm), it may be frozen for months if you wish.

About 15 or 20 minutes before baking, adjust a rack one-third up from the bottom of the oven and preheat the oven to 450 degrees.

To keep the pastry shell in place during baking, cut a 12-inch square of aluminum foil and place it shiny side down in the frozen shell. Press it into place all over. Do not fold the corners of the foil over the rim; let them stand up. Fill the foil at least three-quarters full with dried beans or with pie weights. (I use about 5 cups of a combination of black beans and black-eyed peas that I have been using for the same purpose for about 25 years.)

Bake the frozen shell at 450 degrees for 12 to 13 minutes, until it is set and lightly colored on the edges. Remove the pie plate from the oven. Reduce the heat to 400 degrees. Gently, slowly, remove the foil and beans by lifting the four corners of the foil.

Replace the plate in the oven and continue to bake for 7 or 8 minutes, or longer if necessary. Watch the pie shell almost constantly; if it starts to puff up anywhere,

continues ↘

reach into the oven and pierce the puff carefully with a cake tester to release trapped air. Bake until the edges are golden. Do not underbake. A too-pale crust is not as attractive as one with a good color. The bottom will remain paler than the edges. (During baking, if the crust is not browning evenly, reverse the position of the pan.)

Place on a rack and let cool.

To Form an Extra-Deep Pie Shell

Follow the above directions (rolling the dough ½ inch wider — or 13½ inches) up to folding the hem of the pastry. Fold the hem toward the inside and fold a ¾-inch (rather than a ½-inch) hem. You should have a raised ¾-inch hem standing straight up all around the inner edge of the rim. Form it into a straight, even wall all around. To flute it (keeping it high), leave it upright, lightly flour the thumb and the tip of the index finger of one hand, and pinch from the outside so the outer edge of the raised wall of pastry forms a horizontal V (or a V that has the point facing outside). It seems easiest to me to start at the right side (three o'clock) of the plate. Use the index finger of your other hand to support the inside of the crust while you pinch it.

Pinch again 1 inch away from the first. Continue to pinch and form V's all around the outside of the rim 1 inch apart. Then do the same thing on the inside of the rim, this time starting at the left side (nine o'clock) of the plate, pinching between two out-pointing V's on the outside and forming a nice, neat zigzag pattern all around, standing ¾ inch straight up.

To Patch the Pastry

I was making a recipe in which the pastry is baked empty and then a juicy filling is poured in and the pastry is baked again. But while the crust baked empty, it formed a 3- or 4-inch crack right down the middle. If I had poured the filling in, it would have run through the crack, stuck to the pan, and been a disaster. I stood there looking at it, feeling totally helpless.

My husband walked into the room and I didn't think he even saw what had happened — but he did, and without a moment's pause he said, "Patch it with almond paste." It took a few seconds for his brilliant comment to sink in — it was genius. I still cannot understand how he knew so quickly what was probably the only solution possible, and one I had never heard of before.

Since then I have used this sensational trick many times. Whatever would I have done if I had not known about this?

I have used both marzipan and almond paste. The brand I buy is Odense, which is made in Denmark and is generally available at fine food stores all over America. It seems to last forever (either at room temperature or refrigerated), but do not allow it to dry out. After you open it, be sure to wrap it airtight. I use both plastic wrap and aluminum foil.

Cut off a thin slice or break off a small chunk of the marzipan or almond paste and press it between your fingers to make a thin patch slightly larger than the damaged area. Beat a bit of egg white lightly (only until foamy), then use it as a paste. With your fingertip, brush the white onto one side of the patch and place it, egg white down, over the damage. (I have also used just a bit of water as a paste and it worked, but if you have egg white, I think it might be safer than water.) Flour your fingertips and press gently around the rim of the patch.

Then pour in the filling and no one will ever know, and you will say thank you to Ralph every time you patch pastry this way.

To Make an Aluminum Foil Frame

To prevent overbrowning of the edge of a piecrust, make an aluminum foil frame as follows: Cut a 12-inch length of regular aluminum foil (not heavy-duty foil). Fold in half and then in the opposite direction in half again, making a square. Fold once more, folded corner to corner, making a triangle. To make a 7-inch hole in the middle, measure 3½ inches from the point of the triangle that is in the middle of the foil and cut out a shallow arc from the long side of the triangle to one short side. Open the folded foil frame and lay it over the top of the pie so the edges are covered, and the center is exposed to get brown.

(You might want to make two frames and use them both at the same time, placing one over the other so that the points of the second frame are between the points of the first frame.)

After using the frame, reserve it to use over and over again.

APRICOT TART

Makes 8 to 10 portions This is a favorite dessert that I taught in many cities around the country when I gave cooking classes. And when *Food & Wine* magazine asked me for a recipe for their cover, this was it. It is a wonderful tart made of the best pastry I know. It can be beautifully plain, or creative and artistic with a design on top made of some of the pastry. It is great fun to make and you will be proud to serve it. Plan it for a party (or a magazine cover).

The filling can be made days or weeks ahead—the apricots soak overnight, but if you are in a rush, they need not be soaked, just simmer them longer to soften them. The pastry is best made right before using it. In cooking classes I served this warm, even hot. I have also frozen it for weeks and thawed it to serve. Or I have made it several hours ahead of time and let it cool to room temperature. Any of these ways is fine.

You will need a plain flan ring measuring 9½ inches in diameter and ¾ inch in depth. (The tart can also be made in a 9-inch loose-bottomed cake pan in place of the flan ring; even though the cake pan is deeper, you can make a tart only ¾ inch deep in it.)

I use plain supermarket apricots; they have a nice tart flavor and they generally work better for this recipe than some of the fancier, more expensive apricots. (The more expensive ones sometimes do not fall apart as they should, even after long cooking.) The filling should be made first.

FILLING

- 12 ounces (about 2 cups) dried apricots
- 2 cups water
- 1¼ cups sugar
- ½ teaspoon vanilla extract
- ¼ teaspoon almond extract
- OPTIONAL: 1 tablespoon rum, Cognac, or kirsch
- OPTIONAL: About 2 tablespoons thinly sliced toasted almonds

RICH FLAN PASTRY (PÂTE SABLÉE)

- 2½ cups *unsifted* unbleached all-purpose flour
- Scant ½ teaspoon salt
- ½ cup sugar
- 8 ounces (2 sticks) unsalted butter, cold and firm, cut into ½-inch pieces (it is best to cut the butter ahead of time and refrigerate it)
- 1 large egg plus 2 large egg yolks
- Finely grated zest of 1 lemon
- 2 teaspoons lemon juice

EGG GLAZE

- 1 large egg yolk
- 1 teaspoon water

APRICOT GLAZE

- ¼ cup apricot preserves
- 2 teaspoons water

For the filling:

Soak the apricots overnight in the water.

Place the apricots and water in a heavy saucepan. Add the sugar and stir to mix. Place over moderately high heat and stir until the mixture comes to a boil. Reduce the heat slightly, cover, and simmer for about 10 minutes — stir occasionally to be sure it is not sticking or burning. Then uncover, raise the heat to moderately high again, and stir almost constantly until the apricots are very tender and beginning to fall apart and the liquid has thickened — reduce the heat if necessary to avoid spattering — and remember that the mixture will thicken more as it cools; do not cook until it becomes too dry. It usually takes 8 to 10 minutes, but apricots vary considerably and some may take longer. You can help them along by breaking the apricots with the side of a wooden spoon as you stir them. Do not puree them — you should have thick, chunky apricot preserves.

Remove from the heat. Let cool a bit and then stir in the vanilla and almond extracts and the optional liquor. If you wish, stir in a few thinly sliced toasted almonds.

This can be used as soon as it has cooled, or it can be refrigerated for weeks. (Many of the people who came to the cooking classes told me they liked the apricot preserves so much that they made it to serve with toast — I agree.)

For the pastry:

Fit the food processor with the steel blade. Place the flour, salt, and sugar in the bowl of the processor. Add the butter and process on-and-off (like pulse beats) for about 10 seconds, until the mixture resembles coarse meal.

In a small bowl, mix the egg, yolks, zest, and juice. Then, with the processor going, add these mixed ingredients through the feed tube and process only briefly (just a few seconds) until mixed, not until it all holds together — it should be dry and crumbly.

Turn the pastry out onto a large board, marble, or counter top. Press together to form a ball. Then "break" the dough as follows: Start at the far end of the ball of dough and, using the heel of your hand, push off a small piece (it should be a few tablespoonfuls), pushing it against the work surface and away from you. Continue until all the dough has been pushed off.

Form the dough into a fat sausage shape, cut it in half, and then form into two balls. Lightly flour the balls of dough. With your hands, flatten them slightly into rounds 6 to 8 inches in diameter. Wrap them in plastic wrap and let them stand at room temperature for 20 to 30 minutes. (If the room is very warm, or if the pastry was handled too much, it may be refrigerated for about 10 minutes, but no longer. If it is too cold when it is rolled out, it will form small cracks on the surface and the filling might run out.)

continues ↘

To shape and bake:

Place two racks in the oven, one one-third up from the bottom and one in the center, and preheat oven to 375 degrees. Butter the inside of a 9½ x ¾-inch flan ring and place it on an unbuttered flat cookie sheet (the sheet should have at least one flat edge so you can slide the baked tart off the sheet).

Flour a pastry cloth and a rolling pin. Place one round of the dough on the cloth and roll it into a 12-inch circle.

Drape the dough over the rolling pin and transfer it to the flan ring, centering it carefully as you unroll it.

With your fingertips, carefully press the dough into place without stretching it. The dough will stand about ½ inch above the ring on the sides. If necessary, straighten it with scissors, leaving ½ inch of dough above the rim.

If the dough cracks or tears while you are working with it, it can be patched with a little additional dough.

Spoon the cold apricot filling into the shell and smooth the top of it — it should be flat, not mounded.

Flour the fingers of your dominant hand. Hold a spot on the rim of the dough, holding it with your thumb and the sides of your bent-under index finger. Press on the raised edge of the dough to flatten it and make it thinner. Work all the way around. Then fold the thinner rim of dough down over the filling, pulling it in toward the center a bit in order to keep it slightly away from the flan ring.

Roll the remaining half of the dough until it is a scant ¼ inch thick, then trim it into a circle about 10 to 10½ inches in diameter (use anything that size as a pattern and cut around it with a pizza cutter, a pastry wheel, or a small, sharp knife).

With a pastry brush dipped in water or with your fingertips, wet the rim of the bottom dough that is folded over the filling. Now, to transfer the top crust, drape it loosely over the rolling pin and unroll it over the filling.

With your fingertips, press down on the edges to seal both crusts together. Then cut around the rim with a table knife to remove excess dough; the edge of the dough must not extend over the flan ring or the dough might stick and it will be difficult to raise and remove the ring after the tart is baked. Then press around the edge of the pastry with the back of the tines of a fork to seal it. Again, keep the upper edge of the pastry slightly away from the ring.

For the egg glaze:

Beat the yolk and water just to mix and strain it through a strainer.

Brush glaze over the top of the tart but be careful not to let it run down the sides — that could make it stick to the flan ring. With the back of a table knife, score a diamond pattern in the dough, being very careful not to score the dough deeply; make shallow lines about ½ inch apart, first in one direction, and then on an angle in the opposite direction.

To make a design on the top, press together all leftover scraps of the dough

and roll them out on the pastry cloth with the rolling pin. Roll this a little thinner than the crusts. Cut with a long, sharp knife or a pastry wheel into ½-inch-wide strips. Place them on the tart in a bow design. Then cut the remaining dough with a small scalloped or plain round cutter, or with a heart-shaped cutter, and place these around and on top of the bow.

(When *Food & Wine* magazine made this, it was for their Valentine's Day issue. They cut out the additional dough with large heart-shaped cutters, and placed one heart in the middle and six in a circle around it. It was gorgeous!)

Brush it all well with the egg wash.

With the tip of a small, sharp knife, cut a few small slits (air vents), cutting right up against the bow or other design so the cuts do not show.

Bake on the lower oven rack for about 30 minutes. Then reduce the oven temperature to 350 degrees, raise the tart to the center of the oven, and bake for

20 to 30 minutes more (total baking time is 50 to 60 minutes), until the top is beautifully browned.

When the tart is removed from the oven, if any of the pastry has run out under the flan ring, use a small, sharp knife to trim and remove it.

It is easiest to remove the flan ring if you do it immediately, while the pastry is hot, before it cools and becomes crisper. Use pot holders that are not too thick and bulky (or use a folded towel or napkin) and, very gently, slowly, and carefully, raise the ring to remove it.

(If you have trouble removing the ring, let it stand until the tart is cool. Then slide the tart [still in the flan ring] onto an inverted 8- or 9-inch round cake pan. The ring will then slide down, and the tart can be transferred to a serving plate. All of these directions are HANDLE WITH CARE.)

If you were able to lift the flan ring up off the hot tart, then let the tart cool completely on the cookie sheet.

continues ↘

When cool, use a flat-sided cookie sheet as a spatula and carefully transfer the tart to a flat serving plate. Or carefully loosen the tart by sliding a long, narrow metal offset spatula under it and, if it moves easily, using your hands to slide it off the flat side of the cookie sheet. But don't force it; if it feels as though the tart might crack, use something large and flat (i.e., the bottom of a loose-bottomed quiche pan) to transfer it.

For the apricot glaze:

In a small pan over moderate heat, stir the preserves and water until the mixture comes to a boil. Strain through a strainer.

Brush the glaze carefully all over the top of the tart. (If you plan to freeze the baked tart, do not glaze the top until the tart is thawed — glaze it shortly before serving.)

This tart is delicious as it is, but it is still better with vanilla ice cream; the slightly sour taste of the apricots with the smooth, sweet ice cream is gorgeous!

KEY LIME PIE

Makes 8 to 12 portions The original Key Lime Pie was made with a baked crust because it was created before graham crackers were manufactured. And it was topped with baked meringue, never ever with whipped cream, since the recipe, made with canned milk, came about because of a lack of both refrigeration and grazing land for milk cows in the Florida Keys.

This is the most popular of all my Key Lime Pies; it uses gingersnaps for the crust instead of graham crackers. It is so easy (no cooking) you will think something is missing. It must be made the day before serving or it will be too runny. This recipe can be made with regular green limes or with lemons, but then it is not a Key Lime Pie.

This is the pie that made headlines on the Op-Ed page of the *New York Times*. I made twenty for President Ronald Reagan's Economic Summit in Williamsburg, Virginia. The Secret Service dropped all but four pies. Happily, each world leader got one bite. These things happen.

GINGER CRUMB CRUST

- 1½ cups gingersnap crumbs
- 3 tablespoons granulated sugar
- ½ teaspoon ground cinnamon
- ¼ teaspoon ground nutmeg
- 3 ounces (¾ stick) unsalted butter, melted

FILLING

- 4 large egg yolks
- 1 (14-ounce) can sweetened condensed milk
- ½ cup Key lime juice

WHIPPED CREAM

- 2 cups heavy cream
- ¼ cup granulated or confectioners' sugar
- 1 teaspoon vanilla extract

OPTIONAL: fresh strawberries

For the crust:

Preheat oven to 325 degrees.

Combine all the ingredients and pat and press into a 9-inch pie plate. Bake for 10 minutes. Cool.

For the filling:

You can use an electric mixer, an eggbeater, or a wire whisk. Beat the yolks lightly to mix. Add the condensed milk and mix. Gradually add the lime juice, beating or whisking only until mixed.

Pour the filling into the crumb crust. It will make a thin layer; the color will be pale lemon—not green. It will be fluid now,

continues ↘

but as it stands, a chemical reaction takes place and the filling will become about as firm as a baked custard.

Refrigerate overnight.

Or if you wish, bake the filled pie for 10 minutes in a 350-degree oven, then cool and chill.

Whipped cream is optional on this; natives do not use it — restaurants do (I do).

For the whipped cream:

In a chilled bowl with chilled beaters, whip the ingredients until the cream holds a shape and is firm enough to spread over the pie. If you whip the cream ahead of time, refrigerate it. It will separate slightly as it stands; just whisk it a bit with a wire whisk when you are ready to use it.

Spread the whipped cream over the cooled filling.

Fresh strawberries and Key Lime Pie are a divine combination. If you like, either form a border of the berries standing up around the rim, or serve them separately.

BLACK BOTTOM PIE

Makes 8 portions Marjorie Kinnan Rawlings, the Pulitzer Prize–winning author of *The Yearling*, also wrote a delightful cookbook, *Cross Creek Cookery*, which is a mouthwatering account of the food served in her house in central Florida. In it, she says of her Black Bottom Pie, "I think this is the most delicious pie I have ever eaten…a pie so delicate, so luscious, that I hope to be propped up on my dying bed and fed a generous portion. Then I think that I should refuse outright to die, for life would be too good to relinquish."

My sentiments are the same. This is glorious.

CRUST

- 1¼ cups graham cracker crumbs
- 1 tablespoon granulated sugar
- 1 teaspoon ground ginger
- 1 teaspoon ground cinnamon
- 2 ounces (½ stick) unsalted butter, melted

FILLING

- 2 ounces unsweetened chocolate
- 1 tablespoon (1 envelope) unflavored gelatin
- ¼ cup cold water
- 1 cup granulated sugar
- 1 tablespoon cornstarch
- Salt
- 4 large eggs, separated
- 1¾ cups milk
- 2 tablespoons dark rum
- 1 teaspoon vanilla extract
- ⅛ teaspoon cream of tartar

WHIPPED CREAM

- 1 cup heavy cream
- ¼ cup confectioners' sugar
- 1 scant teaspoon vanilla extract

OPTIONAL: coarsely grated chocolate for garnish

For the crust:

Adjust rack to center of oven. Preheat to 375 degrees. Line a 9-inch pie plate with nonstick aluminum foil, shiny side down, pressing it firmly onto the plate.

In a bowl, mix the crumbs with the granulated sugar, ginger, and cinnamon, and then add the melted butter. Stir with a rubber spatula, pressing the mixture against the sides of the bowl, until completely mixed. The mixture will look crumbly but will hold together when pressed into place.

Press the crumb mixture into the lined pie plate firmly and up the sides. Bake for 8 minutes. Cool to room temperature.

For the filling:

Melt the chocolate in the top of a small double boiler over hot water on moderate heat. Remove the bowl from the hot water and set aside.

Sprinkle the gelatin over the cold water and set aside.

continues ↘

In a small bowl, mix ½ cup of the granulated sugar (reserve remaining ½ cup sugar) with the cornstarch and a pinch of salt. Set aside.

In the top of a large double boiler, stir the yolks lightly with a small wire whisk or a fork just to mix.

Scald the milk uncovered in a small, heavy saucepan over moderate heat until you can see small bubbles on the surface. Stir in the sugar-cornstarch mixture. Pour very slowly, in a thin stream, into the yolks—stirring constantly. Place over, but not touching, hot water in the bottom of the double boiler on moderate heat. Cook, stirring gently and scraping the pot with a rubber spatula, for 12 to 15 minutes, until the custard thickens to the consistency of a medium cream sauce. Lift top of double boiler off the hot water.

Remove 1 cup of the custard and set aside to cool, stirring occasionally, for 5 to 10 minutes, until tepid.

Meanwhile, to the remainder of the custard in the top of the double boiler, immediately add the softened gelatin and stir until thoroughly dissolved. Stir in the rum and set aside.

Gradually add the reserved cup of custard to the chocolate, stirring constantly with a small wire whisk. Mix thoroughly until smooth. Add the vanilla and turn the mixture into the prepared crust. Spread level and refrigerate.

In the small bowl of electric mixer at moderately high speed, beat the egg whites with a pinch of salt and the cream of tartar until the mixture increases in volume and starts to thicken. While beating, gradually add the reserved ½ cup sugar and continue to beat until mixture holds a shape and is the consistency of thick marshmallow sauce.

Gradually fold the rum custard (which may still be warm) into the beaten whites. Pour gently from one bowl to another to ensure thorough blending.

Pour over the chocolate layer, mounding it high in the center. (If there is too much filling and it might run over, reserve some at room temperature. Chill the pie in the freezer for 10 to 15 minutes, or in the refrigerator a bit longer, to partially set the filling. Then pour on the reserved portion and it will not run over.)

Refrigerate pie for 2 to 3 hours.

For the whipped cream:

In a chilled bowl with chilled beaters, whip the cream, confectioners' sugar, and vanilla until the cream holds a shape. Spread evenly over filling, or use a pastry bag with a star tube and form a heavy, ruffled border of cream.

If you like, if the cream was spread over the pie, sprinkle it with coarsely grated chocolate; if it was put on to form a border, fill the center with grated chocolate.

COFFEE BUTTERCRUNCH PIE

Makes 8 portions   This rich creation is the famous Coffee-Toffee Pie from Blum's in San Francisco. I never know what to answer when people tell me, as they often do, that this is better than sex. (What would you say?)

NOTES
↓
Both the crust and filling recipes may be doubled. The extra crust may be frozen by itself, or the filled crust can be frozen.

↓

The pie should be refrigerated for at least 5 to 6 hours before serving.

CRUST

- ½ package pie crust mix (measure the contents of a package into a measuring cup and use half)
- 1 ounce unsweetened chocolate
- ¼ cup firmly packed light brown sugar
- 2½ ounces (¾ cup) walnuts, very finely chopped (must be finely chopped — not ground)
- 1 teaspoon vanilla extract
- 1 tablespoon water

FILLING

- 1 ounce unsweetened chocolate
- 4 ounces (1 stick) unsalted butter
- ¾ cup firmly packed light brown sugar
- 2 teaspoons instant espresso or coffee powder
- 2 large eggs

TOPPING

- 2 cups heavy cream
- 2 tablespoons instant espresso or coffee powder
- ½ cup confectioners' sugar
- OPTIONAL: coarsely grated semisweet chocolate

For the crust:

Adjust rack to center of oven and preheat to 375 degrees. Line a 9-inch pie plate with nonstick aluminum foil, shiny side down, pressing it firmly onto the plate.

Place the pie crust mix in a mixing bowl.

Cut the chocolate into small pieces and place it in the bowl of a food processor fitted with the metal chopping blade. Process for about half a minute until fine. Add the brown sugar and nuts. Pulse briefly and then transfer the mixture to the pie crust mix in the bowl. Mix the vanilla and water and gradually drizzle it over the mixture — don't pour it all in one place — while using a fork to stir and toss. The mixture will be lumpy and crumbly. Do not try to make it smooth; stir it very briefly. It will hold together when you press it into place.

continues ↘

Press the crumb mixture into the lined pie plate firmly and up the sides. Bake for 15 minutes. Cool to room temperature.

Meanwhile, prepare the filling.

For the filling:

Melt the chocolate in a double boiler and set aside to cool. In small bowl of electric mixer, beat the butter to soften a bit. Gradually add the brown sugar and beat at moderately high speed for 2 to 3 minutes. Mix in the cooled, melted chocolate and the instant coffee. Add the eggs individually, beating for 5 minutes after each, and scraping the bowl occasionally with a rubber spatula.

Pour the filling into the prepared crust. Refrigerate for 5 to 6 hours or overnight. (Pie may be frozen now or it may be refrigerated for a day or so. If you freeze it, freeze until filling is firm before wrapping airtight. Frozen pie should be uncovered and thawed overnight in the refrigerator.)

Either shortly before serving or a few hours before, prepare the topping.

For the topping:

In a chilled bowl with chilled beaters, whip the cream with the coffee and confectioners' sugar until firm. Do not overbeat, but it must be firm enough so that it holds its shape when the pie is served.

Spread the topping smooth over the filling, or apply in fancy swirls using a pastry bag with a large star tube.

Sprinkle top with optional grated chocolate. Refrigerate.

APRICOT-APPLE CRUMBLE

Makes 6 portions A delicious casserole of juicy sliced apples and poached dried apricots (a great combination), with a hint of rum and a crisp and crunchy walnut crumb topping. This can wait at room temperature for an hour or two before it is baked. And then it can be served hot, right out of the oven, when it is most sensational. Or it can be served at room temperature.

You need a shallow ovenproof casserole with a 3-quart capacity.

CRUMB TOPPING

- ¾ cup *unsifted* unbleached all-purpose flour
- ¼ cup *unsifted* whole wheat flour
- ½ cup firmly packed dark brown sugar
- 4 ounces (1 stick) unsalted butter, cold and firm, cut into small pieces

FILLING

- 3½ ounces (1 cup) walnuts
- 6 ounces (about 1 cup) dried apricots
- ⅔ cup water
- ⅓ cup apricot preserves
- ¼ cup dark rum (or apple juice or orange juice)
- 3 pounds (about 8 medium-large) Golden Delicious apples
- ¼ cup firmly packed dark brown sugar

For the topping:

Place both flours and the sugar in a large bowl. Rub the ingredients between your fingertips until mixed. Add the butter and, with a pastry blender, cut the mixture until it resembles coarse crumbs and the pieces of butter are about the size of corn kernels. The ingredients should not hold together. Refrigerate.

For the filling:

Adjust a rack to the center of the oven and preheat the oven to 350 degrees. Butter a shallow 3-quart ovenproof casserole (13 x 9 x 2 inches) and set aside.

To toast the walnuts, place them in a shallow cake pan and bake for 10 minutes, stirring occasionally, until very hot. Cool and then break them into medium-size pieces and set aside.

Place the apricots and water in a small, heavy saucepan. Bring to a boil over high heat. Then cover, reduce the heat to moderate, and let cook, stirring occasionally, until the apricots are completely tender when tested with a cake tester or a toothpick. Uncover and stir constantly until there is no liquid remaining. (While stirring, press the apricots against the sides of the pan, breaking them into coarse chunks.) Add the apricot preserves and stir until melted. Remove from the heat. Stir in the rum (or juice) and set aside.

With a vegetable peeler, peel the apples. Cut them from top to bottom into halves. With a melon baller, remove the cores.

continues ↘

With a small, sharp knife, cut a small groove in the top and bottom of each half, removing the fibers and stems. (Or quarter the peeled apples and remove the cores and stems with a small knife.)

Cut each half into about 8 wedges and place in a large mixing bowl. Add the apricot mixture and the sugar. With a rubber spatula, stir to mix well. (Each wedge should be coated with the preserves.)

Turn into the buttered casserole. With your fingers, arrange the apples to level the top layer.

Sprinkle the walnuts evenly over the apples.

Then, with your fingers, sprinkle the crumb topping over the nuts.

If you are not ready to bake the casserole now, cover it with plastic wrap and let it wait at room temperature.

When you are ready to bake, adjust a rack to the center of the oven and preheat the oven to 400 degrees.

Bake the casserole, uncovered, for 30 to 40 minutes, until the apples in the center are tender when tested with a cake tester or a toothpick, the juices are bubbling, and the crumb topping is slightly browned.

Serve hot, warm, or at room temperature. Serve as is or with vanilla ice cream.

STRAWBERRY TART

Makes 8 portions This crisp, cookie-like shell, baked in a flan ring, is filled with strawberries and generously covered with a glaze made of pureed strawberries. It is a picture. And very delicious.

If you wish, the pastry shell may be shaped in the flan ring and frozen for days or weeks. It is best to bake it when you are ready to use it; that should be the day you serve it.

You will need a 9- or 10-inch flan ring, ¾ or 1 inch deep.

PASTRY

- 1 cup *unsifted* unbleached all-purpose flour
- 2 tablespoons sugar
- ¼ teaspoon salt
- 4 ounces (1 stick) unsalted butter, cold and firm, cut into small pieces
- 1 large egg, beaten lightly just to mix

FILLING

- 2 or 3 pint boxes (2 or 3 pounds) fresh strawberries, depending on the size of the berries and the size of the flan ring (if you use the berries whole you will need a large number; but if they are very large, you can cut them in half, and use only half as many)
- 1 cup sugar
- ⅛ teaspoon salt

- 2 teaspoons unflavored gelatin
- ½ cup plus 1 tablespoon water
- 1 tablespoon lemon juice
- 3 tablespoons cornstarch

—

OPTIONAL: 1 kiwifruit, for decorating

WHIPPED CREAM

- 2 cups heavy cream
- ¼ cup confectioners' or granulated sugar
- 1 teaspoon vanilla extract

For the pastry:

In a food processor: Fit food processor with the metal blade and place the flour, sugar, salt, and butter in the bowl. Process on and off for only a few seconds, until the mixture resembles coarse meal. Then add the egg and process only until the mixture barely holds together — be careful not to process any longer.

In a mixer: The same procedure may be followed, using the large bowl of the mixer and low speed. The "coarse-meal" stage will take longer to arrive at in the mixer than in the processor. While you are

mixing, use a rubber spatula to push the ingredients toward the beaters.

Turn the mixture out onto a lightly floured board. Flour your hands, squeeze the pastry together, and form it into a ball. Flour the ball lightly, flatten it to a 6- or 7-inch circle, and put it on a floured pastry cloth. With a floured rolling pin, roll the pastry into a 12-inch circle.

Place the flan ring (see headnote) on a cookie sheet. Roll the pastry loosely on the rolling pin, and unroll it over the flan ring,

continues ↘

centering it carefully. With your fingers, press it into place. With scissors, trim excess, allowing ½- to ¾-inch overlap. Fold excess inside to form a double thickness on the rim and press together firmly. The rim should be upright a scant ¼ inch above the flan ring. If you wish, form a design on the folded edge by pressing the back of a knife blade at an angle across the top of the rim, at ¼-inch intervals all around the edge, or crimp it with a dough crimper.

Place the pastry shell on the cookie sheet in the freezer at least until it is frozen, or longer if you wish (if you do leave it in the freezer longer, cover it well with plastic wrap or foil after it is frozen).

When you are ready to bake, adjust a rack to the center of the oven and preheat the oven to 375 degrees. Line the frozen shell with aluminum foil and fill it with dried beans or pie weights (aluminum pellets made for that purpose) to keep the shell in place.

Bake for 30 minutes. Remove from the oven and carefully remove the foil and beans by lifting the four corners of the foil. Return the shell to the oven and continue to bake for about 10 minutes more, until the shell is thoroughly dry and lightly browned; after removing the foil keep an eye on the pastry — if it puffs up, prick it with a cake tester.

For the filling:

Wash the berries, pick off the stems and hulls, and drain on towels.

In a blender or a food processor, puree 1 box of the berries to make 2 cups puree. Strain the puree through a large strainer set over a large bowl. Place the strained puree in a heavy 2-quart saucepan and add the sugar and salt.

In a small custard cup, sprinkle the gelatin over 2 tablespoons of the water and let stand.

Place the remaining ½ cup minus 1 tablespoon of water and the lemon juice in a small bowl with the cornstarch and stir to dissolve. Add the cornstarch mixture to the strained berries.

Place over moderate heat. Stir constantly but gently with a rubber spatula for about 6 or 7 minutes, until the mixture comes to a low boil, thickens, and becomes rather clear. Then reduce the heat to low, add the softened gelatin, and stir to dissolve. Continue to cook and stir gently for 3 minutes more.

Remove from the heat and gently transfer to a wide bowl to cool.

While the cooked berries cool, place the remaining berries in the baked shell. They may stand upright, in a pattern of concentric circles. Or, if they are large, they may be cut in half and placed on their cut side, overlapping one another in concentric circles. Either way, they should completely fill the shell.

With a teaspoon, gently spoon the cooled berries evenly all over the berries in the tart and the spaces between. If the berries were halved and are overlapping, it may be necessary to raise some of them a bit to allow the mixture to run under and around them, and to fill up all the space.

Refrigerate the tart for at least a few hours.

If you like, just before serving, peel the kiwi (with a vegetable peeler), slice it crossways in very, very thin circles, and place them overlapping in a ring around the top. If there are not enough slices, cut them in half and use half slices.

For the whipped cream:

In a chilled bowl with chilled beaters, whip all the ingredients until the cream holds a soft shape but not until it is stiff.

Serve the cream separately, placing a generous spoonful alongside each portion.

Mississippi Mud Pie

Strawberry Tart (page 225)

MISSISSIPPI MUD PIE

Makes 8 to 10 portions Mississippi Mud (a cold drink) was originally a mixture of vanilla ice cream, strong, cold prepared coffee, and a lot of bourbon, with a sprinkling of nutmeg on top. In honor of the original Mud, and because it tastes so good, I pass a bottle of bourbon to be sprinkled or poured over individual portions.

NOTE
↓

It is best to make the crust a day before filling it, or at least several hours before; the pie should be completed at least a day before serving, or it may be frozen for days. Or longer.

- 7½ ounces (21 cookie sandwiches) chocolate sandwich cookies (such as Oreos)
- 2 ounces (½ stick) unsalted butter, melted
- 2 pints coffee ice cream (of course, you can use any other flavor you prefer)

- 1 ounce unsweetened chocolate
- 2 ounces semisweet chocolate
- 1 tablespoon plus 1½ teaspoons water
- 2 tablespoons light corn syrup (e.g., Karo)

- 1½ tablespoons unsalted butter, cut into small pieces
- OPTIONAL: sweetened whipped cream flavored with vanilla extract or rum, bourbon, Kahlúa, etc.; toasted sliced almonds or other nuts; and/or The World's Best Hot Fudge Sauce (page 242)

To prevent the crust from sticking to the plate when the pie is served, line the plate with aluminum foil: Place a 12-inch square of foil into a 9 inch ovenproof glass pie plate — press the foil firmly into place by pressing against it with a folded towel or a pot holder; fold the edges of the foil tightly out over the rim of the plate. Set aside.

Break the cookies into pieces and place them in a food processor or blender and process or blend until the crumbs are fine — you should have a scant 1¾ cups of crumbs.

In a bowl, mix the crumbs thoroughly with the melted butter.

Turn the mixture into the lined pie plate. With your fingertips, distribute the crumbs evenly and loosely over the sides first, and then over the bottom. Then press the crumbs firmly against the sides — be careful that the top edge of the crust is not too thin — and then press them firmly against the bottom. It must all be very firm — no loose crumbs.

Place in the freezer for at least several hours or overnight; it must be frozen firm.

The ice cream should be softened slightly so you can transfer it to the pie plate. Place it in the refrigerator for about 10 minutes or so, depending on the firmness of the

continues ↘

ice cream and the temperature of the refrigerator.

Meanwhile, to remove the foil from the pie plate, nestle an 8-inch pie plate into the frozen crust. Flip the entire assemblage over and place on a flat surface. Gently remove the 9-inch pie plate and put aside. Peel off the foil, return the 9-inch pie plate to the crust, and turn the assemblage right side up. Remove the 8-inch pie plate.

Now turn the softened ice cream into the crust. Spread it smoothly, mounding it a bit higher in the middle.

Return to the freezer until the ice cream is very firm.

Meanwhile, make the chocolate glaze: Chop both chocolates into small pieces and set aside.

Place the water, corn syrup, and cut-up butter in a small saucepan over moderate heat. Stir occasionally until the mixture comes to a boil.

Add the chopped chocolate and remove from heat immediately. Stir with a small wire whisk until the chocolate is melted, and the mixture is smooth.

Set aside to cool to room temperature.

Pour the cooled glaze carefully over the frozen ice cream to cover the top completely—be careful not to let any run over the sides of the crust. If it is necessary to spread the glaze, do it quickly before it hardens. It will be a very thin layer of glaze.

Return the pie to the freezer for at least a few more hours.

When the glaze is frozen firm, the pie may be wrapped airtight with plastic wrap and may be frozen for any reasonable time.

If you like, serve with whipped cream, toasted nuts, and/or hot fudge sauce.

CHOCOLATE MOUSSE TORTE

Makes 6 to 8 portions Of the many recipes that were born in my kitchen, this was one of the most exciting because it became the *New York Times* 1972 Dessert of the Year. It starts with a chocolate mousse mixture. Part of it is baked in a pie plate. When it cools, it settles down in the middle, leaving a higher rim. Then the remaining unbaked mousse is placed over the baked mousse. And it is topped with whipped cream.

8 ounces semisweet chocolate

1 tablespoon instant espresso or coffee powder

¼ cup boiling water

8 large eggs (see Notes), separated

⅓ cup granulated sugar

1 teaspoon vanilla extract

⅛ teaspoon salt

WHIPPED CREAM

1½ cups heavy cream

1½ teaspoons vanilla extract

⅓ cup confectioners' sugar

OPTIONAL: coarsely grated semisweet chocolate

NOTES

In the interest of safety, use only the best-quality eggs and wash and thoroughly dry them before using.

An alternate and very attractive way of applying the whipped cream: Use a pastry bag fitted with a medium star tube and, as Jean Hewitt did when she prepared this torte to be photographed for the New York Times, form a lattice pattern over the top of the pie and a border around the edge.

When serving, place the pie plate on a folded napkin (on a platter or cake plate) to hold the plate steady.

Adjust rack to center of oven. Preheat oven to 350 degrees. Butter a 9-inch ovenproof glass pie plate. Dust it with fine, dry bread crumbs. Set aside.

Place the chocolate in the top of a small double boiler over hot water. Dissolve the coffee in the boiling water and pour it over the chocolate. Cover and let stand over low heat, stirring occasionally with a small wire whisk, until the chocolate is almost melted. Remove the chocolate from the heat and continue to stir until smooth. Set aside to cool slightly.

In the small bowl of an electric mixer, beat the yolks at high speed for about 5 minutes, until they are pale-lemon-colored and thickened. Gradually add the granulated sugar and continue to beat at high speed for 5 minutes more until very thick. Add the vanilla and chocolate, beating slowly and scraping the bowl with a rubber spatula until blended.

Remove from mixer. In the large bowl of electric mixer, beat the whites with the salt until stiff but not dry. Gradually, in two or

continues ↘

three small additions, fold the whites into the chocolate (do not be too thorough) and then fold the chocolate into the remaining whites, folding only until no whites show. Handling as little as possible, gently remove and set aside about 4 cups of the mousse. Cover reserved mousse and refrigerate.

Turn the balance into the pie plate; it will barely reach the top. Very gently spread level and bake for 25 minutes. Turn off the heat, then leave it in the oven for 5 minutes more. Remove from oven and cool on a rack. (The mousse will rise during baking and then, while cooling, it will settle in the center, leaving a high rim.)

When completely cool, remove reserved mousse from refrigerator. Handling as little as possible, place the refrigerated mousse in the center of the shell of baked mousse. Mound it slightly higher in the center, but be careful to handle as little as possible or it will lose the air beaten into it.

Refrigerate for at least 2 to 3 hours.

For the whipped cream:

In a chilled bowl with chilled beaters, whip the cream, vanilla, and confectioners' sugar until it holds a definite shape. Spread over the unbaked part of the mousse, excluding the rim. Refrigerate.

If you like, coarsely grate some semisweet chocolate over the top before serving.

POLISH WEDDING CAKES

Makes 16 (2-inch) squares, or 32 or 48 small bars These are called *mazurki* in Polish. There are many versions, all rich and moist. This one has a crunchy crust and tart apricot filling. The pastry is not like American pastry; it will resemble a crumb mixture.

APRICOT FILLING

- 4 ounces (about ⅔ cup) dried apricots
- ½ cup water
- 2 tablespoons granulated sugar

POLISH PASTRY

- 1¼ cups *sifted* unbleached all-purpose flour
- ¼ teaspoon salt
- 1 cup firmly packed dark brown sugar
- 6 ounces (1½ sticks) unsalted butter, cold and firm, cut into ½-inch pieces
- 1¾ ounces (½ cup firmly packed) shredded coconut
- ¾ cup old-fashioned or quick-cooking rolled oats
- 2 ounces (generous ½ cup) walnuts, chopped medium fine

OPTIONAL: confectioners' sugar

For the filling:

In a small, heavy saucepan with a tight cover, bring the apricots and water to a boil, uncovered, over high heat. Reduce the heat to low, cover the pan, and simmer until the apricots are very tender, about 30 minutes, depending on the apricots. The fruit should be very soft and the water should be partially but not completely absorbed.

Press the apricots with a potato masher or stir and mash vigorously with a fork. The mixture should be very thick. Add the granulated sugar and stir until it dissolves. Cool to room temperature. (If you wish, this filling may be made ahead of time and refrigerated.)

For the pastry:

Adjust an oven rack one-third up from the bottom and preheat oven to 325 degrees.

Place the flour, salt, and brown sugar in a mixing bowl. With a pastry blender, cut in the butter until the mixture resembles coarse meal. Stir in the coconut, rolled oats, and walnuts.

Place half (3 cups) of the mixture in an unbuttered 8-inch square cake pan. Press it evenly with your fingertips. Cover with a piece of wax paper, and with the palm of your hand, press against the paper to make a smooth, compact layer. Remove the wax paper.

continues ↘

Spread the apricot filling smoothly over the pastry, staying ¼ to ½ inch away from the edges. Sprinkle the remaining pastry evenly over the filling and repeat the directions for covering with wax paper and pressing smooth. Remove the wax paper.

Bake for 60 to 70 minutes, until the top is barely semifirm to the touch.

Cool in the pan for 15 minutes. Cut around the sides of the cake to release it. Cover with a rack or a cookie sheet.

Invert, remove the pan, cover with a rack, and invert again so that the cake is right side up. Let cool completely and then refrigerate briefly — the cake cuts best if it is cold. Transfer it to a cutting board.

Use a long, thin, sharp knife or a finely serrated one to cut the cake into squares or fingers.

If you like, top the bars with confectioners' sugar. Press it through a fine strainer held over the bars to cover the tops generously.

CHARLIE BROWN ICE CREAM SUNDAES

Makes 8 to 12 portions   There may be no sundae better than this.

VANILLA ICE CREAM

- 6 large egg yolks
- 1 cup sugar
- 4 cups milk
- 1 cup heavy cream
- 1 vanilla bean, or 2 teaspoons vanilla extract

PEANUT BUTTER SAUCE

- 1 cup sugar
- 1 tablespoon light corn syrup (e.g., Karo)
- ⅛ teaspoon salt
- ¾ cup milk
- 2 tablespoons unsalted butter
- ⅓ cup smooth (not chunky) peanut butter
- ½ teaspoon vanilla extract

OPTIONAL, FOR SERVING: **Coarsely chopped salted peanuts**

NOTES

The sauce may be kept warm, or reheated, in the top of a small double boiler over hot water on moderate heat, and stirred occasionally.

The peanut butter sauce thickens to a hard caramel consistency when poured over cold ice cream. Delicious.

For the ice cream:

Put the yolks and sugar in a heavy casserole. Beat with a wire whisk until pale yellow.

In a saucepan, combine the milk and cream. If using a vanilla bean, split it down one side and add it now. (Don't add the vanilla extract yet.) Bring the milk mixture just to a boil.

Add about ½ cup of the hot mixture to the egg yolk mixture and beat rapidly. Add the remaining hot mixture, stirring rapidly. Scrape the tiny black seeds from the center of the vanilla bean into the custard. Heat slowly, stirring and scraping all around

the bottom with a wooden spoon. Bring the mixture almost, but not quite, to a boil. The correct temperature is 180 degrees. This cooking will rid the custard of the raw taste of the yolks.

Pour the mixture into a cold mixing bowl. This will prevent the mixture from cooking further. Let stand until cool or at room temperature. If using vanilla extract, add it at this point.

Pour the mixture into the container of an electric or hand-cranked ice cream maker. Freeze according to the manufacturer's instructions.

continues ↘

For the sauce:

In a 6- to 8-cup heavy saucepan, mix the sugar, corn syrup, salt, and milk. Stir over moderate heat until the mixture comes to a boil. Insert a candy thermometer. Adjust heat so that the sauce boils gently, and let boil without stirring for 30 to 40 minutes, until the temperature registers 225 to 228 degrees. The sauce will have caramelized to a light golden color.

Remove from heat. Add the butter and peanut butter. Stir briskly with a small wire whisk until smooth. Stir in the vanilla. Serve warm.

To serve, spoon the sauce over scoops of ice cream and, if you like, sprinkle with the chopped peanuts.

Deep South Chocolate Ice Cream (page 240)

The World's Best Hot Fudge Sauce (page 242)

Charlie Brown Ice Cream Sundae

DEEP SOUTH CHOCOLATE ICE CREAM

Makes 2 quarts This recipe was given to me after I could not stop eating the extraordinary ice cream at a New Year's Eve buffet in a traditional Mississippi plantation mansion, where a bottle of Grand Marnier was passed around for pouring over the ice cream.

I have often made this with Grand Marnier, espresso (Medaglia d'Oro), and Lindt Excellence bittersweet chocolate. The flavor is beautiful — the smooth texture is beautiful. And although I originally made this the way the recipe is written — without an ice cream maker — now I use the ice cream maker.

To use an ice cream maker: Do not whip the heavy cream. Instead, mix it (unwhipped) with the chocolate mixture. Make sure it is all very cold. Freeze according to machine instructions.

P.S.: People often ask me what my favorite dessert is. My answer is that it's like a line in a wonderful Broadway show some time ago, "When I'm not near the girl I love, I love the girl I'm near." That's how I feel about desserts. But frankly, just between you and me, my favorite dessert is chocolate ice cream. Preferably in a cone.

2 tablespoons instant espresso or coffee powder	5 large egg yolks	⅓ cup crème de cacao or Grand Marnier
½ cup boiling water	¼ cup water	3 cups heavy cream
6 ounces semisweet chocolate	½ cup sugar	
	¼ teaspoon cream of tartar	

Dissolve the espresso or coffee in the ½ cup boiling water. Place it with the chocolate in a small, heavy saucepan, or in the top of a small double boiler over hot water on moderate heat. Stir occasionally to melt the chocolate. Remove from heat and set aside to cool.

Beat the yolks in the small bowl of an electric mixer at high speed for several minutes, until thick and light-lemon-colored.

Meanwhile, in a small saucepan, mix the ¼ cup water with the sugar and cream of tartar. With a small wooden spatula, stir over high heat until the sugar is dissolved and the mixture comes to a boil. Let boil without stirring for about 3 minutes, until the syrup reaches 230 degrees on a candy thermometer (light thread stage).

Gradually, in a thin stream, add the hot syrup to the egg yolks, still beating at high speed. Continue to beat for about 5 minutes more, until the mixture is cool.

Stir the crème de cacao or Grand Marnier into the cooled chocolate mixture, and add that to the cooled egg yolk mixture, beating only until blended. Remove from mixer.

In the chilled large bowl of the electric mixer, with chilled beaters, beat the cream only until it holds a very soft shape. Fold 1 cup of the cream into the chocolate mixture and then fold the chocolate mixture into the remaining cream.

Pour into a shallow metal pan, measuring 13 x 9 x 2 inches (or several ice-cube trays) and freeze until firm around the edges (1½ to 2 hours in one large pan). Meanwhile, place large bowl and beaters of electric mixer in the freezer.

Beat the partially frozen cream mixture in the chilled bowl until smooth. Return to pan or trays or any freezer container. Cover and freeze until firm (about 1½ hours in the one large pan).

JEAN HEWITT'S OLD-FASHIONED LEMON ICE CREAM

Makes about 3 cups This was Jean Hewitt's recipe when she was the home economist of the *New York Times*. It started me on a beautiful binge of ice creams and other frozen desserts made without an ice cream maker. Mrs. Hewitt's recipes are infallible—this one is also miraculously easy and delicious.

Finely grated zest of 1 large lemon (or 2 small)

3 tablespoons lemon juice

1 cup sugar

2 cups light cream

⅛ teaspoon salt

Combine lemon zest, juice, and sugar and stir to mix. Gradually stir in the cream and salt, mixing well. Pour into a metal freezing tray or dish and freeze until solid around the outside and mushy in the middle. Stir well with a wooden spoon. Cover and continue to freeze until firm.

THE WORLD'S BEST HOT FUDGE SAUCE

Makes 1 cup This is very thick, coal black, as shiny as wet tar, and not too sweet. It will turn chewy and even thicker when it is served over cold ice cream — great! It may be served hot or warm, but at room temperature or chilled it will be too thick. It may be refrigerated for a week or two before serving.

½ cup heavy cream

3 tablespoons unsalted butter, cut into small pieces

⅓ cup granulated sugar

⅓ cup firmly packed dark brown sugar

Pinch of salt

½ cup strained cocoa powder (preferably Dutch-process)

Place the cream and butter in a heavy 1-quart saucepan over moderate heat. Stir with a small wooden spatula until the butter is melted and the cream just comes to a low boil. Add both sugars and stir for a few minutes until they are dissolved. (The surest test is to taste; cook and taste carefully — without getting burned — until you do not feel any undissolved granules in your mouth.)

Reduce the heat. Add the salt and cocoa and stir briskly with a small wire whisk until smooth. Strain if necessary.

Serve immediately, or cool and reheat slowly (see Notes).

This should be thick, but when it is reheated it may be too thick. If so, stir in a bit of hot water, adding very little at a time.

NOTES

↓

If you plan to store the sauce in the refrigerator, use a straight-sided jar or a container that flares out at the top. The sauce will become too firm when it is chilled to be spooned out of a jar. It is best to place the jar or container in hot water until the block of sauce melts on the outside and can be poured out of the container.

↓

To reheat, pour the sauce into the top of a small double boiler over hot water, or in a small, heavy saucepan over the lowest heat. Stir and cut into pieces with a wooden spatula until completely melted.

FORTNUM AND MASON SAUCE

Makes 2 cups Fortnum and Mason is an upscale department store in London, though now they ship around the world. This is a very fancy sauce made from red currant jelly and oranges; it is delightful over fruit slices or as a topping for homemade vanilla ice cream — or both. Do make your own ice cream from time to time. It's like being a kid again.

NOTE

↓

The sauce will be bitter if the oranges are greenish, or if they are pared too deeply.

- 2 large, bright-colored oranges (see Note)
- 12 ounces (1 cup) red currant jelly
- 1 tablespoon lemon juice
- ¼ teaspoon ground cinnamon
- ¼ cup Curaçao or Grand Marnier
- 2 tablespoons dark rum

Use a vegetable peeler with a swivel blade to peel the very thin, orange-colored zest off the orange — it must be thin. Cut the zest into slivers. Squeeze the oranges to get ⅔ cup juice.

In a saucepan, combine the zest and juice with the currant jelly, lemon juice, and cinnamon. Cook over moderate heat, stirring occasionally, until the mixture comes to a boil. Adjust heat so that the sauce simmers slowly. Simmer uncovered without stirring for 15 minutes. Remove from the heat and set aside to cool.

Stir in the Curaçao or Grand Marnier and rum. Refrigerate and serve cold.

CHOCOLATE MOUSSE HEATTER

Makes 6 portions It has been said that chocolate is the sexiest of all flavors. This is the sexiest of all desserts.

8 ounces bittersweet chocolate (I like Lindt Excellence)

1 tablespoon instant espresso or coffee powder

⅓ cup boiling water

5 large eggs (see Notes), separated

Pinch of salt

MOCHA CREAM

1 cup heavy cream

¼ cup confectioners' sugar

1 tablespoon instant espresso or coffee powder

—

OPTIONAL: coarsely grated dark chocolate

NOTES

↓

In the interest of safety, use only the best quality eggs and wash and thoroughly dry them before using.

↓

I beat the whites with the salt in the large bowl of the mixer, beating at high speed only until the whites thicken or hold a very soft shape. Then I finish the beating with a large wire whisk so that there is less chance of overbeating.

Break up the chocolate into a small, heavy saucepan. Dissolve the coffee in the boiling water and pour over the chocolate. Place over low heat and stir occasionally with a small wire whisk until the mixture is smooth. Remove from the heat and set aside to cool for about 5 minutes.

In the small bowl of an electric mixer at high speed, beat the egg yolks for 3 to 4 minutes, until pale-lemon-colored. Reduce the speed and gradually add the slightly warm chocolate mixture, scraping the bowl with a rubber spatula and beating only until smooth. Remove from mixer.

In a large bowl, combine the salt and whites and beat until they hold a definite shape but are not dry. (See Notes.) Without being too thorough, gently fold about one-quarter of the beaten whites into the chocolate mixture, then fold in a second quarter, and finally fold the chocolate into the remaining whites, folding only until no whites show.

Gently transfer the mousse to a wide pitcher and pour it into six large dessert glasses or wineglasses, each with about a 9-ounce capacity. Do not fill the glasses too full; leave generous headroom in each.

Cover with plastic wrap or aluminum foil and refrigerate for 3 to 6 hours. (The mousse may stand longer — 12 to 24 hours, if you wish. The texture will become more spongy and less creamy. Delicious both ways.)

For the mocha cream:

In a chilled bowl with chilled beaters, beat the heavy cream with the sugar and coffee only until thickened to the consistency of a heavy custard sauce, not stiff. Pour or spoon onto the desserts to completely cover the tops.

If you like, top with a light sprinkling of coarsely grated chocolate.

PLAIN OLD-FASHIONED RICE PUDDING

Makes 3 or 4 portions This takes just a minute or two to prepare and 3 hours to bake.

4 cups milk

¾ cup sugar

Pinch of salt

2 tablespoons unsalted butter

3 tablespoons uncooked rice (not instant, and not washed—I use Uncle Ben's converted rice)

½ teaspoon vanilla extract

⅓ cup raisins or currants

Ground cinnamon and/ or nutmeg (preferably freshly grated)

OPTIONAL, FOR SERVING: heavy cream

NOTES

You might like to use a fine, favorite rice. Jasmine works.

You may use 2% milk and only 1 tablespoon of butter with excellent results.

Adjust rack to center of oven. Preheat oven to 300 degrees.

In a 5- to 6-cup ovenproof casserole, preferably shallow, mix the milk, sugar, salt, butter, and rice, which must be measured carefully. (Just a bit too much will make the pudding heavy.)

Bake uncovered for 2 hours, stirring occasionally—at least three or four times, or more, if you wish.

Add vanilla and raisins or currants. Stir well. Sprinkle a bit of cinnamon and/or nutmeg over the top. Bake 1 hour longer without stirring, in order to let a "skin" form on top.

Remove from oven. The pudding will sink slightly. Cut around the edge so that the "skin" will sink down with the pudding.

Serve while slightly warm, at room temperature, or chilled. Spoon into dessert bowls and pass a pitcher of very cold heavy cream.

AMERICAN CHOCOLATE PUDDING

Makes 4 to 6 portions If you think it doesn't pay to bother making your own pudding when you can buy a box and just add some milk, then you have not tasted the real thing. This has considerably more chocolate than the mix (as well as cocoa, and less sugar, and egg yolks that make it a custard and give it body). It is dense, dark, not too sweet, smooth, semifirm, rich; it is marvelous.

Using cornstarch correctly is a delicate art. Overcooking or overbeating — even the least little bit — can cause the cornstarch to break down and make the mixture too thin.

This recipe is written for good old-fashioned generous portions. But actually they should be smaller if it is to be served after dinner. Try serving this pudding in wineglasses, with the pudding filling the glasses only halfway and the whipped cream filling the remaining space to the top.

1 large or extra-large egg plus 2 egg yolks

2 ounces unsweetened chocolate

3 ounces semisweet chocolate

2¼ cups milk

½ cup plus 1 tablespoon sugar

Scant ⅛ teaspoon salt

2 tablespoons *unsifted* cornstarch

3 tablespoons *unsifted* unsweetened cocoa powder (preferably Dutch-process)

2 tablespoons unsalted butter, at room temperature, cut into small pieces

1 teaspoon vanilla extract

OPTIONAL: 1 tablespoon dark rum

WHIPPED CREAM

1 cup whipping cream

2 tablespoons confectioners' or granulated sugar

½ teaspoon vanilla extract

Have 10- or 12-ounce stemmed wineglasses or dessert bowls ready. Cut rounds of wax paper to place on top of the pudding (actually touching the pudding) after it is poured into the glasses or bowls. Set aside.

In a bowl, beat the egg and yolks to mix and set aside.

On a board, with a long, heavy knife, chop both chocolates (coarse or fine — either is OK).

Place 2 cups of the milk (reserve the remaining ¼ cup) in a heavy saucepan with a 2- to 3-quart capacity. Add ¼ cup of the sugar (reserve the remaining ¼ cup plus 1 tablespoon) and the chopped chocolate.

Place over moderate heat and whisk frequently with a wire whisk until the milk just comes to a boil (flecks of chocolate will disappear by the time the milk boils).

Meanwhile, sift the remaining ¼ cup plus 1 tablespoon sugar, the salt, cornstarch, and cocoa into a mixing bowl. Add the reserved ¼ cup of milk and whisk with a small wire whisk until smooth.

When the milk comes to a boil, pour (or ladle) part of it into the cornstarch mixture, whisking as you pour.

Then add the cornstarch mixture to the remaining hot milk mixture. Stir to mix. Place over moderate heat.

Now, use a rubber spatula to scrape the bottom and sides constantly until the mixture comes to a low boil. Reduce the heat to medium-low and simmer gently, stirring and scraping the pan, for 2 minutes.

Add about 1 cup of the hot chocolate-milk mixture to the eggs and whisk or stir to mix. Then add the egg mixture to the remaining hot chocolate-milk mixture, stirring constantly.

Cook over low heat, scraping the pan with a rubber spatula, for 2 minutes. Be sure that you do not allow the mixture to come anywhere near the boiling stage after the eggs are added.

Remove from the heat. Add the butter, vanilla, and optional rum. Stir very gently until the butter is melted.

Without waiting, pour into the wineglasses or dessert bowls. Cover immediately with the rounds of wax paper, placing the paper directly on the pudding (to prevent a skin from forming).

Let stand to cool to room temperature. Then refrigerate for at least a few hours.

For the whipped cream:

In a chilled bowl with chilled beaters, whip the cream with the sugar and vanilla until it holds a soft shape, not until it is really stiff. (The cream may be whipped ahead of time and refrigerated; if it separates slightly, whisk it a bit before using.) Shortly before serving, spoon the cream on top of the puddings.

APPLE PUDDING

Makes 6 to 8 portions Often when I was working on a new book, I'd make a dessert as our dinner. Some desserts make wonderful meals. Like this Apple Pudding. Try it for your next brunch: a shallow baking dish almost full of a delicious mixture of apples, almonds, and raisins topped with a bit of apricot preserves, then covered with a wonderful crisp, crumbly, and crunchy crust. And it is easy. In Germany the topping is called *streusel* — pronounced "shtroyzel."

TOPPING

- 1 cup *sifted* unbleached all-purpose flour
- ½ cup firmly packed dark brown sugar
- 1½ teaspoons ground cinnamon
- 4 ounces (1 stick) unsalted butter, cut up

APPLE MIXTURE

- 2½ ounces (½ cup) almonds, blanched (skinned) and slivered or sliced
- 3 pounds (6 to 8 medium) apples (preferably Golden Delicious)
- 3 tablespoons granulated sugar
- Grated zest and juice of 1 small lemon
- ¼ cup raisins
- ⅓ cup apricot preserves

For the topping:

Mix the flour, brown sugar, and cinnamon in a bowl. With a pastry blender, cut in the butter until the mixture resembles coarse crumbs. Refrigerate.

For the apples:

Place the almonds in a shallow pan in a 350-degree oven and toast, stirring occasionally, until golden. Remove and set aside to cool.

Adjust rack one-third up from bottom of oven. Preheat oven to 400 degrees. Butter a shallow baking dish with a 2-quart capacity (about 10 x 8 x 2 inches).

Peel, quarter, and core the apples. Cut each quarter the long way into three or four slices. Mix them in a large bowl with the almonds, granulated sugar, zest, juice, and raisins. Turn it all into the baking dish, scraping the bowl clean with a rubber spatula. Dot with small spoonfuls of apricot preserves.

Crumble the refrigerated topping loosely over the apple mixture to cover the apples completely. Do not pack it down. Wipe the edges of the dish. Bake for 30 to 45 minutes, until the apples are tender and the top is lightly browned.

Remove from oven to cool. Serve warm or at room temperature, as is — or even better, with vanilla ice cream.

LEMON BREAD PUDDING

Makes 12 portions   This is a taste thrill when served at any temperature, but it is most spectacular right out of the oven. The lemon curd can be prepared days or even weeks ahead; the bread can be sliced and toasted a day or so ahead if you wish; the pudding can be put together (in about 5 minutes) one hour before it is baked, and it can bake while dinner is being served. It is an easy and foolproof recipe.

LEMON CURD

- 3 large eggs plus 1 egg yolk
- 1 cup sugar
- Finely grated zest of 2 large lemons
- ⅓ cup lemon juice
- 4 ounces (1 stick) unsalted butter, cut into 1-inch pieces

BREAD PUDDING

- 1 loaf (8 ounces) French bread
- 10 large eggs
- 1¼ cups sugar
- 4 cups milk
- ¼ teaspoon salt
- 1½ teaspoons vanilla extract

For the lemon curd:

In the top of a large double boiler, beat the eggs and yolk with the sugar to mix. Stir in the lemon zest and juice. Add the butter. Place over hot water on moderate heat. Cook uncovered, stirring and scraping the pan frequently with a rubber spatula, for 15 to 20 minutes, until the mixture is as thick as mayonnaise; it will register 180 degrees on a candy thermometer.

Remove the top of the double boiler and set aside to cool, stirring occasionally.

You can use the curd as soon as it has cooled, or you can refrigerate it for several weeks.

For the bread pudding:

Preheat the oven to 350 degrees.

With a serrated French bread knife, slice the bread ½ inch thick. Place the slices on cookie sheets and bake for 10 to 15 minutes, until dry but not brown, turning the slices over when half-done. Set aside.

In a large bowl, beat the eggs and 1 cup of the sugar (reserve the remaining ¼ cup sugar). Beat in the milk, salt, and vanilla and set aside.

Butter a shallow, oblong 3-quart baking dish (13 x 8 [or 9] x 2 inches). In the bottom of the baking dish, place a layer of the bread slices touching each other. If necessary, break a few of the slices to fill in spaces. Spread half of the cooled or cold

continues ↘

lemon curd over the bread. Then make a second layer of the bread slices, placing these slices at right angles to the first slices. Again, break a few slices if necessary to fill in space. You may have a few slices left over that you will not need. Spread the remaining curd over the top.

Now ladle the egg-and-milk mixture slowly all over the top. Let stand at room temperature for 1 hour.

Before baking, adjust a rack to the center of the oven and preheat the oven to 350 degrees.

Sprinkle the remaining ¼ cup sugar evenly over the pudding.

Place the baking dish in a large, shallow pan, place in the oven, and then pour hot water into the pan to about half the depth of the baking dish.

Bake for about 45 minutes, until the top is puffed and just barely colored. Testing this with the point of a knife (the way custard is generally tested) is not good, because the lemon curd will cling to the blade even after the custard is done. It is better to tap the side of the baking dish lightly — when the middle of the pudding moves only slightly, it is done. (I have made this many times, and now all I do is test the oven temperature with a portable thermometer and watch the clock carefully.)

If necessary, you may place the baking dish under the broiler for just a few seconds to darken the top, but only until barely golden.

Serve right away — piping hot — or at room temperature.

BROOKFIELD CENTER STRAWBERRIES WITH CUSTARD SAUCE

Makes 4 portions Brookfield Center is a beautiful small town in Connecticut where my parents had a dairy farm. My mother grew many fruits and vegetables there. Her strawberries were fabulous. This is one of the ways she served them.

When strawberries are really good, this is one of the finest of all desserts.

NOTES
↓
For more than three or four people, you can double the sauce recipe.
↓
To use a vanilla bean instead of the extract: Slit a 6- to 8-inch vanilla bean the long way. Scrape the seeds into the milk and cream and add the pod, also, before scalding. Leave it in until the sauce is strained.

CUSTARD SAUCE

1 cup milk

1 cup light cream

4 large egg yolks

½ cup sugar

Pinch of salt

1 teaspoon vanilla extract

—

1 quart fresh strawberries, washed, hulled, and refrigerated

For the sauce:

In a heavy saucepan over moderate heat, scald the milk and cream.

Meanwhile, in the top of a large double boiler off the heat, stir the yolks lightly with a small wire whisk just to mix. Gradually stir in the sugar and salt.

When you see steam rising from the milk and cream, a wrinkled skin forming on top, or tiny bubbles around the edge, remove the pan from the heat and very gradually stir the cream mixture into the yolks.

Place over hot water, which must not touch the upper section of the double boiler and should be simmering gently, not boiling hard.

Stir the custard mixture constantly with a rubber spatula, scraping the sides and the bottom of the pot until the mixture thickens slightly or will coat a metal or wooden spoon. (This rather difficult moment to ascertain is easy with a candy thermometer: 180 degrees. It might take about 10 minutes.)

Remove from heat immediately to stop the cooking and strain into a bowl or container. Stir in the vanilla.

Cool the sauce, stirring occasionally. When cool, if sauce is not absolutely smooth, strain again through a fine strainer. (Makes 2⅔ cups.) Cover and refrigerate. Serve very cold. Stir briefly before serving.

———

Remove the chilled, hulled strawberries from the refrigerator and slice each berry lengthwise into three or four slices.

Serve the berries in individual bowls with a generous topping of very cold custard sauce and pass remaining sauce separately.

TIRAMISU

Makes 12 portions *Mamma mia* — this is something else! It is totally irresistible. An important dessert for an important event. Magnificent. Exciting. Although it can be made with store-bought ladyfingers, you might like to try it (and I hope you will) with homemade chocolate ladyfingers. Make this one to two days before serving.

NOTE

↓

Mascarpone is an unsalted Italian cheese similar to cream cheese, but smoother, richer, and softer. It is extremely perishable and should be used soon after it is purchased.

1¼ cups unsweetened prepared strong espresso (I use 5 tablespoons instant espresso powder in 1¼ cups hot water; it is stronger than brewed espresso)

6 tablespoons Grand Marnier

1 recipe Chocolate Ladyfingers (page 141), or 6 to 8 ounces store-bought ladyfingers (sufficient to make two layers in a baking dish that measures about 13 x 9 inches)

16 to 17½ ounces (about 2 cups) mascarpone (see Note)

¼ cup dark rum

5 large eggs, separated

6 tablespoons sugar

2 cups whipping cream

½ teaspoon vanilla extract

⅛ teaspoon salt

Unsweetened cocoa powder (preferably Dutch-process)

You will need an oblong casserole that measures about 13 x 9 x 2 inches with at least a 14-cup capacity. Set the casserole aside.

Mix the espresso and the Grand Marnier. Place half of the mixture in a shallow bowl large enough to dip the ladyfingers into (reserve the remaining half of the mixture).

One at a time, place a ladyfinger in the espresso mixture. Turn it upside down two or three times until it is well moistened but not until it starts to fall apart. Place the ladyfingers, flat side down, in the casserole, close together to make a fairly solid layer. If necessary, cut some of the ladyfingers to fill in large empty spaces. Reserve enough of the ladyfingers to make a second layer (you will form two layers of ladyfingers alternating with two layers

of the mascarpone mixture). If some of the espresso mixture is left over in the shallow bowl, drizzle it onto the moistened ladyfingers. Set the casserole aside.

Place the mascarpone in a large bowl. Add the rum and beat or whisk until smooth. Set aside.

In the top of a small double boiler over warm water on medium-low heat, beat the yolks using an eggbeater or handheld electric mixer with 3 tablespoons of the sugar (reserve the remaining 3 tablespoons sugar). Beat for 3 minutes, or until light and foamy. Remove from the heat and, without waiting, stir or beat the yolk mixture into the mascarpone mixture. Set aside.

continues ↘

In a chilled bowl with chilled beaters, whip the cream with the vanilla until the cream just holds a firm shape.

In two additions, fold about one-third of the mascarpone mixture into the whipped cream. Then fold the whipped cream into the remaining mascarpone mixture. Set aside.

In the small bowl of an electric mixer with clean beaters, beat the egg whites with the salt on moderate speed until foamy. Increase the speed to high and beat until the whites hold a soft shape. Gradually add the remaining 3 tablespoons sugar and continue to beat on high speed only until the whites hold a straight shape when the beaters are raised, but not until dry. Do not overbeat. Add the beaten whites all at one time to the mascarpone-and-cream mixture and fold together.

Pour half of this mixture over the layer of ladyfingers. Smooth the top.

Pour the remaining espresso mixture into the shallow bowl. To make a second layer of ladyfingers, dip them one at a time — as above — and place them flat side down close together on top of the mascarpone layer.

If any of the espresso mixture is left over, drizzle it onto the ladyfingers.

For the top layer, pour the remaining mascarpone mixture on the ladyfingers. Smooth the top. (The dish will be very full.)

Refrigerate uncovered.

After a few hours in the refrigerator (or longer if more convenient), sift or strain a dense layer of cocoa all over the top (so no white shows through). Wipe the rim of the casserole. Cover with plastic wrap and continue to refrigerate at least overnight.

Just before serving, sift or strain a little more cocoa on top.

The tiramisu should be served very cold, preferably on chilled plates.

To serve:

You can't be "chicken" when you serve this; you have to be gutsy. Cut the tiramisu into oblongs with a small, sharp knife. Then, courageously, slide a wide metal spatula under a portion, lift it and move it over a dessert plate, and with another wide metal spatula push it off, trying to keep it top side up as much as possible.

SAIDIE HEATTER'S POPOVERS WITH HONEY BUTTER

Makes 10 large or 8 very large popovers My mother was called the Popover Queen — she was also the Blintz Queen, the Blueberry Pie Queen, the Queen of the Barbecue, etc. My father bestowed a title on her at almost every meal. Her popovers were incredible. Gorgeous. Amazing. This is truly an heirloom recipe.

Making the popovers is really simple and easy and I don't see how anything can go wrong. But plan ahead. Plan to make the batter a day ahead and refrigerate it overnight. And plan the timing so that the popovers will be served immediately after they come out of the oven.

These are baked in individual china or pottery custard cups with a 4- or 6-ounce capacity that are deep and narrow; do not use cups that are wide and shallow and flare at the tops.

But I have a friend who bakes them in 1-cup ovenproof glass measuring cups and they are quite possibly the most dramatic of all. She uses ½ cup of batter in each cup. She says to use cooking spray, not butter, to prepare the cups. She checks on them after 50 minutes of baking, and she uses words like, "Fabulous! Divine! So exciting!" (And the handles make it so easy to serve.)

---

2 cups *sifted* unbleached all-purpose flour

1 teaspoon salt

6 large eggs

2 cups milk

3 ounces (¾ stick) unsalted butter, melted and cooled

Unsalted butter or Honey Butter (page 261)

You may use an electric mixer, an eggbeater, or a wire whisk. Whichever you use, beat as little as possible to blend the ingredients. (An electric mixer must be used at low speed.)

Place the flour and salt in a large bowl. In a separate bowl, beat the eggs lightly only to mix. Mix in the milk and butter. Very gradually, beat the liquids into the dry ingredients. Do not overbeat; the batter should not be foamy. If it is lumpy, strain it. If necessary, strain it again. Do not worry about the little bits of butter you see. Cover and refrigerate overnight.

The next day, before baking, adjust a rack one-third up from the bottom of the oven and preheat the oven to 375 degrees. Generously butter eight 6-ounce cups or ten 4-ounce cups. Arrange them on a rimmed baking sheet for ease in handling, spacing them as far apart as possible. Stir the batter well without beating to make it smooth and without incorporating any

continues ↘

air. Pour into a pitcher and then pour the batter into the prepared cups, filling them to about ½ inch from the tops.

Place in preheated oven. Bake 6-ounce cups for 1 hour; 4-ounce cups for 50 minutes. Do not open the oven door until the baking time is almost up. However, ovens vary, so check the popovers about 10 minutes before the time is up. They should bake until they are really well browned. If they are not dark enough they will be soggy and limp instead of crisp and crunchy. When done, without removing them from the oven, reach in and with a small, sharp knife quickly cut two or three slits in each popover to release steam. Continue to bake 5 minutes more.

Remove from oven and take the popovers out of the cups immediately. If necessary, use a small, sharp knife to release them from the cups.

Serve immediately in a napkin-lined basket, but do not cover with the napkin or they will steam and soften. Serve with butter or Honey Butter.

Honey Butter

For each ¼ pound butter, use ⅓ to ½ cup honey, depending on your taste and the strength of the honey — some honeys have a stronger flavor than others. Beat the butter and gradually add the honey, beating until smooth. Pack in a crock, jar, or individual butter dishes. Refrigerate until firm. May be refrigerated for a week or so, or may be frozen.

Serve Honey Butter with toast, as you would serve butter, or with pancakes, waffles, or popovers.

CHARLOTTE RUSSES

Makes 6 or 7 portions This brings back memories of days when charlotte russes were sold from pushcarts on the streets of New York. (I was in about the fourth grade.) How did an elaborate and classic French dessert wind up on pushcarts on the Lower East Side? And how did they make them so good?

Before serving, you might want to decorate each charlotte with candied violets or rose petals, a bit of grated chocolate, a piece of glacéed fruit, a few toasted, sliced almonds, and/or...

18 double ladyfingers

OPTIONAL: light rum, framboise, or kirsch

VANILLA FILLING

3 large eggs, separated

1¼ cups milk

1 tablespoon (1 envelope) unflavored gelatin

½ cup granulated sugar

1 teaspoon vanilla extract

Scant ¼ teaspoon almond extract

1 cup heavy cream

⅛ teaspoon salt

TOPPING

OPTIONAL: tart, dark red jam or jelly

1 cup heavy cream

¼ cup confectioners' sugar

1 teaspoon vanilla extract

NOTES

↓

In the interest of safety, use only the best-quality eggs and wash and thoroughly dry them before using.

↓

I beat the whites with the salt in the large bowl of the mixer, beating at high speed only until the whites thicken or hold a very soft shape. Then I finish the beating with a large wire whisk so that there is less chance of overbeating.

↓

These are beautiful if prepared individually in 8-ounce old-fashioned cocktail glasses or other straight-sided glasses that are no deeper than the length of the ladyfingers.

Separate the ladyfingers into individual fingers.

If using the optional rum, framboise, or kirsch, pour 3 or 4 tablespoons into a small dish. With a pastry brush, brush the flat side of each ladyfinger very briefly with a bit of the rum.

Place the fingers, touching each other and with rounded side against the glass, around the sides of six or seven straight-sided wide and shallow glasses (see Notes).

For the filling:

In the top of a small double boiler off the heat, stir the egg yolks just to mix. Gradually mix in the milk and then the gelatin and ¼ cup of the granulated sugar (reserve remaining ¼ cup sugar).

Place over hot water on moderate heat and stir until the custard thickens enough to coat a spoon (175 to 180 degrees on a candy thermometer).

continues ↘

Remove from the heat and stir in the vanilla and almond extracts.

Place the top of the double boiler into a bowl of ice water and stir until the custard is cool. Remove from ice water and set aside.

In a chilled bowl with chilled beaters, whip the cream until it holds a soft shape, not stiff. Set aside.

Combine the egg whites and salt in a large bowl and beat until they increase in volume and barely begin to thicken. Gradually add the reserved ¼ cup granulated sugar and continue to beat only until the whites hold a point, barely stiff (see Note). Set aside.

Place the custard over the ice water again and stir again until the custard begins to thicken slightly. Gradually fold the custard into the whites, then gradually fold that mixture into the whipped cream.

Spoon the filling (or pour from a wide pitcher) into the prepared glasses, mounding them high. Refrigerate for 2 to 3 hours.

For the topping:

Top each dessert with a small spoonful of the optional jam or jelly, if you like. In a chilled bowl with chilled beaters, whip the cream with the confectioners' sugar and vanilla until it holds a shape. With a pastry bag and a large star tube, pipe a heavy ring of the cream around the outer edge of each dessert, letting the jam or jelly show through in the middle. Refrigerate.

COLD LEMON SOUFFLÉ

Makes 6 to 8 servings I'm a Virgo, which means I can't let a recipe go. I have to make it over and over again. I know people who write cookbooks in the time it takes me to do two or three recipes. This is a recipe that requires your careful attention, but if you follow the directions exactly and use the proper equipment and ingredients, the results are sheer perfection. When you take it out and it's gorgeous and everyone says, "This is so wonderful" and "I'm so happy," you will know true satisfaction.

NOTES

In the interest of safety, use only the best-quality eggs and wash and thoroughly dry them before using.

I beat the whites with the salt in the large bowl of the mixer, beating at high speed only until the whites thicken or hold a very soft shape. Then I finish the beating with a large wire whisk so that there is less chance of overbeating.

- 1 tablespoon (1 envelope) unflavored gelatin
- ¼ cup cold water
- 4 jumbo or extra-large eggs or 5 smaller eggs (see Notes), separated
- Finely grated zest of 1 large lemon

- ½ cup lemon juice
- 1 cup granulated sugar
- 1 cup heavy cream
- Generous pinch of salt

TOPPING

- OPTIONAL: 2 to 3 tablespoons tart jam or preserves (sour cherry, currant, raspberry, apricot)

- 1 cup heavy cream
- ¼ cup confectioners' sugar
- 1 scant teaspoon vanilla extract

- OPTIONAL: chopped green pistachio nuts or coarsely grated semisweet chocolate

Prepare a 3-inch collar for a 5- to 6-cup soufflé dish: Use a piece of aluminum foil long enough to wrap around the dish and overlap a few inches. Fold it in half lengthwise. Brush canola oil on the top half of one side or spray it with cooking spray. Wrap it around the dish, oiled side on top and facing in. Fasten tightly with string or straight pins.

Sprinkle the gelatin over the cold water and set aside. Place the egg yolks in top of small double boiler off the heat and stir lightly just to mix. Add the grated lemon zest and then gradually stir in the lemon juice and ½ cup of the granulated sugar (reserve remaining ½ cup sugar). Place over hot water on moderate heat and cook, scraping the sides and bottom continuously with a rubber spatula, until the mixture thickens slightly "to coat a metal spoon" — or about 180 degrees on a candy thermometer. Remove top from heat. Add the gelatin and stir to dissolve. Let stand, stirring occasionally, until completely cool.

continues ↘

In a chilled bowl with chilled beaters, whip the cream until it holds a soft shape.

In small bowl of electric mixer, beat the egg whites and the salt until the whites have increased in volume and have started to thicken. While beating, gradually add the reserved ½ cup granulated sugar and continue to beat at moderately high speed until the whites stand in peaks — do not overbeat; the meringue must not be dry.

Gradually, in several additions, fold the cooled lemon mixture into the whites and then, in a large bowl, fold together the lemon mixture and the whipped cream.

Pour the lemon chiffon mixture into the prepared soufflé dish. Refrigerate for 5 to 6 hours.

For the topping:

If using preserves, stir to soften and then spread over the top of the soufflé, or just place on at random by small spoonfuls.

In a chilled bowl with chilled beaters, whip the cream with the confectioners' sugar and vanilla until it holds a definite shape.

Remove the collar from the soufflé. Either smooth the topping over the top or apply it with a pastry bag and a large star tube, making heavy, rippled lines.

If you wish, sprinkle with chopped pistachio nuts or grated chocolate.

Refrigerate for several hours.

ORANGES IN RUM, CUBAN STYLE

Makes 4 to 6 portions In Havana, each portion is topped with a few small pieces of guava paste.

6 large seedless oranges

2 tablespoons sugar

¼ cup dark rum

⅓ cup guava jelly, red currant jelly, or marmalade

Peel and section the oranges. Place the sections in a wide bowl. Sprinkle with the sugar and rum. Turn gently to mix and let stand for about 1 hour, turning occasionally. Drain the fruit and reserve the syrup.

In a small pan over moderate heat, stir the jelly or marmalade to soften. When smooth, mix it with the reserved syrup and pour over the orange sections.

Cover and refrigerate, stirring occasionally.

Serve in large brandy snifters or wineglasses that have been in the freezer for about ½ hour. Serve quickly, while glasses are still frosty.

PÊCHES MELBA WITH SAUCE MELBA

Makes 6 portions "Melba" was the great Australian opera star Dame Nellie Melba. Escoffier was the chef at the Savoy Hotel in London. The year was 1892, when Escoffier created the famous dessert in Dame Melba's home. (Melba toast was also named in honor of this same lady.)

In the original version, a swan carved of ice (symbolic of the swan in the opera *Lohengrin*) was in the center of a platter and the peaches and ice cream were arranged around it.

At Maxim's in Paris, this is served with whole, fresh raspberries, not a sauce.

Vanilla ice cream

Stewed Peaches (below)

Fresh raspberries or Sauce Melba (below)

Toasted, sliced almonds

For each portion: On a chilled, flat dessert plate, place a scoop of vanilla ice cream and a drained, whole, stewed peach. Top with either fresh raspberries or Sauce Melba, and sprinkle lightly with toasted, sliced almonds.

Stewed Peaches

Makes 6 peaches

When peaches are wonderful and full of flavor, this is super-delicious — and beautiful. By the way, these stewed peaches freeze perfectly. The peaches should be stewed only until barely tender; they should remain slightly firm.

6 large freestone peaches, ripe but firm

1½ cups water

1 cup sugar

1 vanilla bean, 6 to 8 inches long

To peel the peaches: Have ready a large bowl of ice water, a slotted spoon, and a saucepan of boiling water deep enough to cover the peaches.

With the slotted spoon, place the peaches in the boiling water, two or three at a time. If the peaches are fully ripe they will need only about 15 seconds in the boiling water; if not quite ripe they will need more. With the slotted spoon, raise a peach from the boiling water and move your thumb firmly over the skin. If the skin has loosened enough it will wrinkle and feel loose from the fruit. At that point transfer to the ice water.

Peel with your fingers, starting at the stem end, and return the peeled fruit to the ice water. Partially peeled peaches may be returned to the boiling water for additional boiling if necessary. Continue blanching and peeling the remaining peaches.

In a saucepan large enough to hold the peaches in a single layer, combine the water and sugar. Slit the vanilla bean and scrape the seeds into the water; add the pod also. Bring to a boil, stirring, and let boil for about 5 minutes to make a syrup. With the slotted spoon, add the peaches and adjust the heat so that the syrup simmers gently. Cook covered, turning the peaches a few times with two rubber spatulas in order not to mar them and basting occasionally with the syrup. Test for doneness with a cake tester. Do not overcook. When just barely tender, transfer peaches gently with the slotted spoon to a large wide bowl or casserole.

Raise the heat and boil the syrup rapidly for a few minutes to reduce slightly. Taste the syrup, and continue to boil until it tastes right — sweet enough and not watery. Pour the hot syrup over the peaches. Do not remove the vanilla bean. Set

aside to cool, basting occasionally with the syrup.

Cover with plastic wrap or transfer to a covered freezer container. Refrigerate and serve very cold.

Serve in dessert bowls with a generous amount of the syrup.

Sauce Melba

Makes 2 generous cups

2 cups fresh raspberries
½ cup red currant jelly

Either mash and force the berries through a strainer, or puree in a food mill and then strain to remove seeds.

Stir the jelly in a small pan over moderate heat to melt. When smooth, mix with the raspberry puree. Chill and serve cold.

CANDIED GRAPEFRUIT RIND

Makes about 2½ pounds This is fabulous — classy — elegant. It takes a while to make it (and it might take a day or two for it to dry sufficiently). But then, if you can resist eating it all, it will last for many weeks. I'm guessing — I was never able to keep it that long.

A jar of this makes a beautiful and much appreciated gift, especially at Christmastime, when grapefruits are at their best.

3 large, thick-skinned grapefruits (the very thick-skinned fruit is best for candying, although it will take more time to get it dry enough)

About 5 cups sugar

Cut each grapefruit from top to bottom into large wedges. Peel off the rind and slice each wedge of peel the long way into pieces about ½ inch wide at widest point.

Place the peels in a large saucepan and pour boiling water over to cover. Boil for 5 minutes. Drain and repeat three more times, using fresh boiling water each time (four waters, or blanchings, in all).

In a wide, deep frying pan or a wide, shallow saucepan, mix 2½ cups sugar and 1½ cups water. Place over high heat and stir until the sugar dissolves. Let boil until the syrup spins a thread (230 to 234 degrees on a candy thermometer). Add the drained peels and stir well. Reduce the heat so that the syrup boils gently. Stir occasionally and let simmer, partially covered, for about 1 hour, until the peels are tender and have absorbed almost all of the syrup. Then uncover and cook slowly, stirring gently, until all the liquid has been absorbed or evaporated. Place the peels in a single layer on cake racks set over a large piece of aluminum foil.

Without waiting, place 2 to 3 cups of sugar in a shallow bowl or tray and roll each piece of warm peel in the sugar. Then place on cake racks and let stand overnight to dry, only loosely covered, at room temperature.

If the peels are still a little too wet, let them stand longer until dry. But if they are still very wet, place the racks on cookie sheets in an oven set at the lowest temperature for 30 minutes to 1 hour, but no longer than necessary. Candied peel is best when still moist inside. Reroll in sugar and let stand again to cool. Store airtight.

BLUEBERRY MUFFINS

Makes 12 muffins Especially light, tender, and delicate, these pale golden muffins are generously spotted with deep purple berries. Quick, easy, delicious, and they freeze well. Serve hot or cooled, either as a sweet bread with a meal, or between meals with tea or coffee.

1 cup fresh blueberries	½ teaspoon salt	½ cup milk
1½ cups *sifted* unbleached all-purpose flour	½ cup sugar	Finely grated zest of 1 medium lemon
	1 large egg	
2 teaspoons baking powder	2 tablespoons unsalted butter, melted	

Adjust a rack to the center of the oven and preheat the oven to 400 degrees. These can be baked in the cups of a muffin pan lined with paper liners. However, without the liners, buttered pans give the muffins a nicer crust. I use a buttered, standard 12-cup nonstick muffin pan.

The berries must be washed and thoroughly dried; rinse them in cold water, drain, and spread them out in a single layer on paper towels. Pat the tops with paper towels and let stand until the berries are thoroughly dry.

Into a very large mixing bowl, sift together the flour, baking powder, salt, and sugar. Add the dry berries and stir to mix without breaking the berries.

In a mixing bowl, beat the egg lightly with a whisk or eggbeater just to mix. Mix in the melted butter and then the milk. Stir in the grated zest.

The secret of muffins is not to overmix. Add the liquid ingredients all at once to the dry ingredients and, with a large rubber spatula, stir/fold very little — only until the dry ingredients are barely moistened. It should take only a few seconds. If you do not handle it too much the batter will be lumpy, which is the way it should be.

Spoon into the muffin cups, filling them two-thirds full. Bake for 20 to 25 minutes, until golden.

Cool in the pan for 2 or 3 minutes. Then cover with a rack, turn over the pan and the rack, and remove the pan. Turn the muffins right side up.

BONE APPÉTIT

Makes 12 to 18 dog biscuits These are gourmet dog biscuits.

Bonkers was a special dog who belonged to my brother and sister-in-law, Basil and Connie Heatter. Bonkers was the boss and he knew it. He lived to be nineteen years old. Connie regularly made these dog biscuits for him, and I don't know if they contributed to his remarkable age, but I do know that he adored them and could never get enough.

Although Connie cut them with a heart-shaped cookie cutter — to express her sentiments — you can buy cutters shaped like dog biscuits, in different sizes, in most kitchen shops (Williams-Sonoma has them), or you can cut them into bars with a knife.

Incidentally, I've been told that the nutritional yeast in these will repel fleas (but the dog must eat it, not have it rubbed over his body). The other ingredients will, of course, make your dog healthy and happy and the smartest and strongest dog on the block.

All of the following dry ingredients are available in health food stores.

¼ cup unprocessed bran

1 cup *unsifted* whole wheat flour

¼ cup raw wheat germ

1 tablespoon powdered bone meal

1 tablespoon nutritional yeast

¼ cup dry powdered milk

2 large egg whites

1 (6-ounce) jar (about ⅓ cup) chicken or beef and vegetable baby food

NOTE

If you are making these for a small dog, the dough should be rolled thinner, in which case they don't have to bake as long.

Adjust a rack to the middle of the oven and preheat oven to 300 degrees.

Place all the ingredients in a large bowl and stir — and stir — until completely mixed.

Flour a pastry cloth and a rolling pin.

Form the dough into a mound and roll it out on the pastry cloth with the rolling pin until it is about ⅓ inch thick. Cut with cookie cutter (see headnote). Or, with a long, sharp knife, trim the edges and then cut the dough into slices about 1¼ inches wide; then cut the slices into 3-inch lengths. Place the biscuits on a cookie sheet; they can be close to one another.

Bake for 1 hour, reversing the sheet front to back and turning the biscuits upside down once during baking.

continues ↘

After 1 hour, turn off the oven but let the biscuits cool in the oven for about ½ hour. Remove from the oven and let stand until cool.

Bowwow!

P.S. I don't have a dog. After I wrote this recipe I gave samples of the biscuits to all my friends who have or know some dogs. During the next few days everyone except a certain gentleman friend called to tell me how much the dogs enjoyed them...the dogs barked and ran around looking for more.

Finally, I called the gentleman and asked, "What about the dog biscuits?" He answered, "Oh, I just ate them today. I love them. They're wonderful."

"But they were dog biscuits — they were for a dog."

"But I got hungry, and they were delicious."

acknowledgments

Everyone who contributed to bringing this book into the world knows that happiness is baking...and sharing. In the Heatter family, we call it "cookie diplomacy."

Very special thanks to our neighbor, Hope Fuller, and her super-Maida-fan cousin, Stephen Wander, for copious thoughts on many recipes. They both have known her for many years, and Hope has spent more hours taking meticulous notes in Maida's enchanted kitchen than anyone on Earth.

Thank you to those at Little, Brown and beyond who were instrumental in publishing this volume, including Ira Boudah, agent extraordinaire Janis Donnaud, Lisa Ferris, Nicky Guerreiro, Jules Horbachevsky, Alice Oehr, Deri Reed, Michael Szczerban, Toni Tajima, Elora Weil, and Jayne Yaffe Kemp.

We are very grateful to others whose contributions went beyond the simple request for a favorite recipe or story, including Dorie Greenspan, Linn Hadden, Barbara Lazaroff, Olga Massov, Bruce Munter, and Joan Sutton.

Votes for family favorites and wonderful anecdotes came to us in an avalanche of texts and tweets, hand delivery and snail mail. Everyone wanted "a piece of the pie"—so to speak. Much gratitude to Jessica Battilana, Suet Chong, Erica Gelbard, Gabriella Gershenson, Peter Gethers, Zachary Golper, Cathy Gruhn, Christopher Hirsheimer, Julia Kramer, Catherine Newman, Wolfgang Puck, Michael Schwartz, Lauren Shakely, Nancy Silverton, Leslie Stoker, Marcia Tennyson, Mary Tondorf-Dick, and Julia Turshen.

One amusing skirmish ensued among fans: Which is better, the Best Damn Lemon Cake or the East 62nd Street Lemon Cake? (An argument reminiscent of the hilarious "I can't believe it's not butter" scene from the Britcom *The Vicar of Dibley*.)

You'll just have to decide for yourself.

— **Connie and Maida Heatter**

index

Page numbers in *italics* refer to illustrations.

about the author

Maida Heatter, dubbed the Queen of Cake by *Saveur,* is the author of several classic books on dessert and baking. She is the recipient of three James Beard Foundation Awards and has been inducted into the organization's Hall of Fame. Born on Long Island, she is now 102 years old and lives in Miami Beach. She was assisted in the preparation of this book by her sister-in-law, Connie Heatter.